Published & Edited by
Paul Connolly

Manufactured & Printed by Westsidepress 2014
Unit 1, Greenhills Road Industrial Estate
Tallaght, Dublin 24, Ireland

ISBN 978-0-9930979-0-4

For

Martina

PREFACE

I grew up in Bushy Park, Mount Talbot, County Roscommon and crossed the worn limestone step at the entrance to Mount Talbot National School for the first time in September 1979. My father and grand-father had crossed this very same stone step before me as did my older siblings. I sat down in the 'small room' beside a fair haired boy called Brian Kelly who lived next door to the school. This is the day for me that started my lifelong fascination and appreciation of the village of Mount Talbot. I spent all my youth in Mount Talbot with Brian, fishing, skipping stones, observing nature, observing people, even then I realised that this place was special, there was something about it that drew me back. I left Mount Talbot National School and began my secondary education in Saint Mary's College, Ballygar and after finishing secondary school I obtained a Bachelor of Engineering in Cork. I subsequently moved to Galway and began working with a Consulting Engineering Company and from there I moved to Galway County Council where I still work today. I have no direct qualifications relating to History but I have read extensively on this subject. I did however complete a Diploma in Archaeology a number of years ago at the National University of Ireland in Galway under Dr Carleton Jones and this has helped enormously with the earlier content of this book.

The concept of writing a book on the history of Mount Talbot only really materialised in 2009. I had just finished playing senior hurling with Four Roads hurling club and I found that I had a lot more free time on my hands particularly in the evenings and at weekends. I began to fill this time by gathering additional historical information relating to Mount Talbot and its environs. I had been gathering information practically all my adult life but never had sufficient time to make the necessary trips to the libraries and archives throughout the country to view additional documents. The book really started as a tidying up exercise for all the material that I had gathered, I wanted to put some sort of order to my research so I started writing explanations and notes to accompany each document or photograph that I possessed and when I started I couldn't stop! I found myself carrying out further research to fill in the blanks that existed between the various eras and after a very short time I realised that an extraordinary history was unfolding in front of me. I felt that this history needed to be shared with the people from the area and beyond.

For me Mount Talbot has always been a special place, it has a pulse, a heartbeat and a sense of history. The area breathes heavy from a long and turbulent past, every ruin, every hill and hollow, every part of the river has a story to tell. It seemed to cry out for its story to be told, this is its story.

INTRODUCTION

One of the most difficult decisions I had to make when I commenced writing this book was deciding what townlands in the area around Mount Talbot would be included in the text. I decided to concentrate on the townlands that are located directly adjacent to Mount Talbot, townlands that we all associate with being part of the fabric of Mount Talbot. The townlands in question are: Garrier, Thornfield, Cloondara, Lismaha, Lisgillilea (Bushy Park), Cloonca, Cartron, Cloonlaughnan (including Corrocot) and Cloonakilleg. I have concentrated on these townlands when writing about land ownership, the various local and national census and other surveys that were carried out throughout the centuries. Various references are made however throughout the book to other townlands in the area including Cloonruff, Araghty, Correbeg, Attiknockan, Cloghan, Turrock and Scrine.

The first chapter examines pre-history covering from the late Stone Age to the 5th century AD. Chapter 2 looks at events that occurred during the Medieval Period. This chapter deals with events from the 5th century up to the end of the 16th century including the rise of the powerful O'Kelly family. Technically the Medieval Period finishes in the mid 16th century but I included the second half of this century in Chapter 2 to avoid confusion. Chapter 3 examines the three major conflicts that occurred throughout the 17th century, people from the area were directly involved in all of the bloody wars of this century. Chapter 4 deals with the 18th century, the foundation of landlordism occurs in this century and the village of Mount Talbot was founded. Chapter 5 looks at the 19th century, parts of this chapter very difficult to write because of the terrible suffering that occurred in the area during the famine. Chapter 6 deals with the 20th century, this century saw major changes in the area with land ownership reverting back to the people and the creation and consolidation of the Irish Free State. This chapter also contains numerous photographs including many from the 'Cronin Collection' taken by the late Tim Cronin throughout the 1960's and 70's. Chapter 7 gives a brief account of the 21st century so far and includes modern photographs of places of interest in the area. As may be seen in the content listed above there is no section in this book that deals directly with the Iron Age as scant archaeological evidence exists in the area relating to this period. The lack of information relating to the Iron Age is not unique to Mount Talbot and is replicated throughout the country. There are some historical sources available but most sources are not contemporary with the time and were written in later centuries. Many Irish families wrote their histories during the Medieval Period and often embellished their pedigree to increase the families status. I have used some of these non-contemporary sources in the first part of chapter 2 when discussing the arrival of the O'Kellys in the area during the Iron Age.

The O'Kellys of Aughrane owned the townlands of Garrier, Thornfield, Cloonakilleg and Cartron from Medieval times up to the late 19th century. Aughrane Castle or Castle Kelly, was located to the north west of Mount Talbot, near the modern town of Ballygar. Another branch of the O'Kellys owned Mount Talbot and the other remaining townlands in the area during the Medieval period, this family fought against Cromwell and subsequently lost their ancestral lands, they were replaced as landowners by the Talbot family of Templeogue who were transplanted to the area. These 3 families are examined in detail in the relevant chapters of this book as they effectively controlled all the areas within the catchment until the implementation of the Land Acts in the late 19th and early 20th centuries.

This book as the title suggests is written as a journey, a journey that begins in the late Stone Age and ends in the present time. To go on this journey it is necessary to arrange the chapters in chronological order from earliest to modern times. I wanted to allow the reader to travel unimpeded through the centuries, I wanted this journey to flow without the need to be checking timescales or wondering what century you were reading about. I would have liked to have completed one chapter on the Talbots but they were in Mount Talbot for three centuries. I have therefore brought the Talbots through the book with everyone else and for clarity I have included an appendix at the end of the book showing a full lineage of the leading family members through the centuries. This arrangement was difficult to complete successfully but I hope my intentions have been achieved and the reader may find that the journey they embark on through the ages of Mount Talbot free flowing and enjoyable.

Variations in surnames and in the name of townlands may be noticeable throughout the book but these names have been printed as they were found in the various census and other documents that they are taken from. I have made every effort to ensure that the information contained in this book is accurate however there may be some mistakes or omissions that were not found during editing and were inadvertently included. I have included footnotes where necessary to highlight a source or to further explain a particular item included in the textb and a full bibliography is included at the end of this book.

The historic houses, sites and monuments examined in this book are located within privately owned lands. Permission must be sought from individual house and landowners prior to entering private property.

ACKNOWLEDGEMENTS

This book would not have been possible without the tremendous help and assistance I received from so many people before and during the writing process. The book would not even have started without the complete and unwavering support of my wife Martina. She gave me the belief to commence this wonderful journey and gave me the encouragement and support that I needed to keep going until the very end. I also received fantastic support from other family members. My mother, as always, was very supportive and was particularly excited about the parts of the book that related to her birthplace near Ballygar. My four older brothers were all very helpful, I received a large amount of material from Ger who also gave great advice on parts of the book that were proving difficult to complete. Michael accompanied me on many occasions to the National Library of Ireland, the National Archives of Ireland and other interesting places where we came across many wonderful original documents and photographs relating to the area. Tommy edited the book and together with Hubie, gave great advice on what to include in the book and also provided information that is included within the text. My sister Sheila helped enormously with editing and also gave much needed encouragement during times when histories and more particularly chronologies were not fitting together. I received great support from all other family members who helped out in various ways throughout the writing and editing processes.

The reaction I received from the people of Mount Talbot was phenomenal and overwhelming. I knocked on many doors and phoned and e-mailed many people and I was completely over awed by the reaction of the wonderful people of Mount Talbot and its environs. I also contacted emigrants and other people with links to the area and found that everyone I contacted wanted this amazing story to be told as much as I did.

Emma Cronin was very helpful and gave me unrestricted access to the 'Cronin Collection' of slides and other documents of importance relating to the area. Tim Cronin was an historian of immense stature and he was ahead of his time in many ways. His writings were of enormous benefit to me particularly his text relating to the Elizabethan era. I enjoyed my visits to Emma from a research point of view but I enjoyed them even more for their social enjoyment. Emmy Eustace provided a fantastic array of photographs, letters and other documents relating to Johnnie Talbot and his wife Julia and I have included many items from this private collection in this book. Tom Kelly was very helpful to me particularly in relation to his uncle, Commandant Tommie Kelly. Marty Smith provided excellent information on the forges and other workshops that existed in Corrocot in the early and mid 20th century. Tommie Kenny provided fantastic information relating to various eras but particularly relating to the War of Independence and Civil War. I received wonderful photos and material relating to Bushy Park House from Helga Mullins. Mary Bridget and Shay Galvin provided important material relating to Joe Galvin of Cloonlaughnan. Mary Francis Turley gave me permission to include her wonderful poetry in this book. Mickey McConn provided some fascinating information relating to the last years of the Talbots and the War of Independence. Willie Gacquin was very helpful and guided me towards some excellent sources in Roscommon County Library. John English provided copies of beautiful photographs of Thornfield House and I was also permitted access to an original rent book from the Talbot estate. I obtained copies of photographs relating to Naughtons shop from Pat Naughton. I received an enormous amount of information relating to the area from mid 20th century from Brian Scanlon and a copy of his beautiful painting of Mount Talbot House is also included in this book. Marie Mannion, the Heritage Officer in Galway County Council gave excellent guidance at the initial stages of writing and provided encouragement throughout. Gerry Beggan provided very interesting information on the O'Kellys of Hy-Many and also on the Cromwellian War. Martina Connaughton took some wonderful modern photographs of the area and many of these are included in this book. Martina also transferred the slides from the Cronin Collection into digital images. Michael McDonnell gave unrestricted access to the ruins of Mount Talbot House and gave permission to take photographs within the former demesne. George Gossip provided very helpful information relating to the architecture and to the construction of Mount Talbot House and the Protestant Church. George also gave permission to use a collection of his historic photographs of the house that are located at the Irish Architectural Archive. Donald Cameron provided an extraordinary array of photographs from his private family collection. Donald is a descendent of the Talbot, Talbot-Crosbie family, his material included family portraits going back to the mid 18th century and he also provided an excellent array of rare photos of Cloonca House. Gerry Waldron gave permission to examine and photograph an original James Nolan hurley from the early 20th century.

I would like to thank the National Library of Ireland for granting reproduction rights for a number of items relating to Mount Talbot held in their Library. I would also like to acknowledge the National Archives of Ireland and its Director for granting permission to reproduce items from their Famine Relief Commission collection. I also wish to thank the National Architectural Archive for allowing the reproduction of photographs relating to Mount Talbot House and the Special Collections section of the James Hardiman Library at NUIG who allowed the reproduction of a document from their collection relating to Galvins nurseries. Eleanor Cracknell, College Archivist at the Eton College Library in the UK, provided details of Johnnie Talbots time at Eton. Patria McWalter, Senior Archivist with Galway County Council gave access to the amazing 'Kelly Collection' in the Archives section of Galway County Library at Nuns Island, this collection is of huge importance and relates to the Kellys of Aughrane from the early 17th century to the late 19th century. I also received important information from the Public Records Office of Northern Ireland, Roscommon County Library, the National Museum of Ireland, the John Rylands Library in Manchester and the Irish Georgian Society.

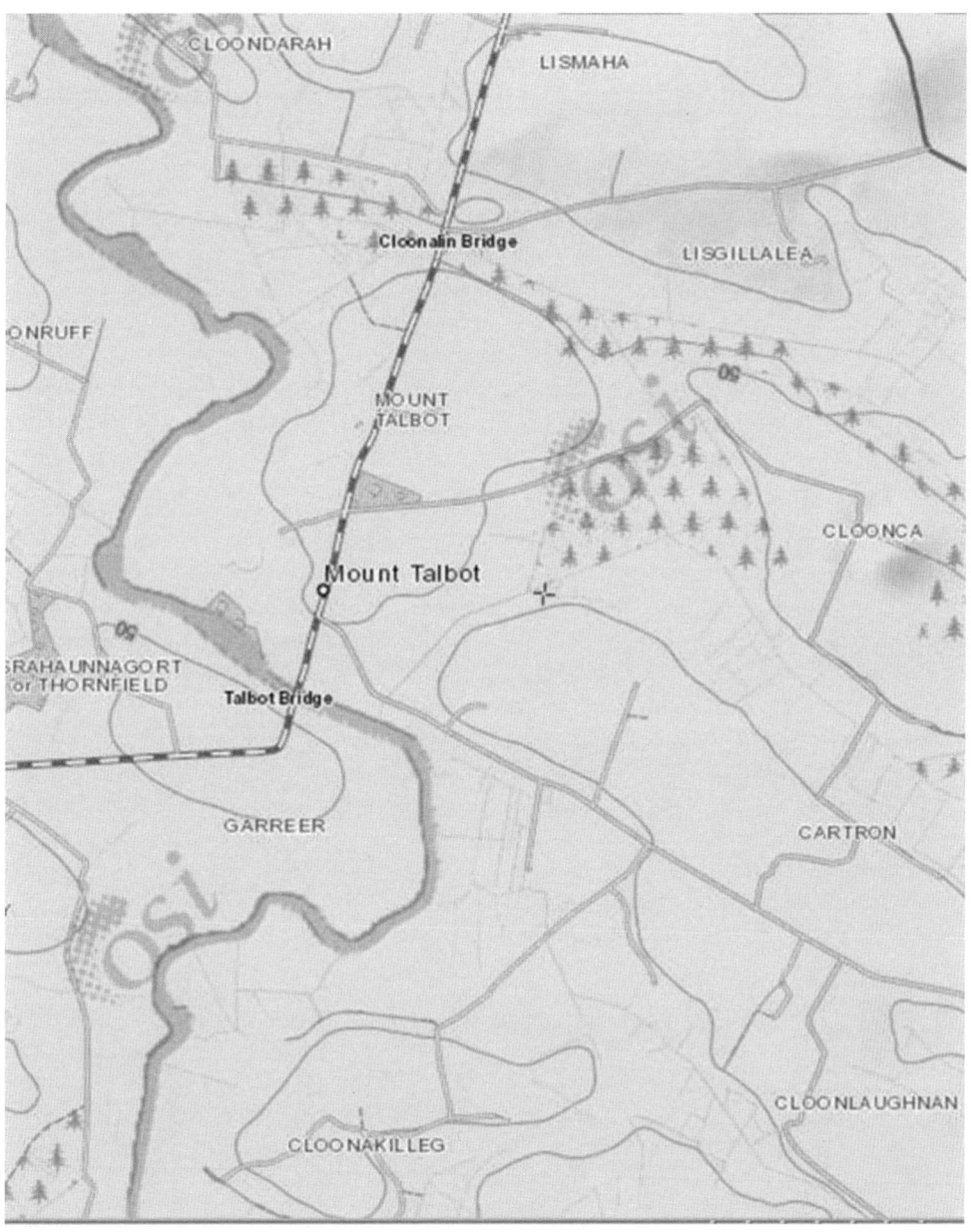

Modern map showing Mount Talbot and the surrounding areas. Mount Talbot is located in South Roscommon adjacent to the river Suck that divides the Counties of Roscommon and Galway. In this book I have used different spelling when referring to some of the townlands shown above. I have used Cloondara for Cloondarah, Clooneleen for Cloonalin and Garrier for Gareer. I have used the same spelling for Cloonlaughnan and Cloonakilleg as shown above but these townlands are pronounced differently locally i.e. Cloonlaughlin and Cloonykilleg. The spelling of the townlands are consistent throughout the book and were primarily chosen to allow referencing to the available sources.

CONTENTS

Chapter 1   Prehistory

Chapter 2   The Medieval Period

Chapter 3   The 17th Century

Chapter 4   The 18th Century

Chapter 5   The 19th Century

Chapter 6   The 20th Century

Chapter 7   The 21st Century

Appendix 1   Lineage of the leading historic families in the area

Appendix 2   Townlands and Placenames

Chapter 1 – Prehistory

The First Inhabitants

It is unclear when the first people arrived in Mount Talbot or the surrounding areas as no archaeological evidence exists to suggest habitation prior to the late Stone Age or Neolithic. A portal tomb was recorded on the first edition ordnance survey maps at a site in Four Roads. The portal tomb is referred to in the map as a *'Druids Altar'* and this was a common name used for such monuments prior to the current name classification that developed later in the 19th century. Although the monument was recorded four and a half kilometres east of Mount Talbot its presence confirms that a settled community was in existence in the vicinity during the late Stone Age. The land at Mount Talbot was always of excellent quality and it is reasonable to assume that this land was cleared of forestry and farmed by people in the Neolithic. The people at this time still relied to an extent on the natural environment for food and the presence of fish in the river Suck at Mount Talbot further enhances the chances of habitation within the townland. Portal-tombs are also known as dolmens and were used as burial chambers. The majority of these monuments date from the third millennium BC. Portal tombs are generally constructed using between three and seven upright stones carrying one or two heavy capstones that slope downwards towards the back. Archaeological excavations carried out throughout the country have revealed that both cremation and inhumation burials were used within the tomb. The portal tomb at Four Roads was removed during the mid 19th century but an impressive replica has been constructed close to the monuments original location to the rear of the present day community centre.

The first edition Ordnance Survey maps depict a large mound almost circular in shape located a short distance north of the walled gardens within the former demesne of Mount Talbot House. This mound still exists today suggesting that the Talbots made every attempt to preserve the monument when constructing their large residence and ornate gardens in the 18th century. The subsequent owners of this land have also preserved the mound in its entirety. The Record of Monuments and Places (RMP) for County Roscommon list this mound as a Tumulus. Without an archaeological excavation, this monument is difficult to accurately date as they were in use for many centuries from the Late Stone Age through the Bronze Age. In 1966 a similar tumulus was excavated north of Mount Talbot village within the barony of Ballintober South in County Roscommon. This excavation revealed that the mound contained eight cist graves and six secondary pit burials. Six of the cists contained Bowl-type funery vessels and human remains. Cremations were the principal bone deposit in six cists with unburnt skeletal material contained in the remaining two cists. In three instances they were accompanied by vessels of the Vase Urn class. Other finds within the mound included a perforated bone pendant, a miniature cup and a bronze dagger. The mound was radiocarbon dated to the 18th century BC.

No dating evidence has been unearthed to date the mound at Mount Talbot but it seems logical that the monument is contemporary with the mound excavated at Ballintober South. It is probable that the mound was used during the Early Bronze Age as a burial place for the deceased members of the local clan. The presence of such a large burial mound within the townland of Mount Talbot suggests that an important clan lived close by. Large mounds or tumulus took time and effort to construct and they were only constructed when the people that were to be interned within the mound were of sufficient high status to justify its construction. These monuments pre-date the coming of Christianity and the burial of local Kings and Chiefs would have been overseen by druids attached to the local clan.

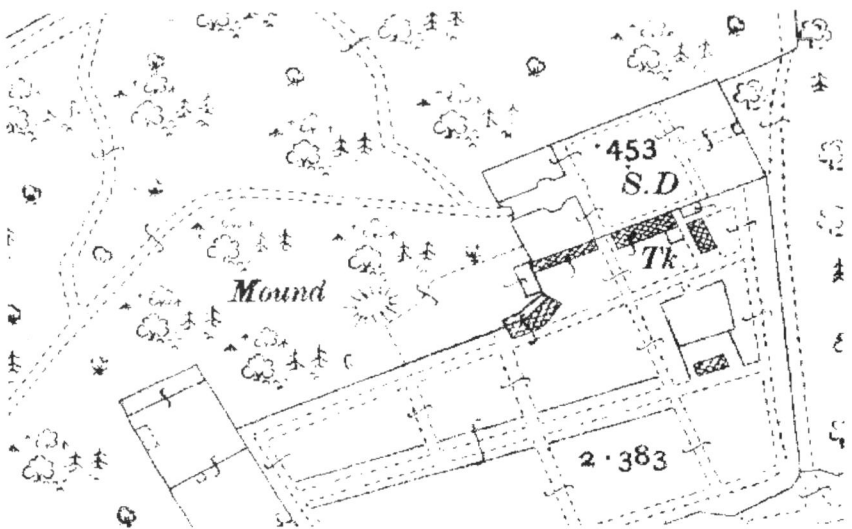

Early Ordnance Survey map showing the position of the 'Mound' within the Talbot demesne (licence number 2010/15CCMA/Galway County Council).

Modern photo of the mound at Mount Talbot (M. Connaughton, June 2014).

2

An interesting follow-on from the examination of this mound is the possibility of the 'Mount' in Mount Talbot being named after it. There are no mountains, hills or raised areas anywhere in the townland of Mount Talbot, the land is flat and no visible features exist in the landscape other than the mound. The fact that the Talbots preserved the mound and built their large mansion nearby suggests that they believed it was of importance. There are of course other possibilities for the use of the word 'Mount' that are unrelated to any feature in the local landscape including the possibility that the word had historical significance for the Talbot family prior to their arrival in the area.

Three artefacts discovered in the area confirm the existence of a settled community in Mount Talbot during the Late Bronze Age. The first datable item was discovered in the river Suck by two 11 year old boys from Mount Talbot during the hot summer of 1985. The two boys in question were Brian Kelly from Mount Talbot village and the author of this book, Paul Connolly from Bushy Park. We were skipping stones in the water approximately 100 metres downstream of Mount Talbot bridge, Brian was looking for the perfect round flat stone at the edge of the water when he discovered a strange looking object nestled in the river bed. It was the perfect shape for 'skipping' but luckily we decided to examine our find. We quickly realised that we needed to show the object to someone else as it seemed very old. My brother Tommy was Principal of Mount Talbot National School at this time and after examining the object he immediately sent it to the National Museum of Ireland in Dublin. Raghnall O'Floinn of the Irish Antiquities Division of the National Museum appraised the object and informed us that we had discovered a Late Bronze Age axehead datable to 800-500 B.C. The axehead was used for cutting saplings and for woodworking rather than as a weapon. It contained a socketed end to allow a handle to be attached and it also contained a minute circular loop underneath to allow a string to be tied around the handle for added strength. Although the axehead did not contain any elaborate decorative markings it was beautifully made and perfectly designed for its purpose. Nationally there have been many discoveries of Bronze Age materials in rivers suggesting that these objects may have been deposited as votive offerings. The summer of 1985 was particularly hot and the river was very low at the time of our discovery. Otherwise we would never have found this historically important object.

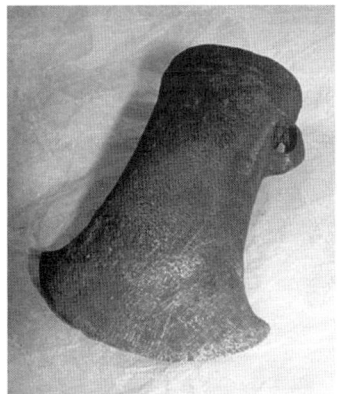 

Late Bronze Age Socketed Axe head (left) and a photo showing how these Axe heads were attached to their wooden handles (right).

A fibula weighing 16 oz. 16 dwt. of very fine gold was discovered on the estate of Reverend Armstrong Kelly of Castle Kelly (Aughrane) in 1819 during the excavation of gravel under a cut away bog a short distance from Mount Talbot village. The exact location is not known but a description exists in Lewis Topographical Dictionary from 1837, in his description of the parish of Athleague Lewis states that it was discovered on the estate then owned by Rev. Armstrong Kelly in County Galway suggesting that the artefact was found in either Garrier, Thornfield or Cloonruff as they were all part of the parish of Athleague and they were part of the Castle Kelly estate that was in Co. Galway. Labourers discovered the artefact imbedded approximately one foot into the limestone gravel sub-stratum and it was estimated that 20 feet of peat-bog had once covered the location of the find[1]. Gold Fibulas date to the late Bronze Age and the object discovered consisted of two hollow conical terminals connected by a curved bow, it is widely believed that they were worn on the chest to fasten two sides of a cloak or dress together but the size and weight of the Castle Kelly fibula suggest that it may have served as a physical representation of wealth and power rather than as an ornament of personal adornment. The fibula was perfectly preserved and in excellent condition, the object has remained undisturbed under the bog for over 2,500 years. Nationally many more gold objects from the Bronze Age have been discovered in bogs and it is believed they were deposited in these places for the purpose of ritual deposition. After its discovery Reverend Armstrong Kelly sent the object to Reverend H.R Dawson who was the Dean of Saint Patrick's Cathedral in Dublin for safekeeping and it subsequently became part of the collection at the National Museum of Ireland. It remains an important part of their collection today.

Gold Fibula from the Late Bronze Age discovered near Mount Talbot in 1819.

---

[1] Cahill, M. (1998) Large gold dress-fasteners of the Irish later Bronze Age. In M. Ryan (ed.), Irish Antiquities – a memorial volume for Dr. Joseph Raftery, 27-58. Dublin.

A sword dating from the late Bronze Age was discovered in the river Suck between the townlands of Cloonakilleg and Tully by Sean Naughton NT from Ballygar in May 1995. Sean was carrying out drainage works on his land in Tully when his son Shane who was then 5 years old, asked to go fishing in the river Suck nearby after noticing a fishing rod in the boot of his father's car. Sean was wearing waders to carry out the land drainage so he agreed to bring Shane and his daughter Aoife fishing for half an hour. After twenty minutes of fruitless casting Sean noticed an object protruding from the river in approximately 18 inches of water. He lifted the object from the river bed and immediately realised that the object was of historical importance. Sean had found a beautiful Late Bronze Age sword weighing two pounds. The sword is sixty centimetres in length with nine rivet holes still visible in the handle, the entire sword was in remarkably good condition and still had a relatively sharp blade. The sword made its way to Professor Rynne of University College Galway (now NUIG) who dated the find to 700 B.C. The sword was subsequently handed over to the National Museum where it remains today. This find dates to the same time as the axehead that was found in the river Suck ten years previously a few hundred metres up-stream. Both objects confirm human habitation in the area but they had two very different functions. The axehead was a domestic tool but the sword confirms that the people in the area needed to arm themselves against potential attack. The sword found at Tully is quite short but it has a broad blade and is very similar to the swords that allowed the Roman armies to create an Empire. In the right hands these swords were a very effective weapon. Swords were to remain an essential accessory to the people of Mount Talbot for the next 1,000 years as internal and external forces battled to control the area.

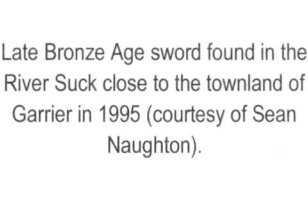

Late Bronze Age sword found in the River Suck close to the townland of Garrier in 1995 (courtesy of Sean Naughton).

Chapter 2 – The Medieval Period

The people of Mount Talbot in the early medieval period lived in what are now described as Ringforts. These homesteads are often locally referred to as 'Fairy Forts'. Ringforts are referred to as Rath, Dun or Lios in ancient texts and modern townlands containing any of these words in their names generally signify the existence of a ringfort within the townland. Ringforts were circular structures that contained an outer embankment (rath) and an inner area (lios) that was used for habitation. These forts were partly designed for defensive purposes and were generally located in areas where a good view of the surrounding land was available to allow potential attackers to be seen in advance. Excavated ringforts in other parts of Ireland have revealed a date range of between 550 AD and 900 AD but some remained inhabited into the later and post medieval period particularly in areas outside Anglo-Norman control. A large ringfort existed close to Mount Talbot village along the banks of the river Suck in the townland of Garrier. It was built for an important member of the local clan as the outer dimensions from north to south measured 90 metres. This ringfort is shown in the first edition Ordnance Survey Maps from 1838 but it had been removed prior to the later OS maps from the 1880's. This ringfort seems to have protected a very important 'ford' that existed over the River Suck near the present day bridge at Mount Talbot. The ford provided a safe crossing point of the river and was passable during high winter floods, it was one of only three such crossing points along the entire length of the river suck. This ford gave Mount Talbot its first recorded name: *'Beal an Atha'* or *'Beal an Atha Ui Cheallaigh'*[2] and this translates as 'the mouth of the ford' or 'the mouth of the O'Kelly ford'. Deepening of the riverbed during the Suck Drainage Scheme of the late 19th century removed any trace of this original ford. Another ford existed south of the large ringfort at Garrier, providing access from the townland of Cloonakilleg to Garrier. As the land on the Cloonakilleg side floods over the winter months, stepping stones were installed through the flooded areas to allow access to the ford at almost all times of the year. The townland of Cloonakilleg translates as 'the meadow of the place of the flag stones'. This ford ceased to serve a function when the 'togher' was built in later centuries linking Cloonakilleg to the main road. However, the ford still exists albeit at a much reduced height and it was used in living memory by a local man in Cloonakilleg to cross the river when walking to Ballygar during the dry summer months.

Cloondara, as the name suggests, contained a double ringfort and this settlement was also located on the banks of the river Suck. Modern aerial photography of Cloondara clearly shows the outline of these forts and the outer diameter dimensions also suggests a fort of importance. The townlands of Lismaha, Lisgillilea and Cloonca contained many ringforts of various sizes and these seem to have been settlements for the regular members of the local clan as none of the forts are of a substantial size. There are also a number of ringforts shown on the first edition Ordnance Survey maps within the townland of Cloonlaughnan and a relatively large diameter fort in Cartron. There are no ringforts shown within the townland of Mount Talbot in the first editions OS maps but it is possible that the building of Mount Talbot House and the development of the village may have resulted in any forts in the area being removed. However a very interesting feature is shown in the first Ordnance Survey maps within the grounds of the Talbot demesne, this feature is called *'cumberlands cave'* and it was described as *'an old building'* by the Ordnance Survey name books from the 1830's. It seems that

---

[2] Ordnance Survey name books for Co. Roscommon, p215.

this feature was a man-made underground structure. The most probable function of this 'cave' was as a soutterain. These underground chambers were generally located within ringforts or other places of habitation during the medieval period to store food and to act as a place of refuge during attack. The existence of a soutterain suggests that an important local family lived within a ringfort at this location at some point during the medieval period. The surrounding embankment that made up the ringfort is no longer visible and must have been removed in later centuries. However another possibility exists, oral history recalls that the eastern part of Mount Talbot or western part of Cloondara contained a Monastery. Souterrains were commonly used in monasteries as they offered protection to the local monks during raids, valuable items within a monastery were also hidden in souterrains during times of volatility. No record exists however within the primary historical sources of a monastery ever existing in this location but oral history must never be discounted. If a monastery did exist here it would have been relatively small and may not have existed for very long.

Location of large ringfort in Garrier from the first edition Ordnance Survey maps. This fort was removed later in the 19th century as it does not appear in maps from the 1880's onwards (OSI, Licence number 2010/15CCMA/Galway County Council).

Modern Aerial Photograph showing Location of the 'double' Ringfort in Cloondara (OSI, Licence number 2010/15CCMA/Galway County Council).

Throughout the medieval period Mount Talbot was part of the kingdom of Hy-Many (Uí Maine), ancient texts recall that this territory had been taken from the local 'firbolgs' at the start of the fourth century by the O'Kellys who had come to the area from the north. The firbolgs were believed to have come to Ireland from Greece prior to or during the Iron Age, they were described in later centuries as having black hair and a dark complexion. Lady Francesca Wilde described them in the 19th century as *'a small, straight haired, swarthy race who have left a portion of their descendants with us to this very day'.* Antiquarian John O'Donovan in the 19th century believed that South Roscommon and East Galway was one of the last strongholds of the firbolgs in the Country, he also believed that some of the local people from these areas were direct descendents of the Firbolgs as they had many of the physical characteristic associated with this ancient race. The sword found in Tully that is mentioned in chapter 1 dates to the time of the firbolg people and may have been used during this volatile time when Gaelic families began to populate the area. The neighbouring townland of Cloonca may also have got its name during this time, the name translates as the 'meadow of the battle'.

After their establishment in the area, the O'Kellys set about consolidating and expanding their newly acquired lands. At its peak Hy-Many extended through south and east Galway, south and mid Roscommon, a small part of north Clare and even extended for a time into Lusmagh in County Offaly. There are numerous references to Hy-Many in the primary historical sources relating to this time including the Annals of Connacht, the Four Masters, the Annals of Loch Ce and the Book of Lecan. In 1843 John O'Donovan edited the book: *'Tribes and Customs of Hy-Many, Commonly Called O'Kelly Country'*, this publication gives a detailed account of the kingdom of Hy-Many including a lineage of the O'Kelly chiefs throughout the late Iron Age and the Medieval Period. The O'Kellys were a very powerful Gaelic family and they built at least 12 large castles in their territory including the local castles at Turrock, Scrine, Aughrane, Correbeg and Attiknockan. They embraced Christianity in the 5th century and built a Monastery at Kilconnell in 1353, they also gave patronage to other religious houses within their territory and beyond. When Conchobar Noenmoy O'Ceallaigh was chief of Hy-Many a church was built specifically for the O'Kellys within the Clonmacnoise Monastery. The O'Kellys are one of only a small number of families in the entire country that had a Church located at Clonmacnoise signifying the family's importance in Medieval Ireland.

The 'Registry of Clonmacnoise' makes reference to the Chief of Hy-Many bestowing seventeen townlands and three houses within his territory to Saint Kieran of Clonmacnoise during the 6th century, this land grant included the townland of Cloonakilleg: *'Cairbre Crum...bestowed unto St Kyran... the proportion of three ungaes and 5d in Cluain acha Leaga* (Cloonakilleg) [3]. Cloonakilleg seems to have remained a religious area up until at least the early 14th century as a tax list from the diocese of Elphin for the years 1302 – 1307 shows that a church existed in a part of the diocese known as 'Clonagaleg'[4], the townland seems to have reverted back to secular ownership after this time. The townland of Carrowntemple in Tisrara contains the remains of a religious settlement and it is believed that the bearers of deceased leaders of the O'Kelly and other leading Gaelic families

---

[3] The Journal of the Kilkenny and South-East of Ireland Archaeological Society 1856-67,Vols 1-6, Royal Society of Antiquaries of Ireland, p455 (contained in the chapter entitled: The Registry of Clonmacnoise with Notes and Introductory Remarks, by J O'Donovan).
[4] H.S Sweetman (ed.), *Calender of Documents relating to Ireland, Her Majesties Public Record Office, London 1302-1307.* 1896.

rested here for a night prior to continuing on to Clonmacnoise for burial. A reference is made in the Registry of Clonmacnoise to the townland of Coolderry which is located close to Mount Talbot, '*and this was the graunt and gift of Tyrmaine unto the comeing of the O'Dubhagaine of Culdaire (Coolderry)*'[5]. The O'Dubhagaine (or Duggan's) were the hereditary Seanchaidhes (historians) of Hy-Many, the surname Duggan was recorded in Coolderry up until the 18th century and in Lisduff throughout the 19th century.

The kingdom of Hy-Many performed many important functions under the Kings of Connacht including the role of treasurers. The O'Kellys also received a percentage of fines levied on convicted criminals under the Brehon Law and were not impelled to provide soldiers to the King of Connacht in times of war. The battle of Clontarf in 1014 is a significant milestone in the history of Hy-Many when Tadhg Mor O'Ceallaigh Chief of Hy-Many joined with Brian Boru the High King of Ireland in his march to Clontarf to face the Danes. Both Tadhg and Brian Boru were killed on the day of the battle of Clontarf (Good Friday 1014) but overall victory in this battle began a long friendship between the O'Kellys and the O'Briens of County Clare that lasted until the battle of Knockdoe in 1504. It was Tadhg Mor's father that first began using the surname O'Kelly, prior to this time clan leaders were called directly after the previous chief and no names were permanent.

The townland we now call Mount Talbot changed its name during the mid to late Medieval Period, up to this time it was known as 'Beal an Atha Ui Cheallaigh' and it subsequently became known as 'Cluain na gCloidhe' (in modern Irish - Cluain na gClaí) and this name translates as the 'meadow of the ditches/hedges' or 'the walled meadow'[6]. It is presently unknown where the name came from but it seems a large stone wall or ditch enclosed an area of land somewhere within the townland. Walled enclosures were very rare in this part of the County at this time. An earthen embankment was the preferred option for enclosing an area for farming purposes or for habitation as may be seen in the remaining ringforts in the area. The possibility of the existence of a walled enclosure increases the likelihood of a monastic settlement existing in the area at some stage during the Medieval Period but as stated previously in this chapter no written record of a monastic settlement in the area has been discovered thus far. The stone souterrain mentioned previously in this chapter may be contemporary with this walled enclosure, no trace of any enclosure exists within the townland today.

The Normans arrived in Ireland in 1169 and quickly gained a strong foothold in the south of the country. In May 1227 almost the entire province of Connacht was handed over to Norman Baron Richard de Burgo by the King of England. The local Gaelic families resisted this intrusion resulting in an enormous force of heavily armed and mounted Norman Knights assembling at Athlone in 1235. They swept through the province with brute force crushing all opposition and Hugh O'Connor, King of Connacht had to seek refuge with the O'Donnells of Donegal. Hugh O'Connor eventually returned to the province but was left with no choice but to accept the new political landscape that was now in place. In the years that followed, parcels of land in Connacht were handed out to various Norman Barons and in 1283 the Parish of Tisrara and other neighbouring lands were given to the Norman

---

[5] The Journal of the Kilkenny and South-East of Ireland Archaeological Society 1856-67,Vols 1-6, Royal Society of Antiquaries of Ireland, p455 (contained in the chapter entitled: The Registry of Clonmacnoise with Notes and Introductory Remarks, by J O'Donovan), p456.
[6] From www.focloir.ie , and from conversation with native Irish speakers and local historians.

Knight Sir Theobald le Botiller, *'Philip de Rupella grants to Sir Theobald le Botiller and his heirs all his land of the cantred in Omany* (Hy-Many) *in Cornacia...and all his lands of Croun, namely the villates of Unchen without Eschean (*Funshinagh*), Tasrather (*Tisrara*), Dundermond (*possibly Bushy Park*), Thobural Gyly on the east of the Suck, and three villates of land nearer said suck on the west, to hold of the Lord Edward, King of England[7]'.* As Cluian na gCloidhe was entirely located within the parish of Tisrara the townland was therefore now in the possession of Sir Theobald le Botiller, it seems the neighbouring townland of Funshinagh was excluded from this land grant. It is possible that the three 'Villates' of land on the west of the Suck that is mentioned in the text may refer to Garrier, Thornfield and Cloonruff.

Document from 1283 stating that the lands at Tisrara (Tasrather) and Dundermot have been given to Sir Theobald le Botiller by Philip de Rupella to hold for the King of England, see right hand side of the fourth line (courtesy of the National Library of Ireland).

It seems that the Le Botiller's took possession of their lands as the 'Calendar of Documents relating to Ireland 1302 to 1307' record that rent was owed to the crown by Theobald le Botiller (Butler) for his lands at 'Omany'. It is worth noting that two families with the surname Butler are recorded within the townland of Lismaha in the Elphin census of 1749. Part of Lismaha was within the old

---

[7] From a translation of the original manuscript by Edmund Curtis, *Calendar of Ormond Deeds 1172-1350 A.D*, IMC, Dublin 1932, p102. Curtis states in his footnotes that 'Dundermond' is in Ballymoe, there was a Dundermond (or Dundermott) in Ballymoe but he was not aware of a townland of this name existing in Tisrara in the late medieval period. Part of Dundermot was within the parish of Athleague and that may explain why it was listed separately to Tisrara. The original manuscript is held at the National Library of Ireland, ref: D.2803.

townland of Dundermott that seems to have been granted to the Butlers in the document shown above. The O'Kellys however regained full control of most of South Roscommon and East Galway within the following century. The Bruce invasion from Scotland in 1315 and the arrival of the Black Death in 1348 allowed many of the Irish families regain possession of much of their former lands. Generally only towns, cities and coastal areas remained under Norman control together with an area known as the Pale that developed around the administrative centre at Dublin.

In 1351 William 'Boy' O'Kelly invited all the poets and bards of Ireland to a feast at his home at Gailey Castle near present day Knockcroghery. The feast occurred at Christmas and lasted for over a month with many poems and songs written to mark the occasion. The annals of Connacht record that *'a general invitation was issued by Uilliam son of Donnchad Muimnech O Cellaig, at Invitation Christmas, to the schools of poetry of all Ireland, and they all came right thankfully, both great and lowly'*. The term the 'O'Kellys of the welcomes' comes from this event and William 'Boy' O'Kelly is a direct paternal ancestor of both the O'Kellys of Cluain na gCloidhe and Aughrane. William's great grandson was Hugh O'Kelly of Athleague who was born in 1427 and later became the 27th chief of Hy-Many. One of Hugh's great grandsons was Malachy O'Kelly of Turrock who had two sons Conor and Brian. The O'Kellys that resided at Turrock were kinsmen of the O'Kelly family that lived at this time at Cluain na gCloidhe. The Annals of Connacht refer to an attack by the O'Conchobair of Sligo on the O'Kelly castle of Turrock' in 1536: *'This army took Turrock Castle and demolished it; and Donnchad son of Emann O Cellaig came to them as a hostage, for fear of his own territory being devastated ...and they carried with them the ornamented door of Turrock (castle) to Sligo'*. A further attack was made on Turrock Castle in 1545, this time by the McDermott's of Boyle who were allied with the O'Kelly chief of Hy-Many. Malachy O'Kelly of Turrock was killed in the attack and his son Brian sought revenge and made an audacious raid on the O'Kelly Chief's castle of Lisdalon near present day Knockcroghery. This action by Brian started a very bloody and bitter O'Kelly Civil War that weakened the overall strength of the O'Kellys in the subsequent years which did not go un-noticed by the observing eyes of the crown. Turrock castle and lands were subsequently lost by the weakened O'Kellys in 1588 when John Byrt received a gift of the lands from the President of Connacht, Sir Richard Bingham. Brian O'Kelly had to vacate Turrock and he was given the lands of Cluain na gCloidhe, Cloondara and Attiknockan by his kinsman Hugh McRory O'Kelly. The 'inquisition' that records this event is still available to view today, this document is written in Latin and is dated the 2nd of February 1589. As part of his inheritance Brian O'Kelly was expected to look after Hugh McRory on certain occasions, the inquisition states that Brian *'shall receive me every Christmas and Easter, or if he cannot do that he shall send me a hog..'*[8]. Brian later took possession of the additional neighbouring town lands of Cullawinna, Cornapallis, Cloonca, Garrier, Tully and Cloonruff. Brian's older brother Conor also had to vacate Turrock but it is unclear where Conor resides after this time[9]. Brian died in 1600 and gave Cluain na gCloidhe and all his other townlands to his son Brian Og Mac Brian O'Kelly.

---

[8] National Archives of Ireland, RC 4/15.

[9] Direct descendents of Conor O'Kelly were reinstated to Turrock Castle and to their ancestral lands in the early 18th century. The convert rolls show a Daniel Kelly of Turrock being enrolled into the Protestant faith on the 8th of June 1718 with his daughter Catherine being enrolled on the 6th of Nov 1746. (E. O'Byrne, The Convert Rolls, Dublin 1981). The Kelly's remained in Turrock until the late 19th century.

Two events towards the end of the 16th century allowed the British Crown to gain complete control over the lands of Hy-Many. The first event was the establishment of the Presidency Council of Connacht in 1568 and the second event was the Composition of Connacht by Queen Elizabeth in 1585. The Composition sought to replace charges and military exactions that Irish Lords and English garrisons imposed on the province by converting them into a rent charge levied on land. From this time onwards Hy-Many and the O'Kelly lands at Cluain na gCloidhe were held by letters patent from the English Crown. An annual rent of 10 shillings per quarter of land was now payable to the crown with the revenues going directly to the Presidency of Connacht. The last vestiges of Gaelic authority had been swept away and it seems that Brian Og O'Kelly of Cluain na gCloidhe resented this imposition of English law. When Brian came to fighting age he immediately offered his services to the powerful Ulster Lords who were engaged in a full scale rebellion against Queen Elizabeth I of England, this rebellion is known as the Nine Years War. In 1601 Brian Og took an active and significant part in the pivotal engagement of this war and one of the most important battles in Irish History, the battle of Kinsale.

Chapter 3 – The 17th Century

The Battle of Kinsale

The battle of Kinsale occurred in 1601 and it was the most important engagement of the Nine Years War as it effectively decided the wars outcome. Hugh O'Neill, Red Hugh O'Donnell, the Maguire's and other allies were engaged in a long drawn out war with Queen Elizabeth's armies. In the early engagements the Irish chieftains won some notable victories but the arrival of Mountjoy as Lord Deputy in 1600 reinvigorated the flagging English resistance. Hy-Many had capitulated to Elizabeth's forces in 1585 but over the following ten years Red Hugh O'Donnell gained control of practically the entire province. O'Donnell even inaugurated an O'Kelly chief of Hy-Many in his quest to return the province to the Gaelic chiefs. Brian Og O'Kelly of Cluain na gCloidhe became an ally of O'Donnell and towards the end of the century they struggled to keep control over the province as they were put under enormous pressure by the resurgent English forces. Catholic Spain had promised assistance to the northern chieftains but did not send a substantial force to Ireland until 1601 and they landed in the worst possible location for their weary armies, Kinsale in County Cork. O'Neill and O'Donnell had to march their armies from the North to the South in terrible weather conditions and through hostile territories. O'Donnell marched from Donegal through Connacht, his chosen route passed through Co. Roscommon and Brian Og O'Kelly and his army joined O'Donnell's forces as he was marching through. We do not know the surnames of the soldiers in the army raised by Brian Og but it is probable that many of these surnames still exist in the area today. After a tortuous march they eventually arrived at Kinsale and found that the English forces had already surrounded the Spanish army that had taken possession and fortified the coastal town of Kinsale. O'Neill arrived with his army and together with O'Donnell's soldiers and other Irish allies, including Donal Cam O'Sullivan Beare, they engaged Mountjoy's army on the night of the 23rd of December 1601. The battle was badly planned and badly fought by the Irish forces with Mountjoy repelling the Irish attack and restraining the Spanish in Kinsale and not allowing them to join the engagement. A complete victory for the Crown forces necessitated surrender from the Spanish and terms were agreed. O'Neill began the perilous journey back to Tyrone and O'Donnell set sail with the Spanish from the nearby port of Castlehaven. Brian Og remained in Munster and stayed with Donal Cam O'Sullivan Beare in County Kerry. The war continued but the battle of Kinsale had weakened the Irish resolve. O'Sullivan Beare lost his castle at Dunboy in early June 1602 after a long siege, the entire company of defenders were killed or later executed. He moved 300 of his people to a stronghold on Dursey island, these people were all non-combatants and included women, children and the elderly. The island was subsequently attacked and all the inhabitants were massacred. Donal Cam O'Sullivan Beare was forced to seek further aid from the Spanish who immediately sent a ship called the 'Patache' to Ardea in County Kerry. Shortly after its arrival O'Sullivan boarded the ship accompanied by Brian Og O'Kelly and brought the provisions that were on-board back to his castle. He then wrote letters to the King of Spain pleading for large scale military assistance[10]. On the 7th of June 1602, Brian Og

---

[10] Public Records Office, *Calendar of State Papers relating to Ireland 1601-03*, B.F Mahaffy (ed), pp 424-425. Brian Og O'Kellys stay with the O'Sullivan Beare is recorded in an 'examination' by the English forces of a captured Irish combatant from Co. Clare, dated the 12th of June 1602.

O'Kelly of Cluain na gCluide sailed on the 'Patache' from Ardea accompanied by Donnough McCarthy and Donnough McMahon O'Brien McEnaspicke of Thomond[11]. They brought with them letters written by O'Sullivan Beare, William FitzGerald (the Knight of Kerry) and Richard Tyrrell to the Spanish King but they found on arrival in Spain that no military assistance was forthcoming. The English forces were closing in on O'Sullivan Beare and he had to act, he gathered his remaining followers that numbered 1,000 and began the now infamous journey from their base in County Kerry to their allies in Ulster, they passed on their way within two miles of Cluain na gCluide, the lands of their ally Brian Og O'Kelly. After two weeks hard marching through hostile terrain in terrible weather O'Sullivan Beare and his followers arrived in County Leitrim, the home of their allies the O'Rourkes. Only 35 of the original 1,000 people had survived the trek, many were lost in skirmishes along the way and to starvation. O'Sullivan Beare decided to remain in Leitrim with his remaining followers and not continue on to Ulster. He eventually made his way to Spain to join Brian Og O'Kelly and the ever expanding exiled Irish community on the continent. He was personally welcomed by the King of Spain and was subsequently made Knight of Santiago. O'Sullivan Beare's past caught up with him however, he was murdered by an English spy just as he was leaving Mass in the Plaza de Santo Domingo in Madrid in 1618, the spy received £500 for this deed, an enormous amount of money at the time. Parts of modern day Mount Talbot, Athleague and other surrounding villages contain people with surnames associated with East Kerry and West Cork, these names include Murphy, Galvin, Leary, Cronin, Carr, Quigley and Connell (from O'Connell). The majority of these surnames can be traced back to O'Sullivan Beares march through the area as some weary travellers in his entourage decided to settle in the locality rather than to march onwards to an unknown fate.

Donal Cam O'Sullivan Beare of South Kerry, Brian Og O'Kelly of Cluain na gCloidhe stayed with O'Sullivan Beare for over 5 months after the battle of Kinsale and brought letters from him to Spain on a ship called the 'Patache'.

---

[11] Hiram Morgan (ed), *The Battle of Kinsale*, Cork, 2006, p377.

Brian Og O' Kelly joined the Spanish army shortly after arriving in Spain and within a couple of years he was deployed to the Netherlands, during his time in the Netherlands Brian Og joined the Army of his old enemy, England. This switching of allegiances may be difficult for the modern observer to understand but it must be remembered that no further assistance from Spain was forthcoming to the Irish and Hugh O'Neill had surrendered to the English in March 1603. Spain and England had signed a non-aggression pact in 1604 (the Treaty of London) bringing an end to the long Anglo-Spanish War and effectively ending any hope that Ireland would receive further military assistance from Spain. A soldier of the calibre of Brian Og O'Kelly was a welcome addition to the English Army and he proved his valour in numerous engagements. Brian received a certificate of army service from his commanding officers Sir Collisthenes Brooke and Colonel Sir Robert Cecil, Earl of Salisbury and he returned to Ireland and made his way to his lands at Cluain na gCloidhe. When Brian arrived home he found all of his lands under occupation and he was prevented from taking possession of them. A petition was subsequently prepared on behalf of Brian and sent to Lord Deputy Sir Arthur Chichester on the 20th of June 1609 by the Earl of Salisbury and other lords requesting that the lands be returned to their rightful owner. This petition states that Brian 'hath been in the service under the states of the Low Countryes. The said land hath been and still is unjustlie withholden from him by unlawfull means...he hath always since his infancie ben true and loyall to the Crowne of England and hath served in the warres in the low countryes[12]'. The petition understandably fails to mention Brian's involvement in the Battle of Kinsale where he fought against the armies of Queen Elizabeth. The petition was a success as the lands were subsequently returned to Brian by King James I with the exception of Tully, Garrier and Cloonruff. However, Brian and his brother Teige of Attiknockan each received one eights of a quarter of land in Cloonruff from the King a few years later.

At the same time as Brian Og O'Kelly marched with Hugh O'Donnell to Kinsale his near neighbour Colla O'Kelly of Scrine, the '6th Lord of the Manor of Screen' also made his way to Kinsale. The purpose of Colla's march to Kinsale however was very different to his relative Brian Og's as he was joining forces with Elizabeth's army under Mountjoy. Colla's father was Roger O'Kelly of Aughrane who was Sheriff of Roscommon in 1590. This O'Kelly family were loyal to the crown and Colla's great grandfather Hugh was granted the freedom of England by Philip and Mary by letters patent in 1557. They were given the English title 'the Lords of the Manor of Screen' in the early 16th century, Screen was a townland not far from Cluain na gCloidhe where Colla O'Kelly owned a large castle and lands, this area is now known as Scrine. Due to their loyalty to the crown it seems that this family temporarily lost control of Aughrane Castle and lands during the Nine Years War as an Irish soldier named Melaughlin O'Kelly had possession of Aughrane at this time[13].

Colla O'Kellys great great grandfather was Maghnus O'Kelly of Scrine who was a brother of Hugh O'Kelly of Athleague, the 27th chief of Hy-Many. Brian Og O'Kelly of Cluain na gCloidhe is directly descended from this Hugh O'Kelly of Athleague making these two opposing soldier's kinsmen and relatives.

---

[12]NAI, PRO M.2748, this document is a hand written copy of the original petition sent from Whitehall, England to Lord Deputy Chichester.
[13] Irish Patent Rolls of James I, Irish Manuscripts Commission, p162. The area was under the control of Red Hugh O'Donnell at this time and Colla would have been considered a traitor to the Irish Chieftains.

Colla O'Kelly rejected the letter 'O' from his surname after receiving a personal request to do so by Queen Elizabeth[14]. He served as a captain of foot under Lord Clanricarde at the battle of Kinsale. After the overall English victory in the nine years war Colla O'Kelly was rewarded for his loyalty by an extensive grant of land amounting to 9,000 acres in South Roscommon and East Galway[15]. A patent roll of James I from 1612 show all the lands and castles given to Colla and it also gives details of extra profitable business enterprises bestowed to him including a weekly market and a yearly fair at Knockcroghery and the right to run a ferry across the river Suck between Ballyforan and Muckloon[16]. This patent also confirms that Colla had regained possession of the lands at Aughrane and it also confirms that he owned Cloonakilleg, Tully and Garrier at this time. The townlands of Garrier and Tully were part of Brian Og O'Kellys lands prior to the Nine Years War and it seems possible that the person occupying all of Brian Og's land when he returned from serving with the British military in Holland was Colla O'Kelly of Scrine. Colla had an older brother called William Reagh who as the oldest sibling had a hereditary claim to the ancestral lands and the castle of Scrine. Colla subsequently convinced his brother to sign away his rights to this land and this document is preserved among the O'Kelly documents in the Archive section of Galway County Council.

Deed dated the 8th April 1608 confirming that William Reagh O'Kelly forfeits all rights to the lands of Scrine and other townlands in the area to his brother Colla O'Kelly (courtesy of Galway County Council Archives, Kelly Papers, G004/04/33).

---

[14] This autographed letter from Queen Elizabeth was preserved with the family documents at Castle Kelly but was lost in the early 19th Century. It was written 'in a very cramp hand on a small piece of greenish coloured paper'-Quote from Denis H. Kelly 19th October 1842 in the 'Tribes and Customs of Hy-many' by John O'Donovan.

[15] T. Cronin, *The foundations of landlordism in the barony of Athlone, 1566-1666*, MA thesis, UCG, 1977, p176

[16] Irish Patent Rolls of James I, Irish Manuscripts Commission, p241.

The Patent Rolls of James I also give details of lands taken by the crown from Irish Soldiers after the Nine Years War, some of these soldiers had been killed in the rebellion. One such patent roll gives details of lands at Garrier and Aughrane that were confiscated by the King: '1 qr parcel of the lands of Melaughlin O'Kelly McEdmund McLaughlin Moyle of Aghrane, slain in rebellion, in Dowlagh, 1 cart in Naghrough, ½ cart. parcel of the lands of Teige Hugh McDonagh O'Kelly of Garrower, Slain in Rebellion'[17]. This patent confirms that another branch of the O'Kellys had replaced Colla as owners of Aughrane prior to the war and this family had rebelled with the Ulster lords against the Queen. The Teige O'Kelly of Garrier that is mentioned had died in battle fighting against the crown. Garrier was owned at this time by Brian Og O'Kelly and this suggests that Teige was a kinsman of the O'Kellys of Cluain na gCloidhe.

Land Ownership

A Patent Roll from 1617 lists the landowners of almost the entire parish of Tisrara providing an invaluable record of the leading families in the area at this time. Landowners in Cluain na gCloidhe and its environs are listed as follows: 'Miles Cavanaugh of Clachan, gent.... The castle, town, lands and qr of Clachan; three-fourths of the qr of Cloonloghnan.....To Teige McBryan O'Kelly of Attiknockan, Bryan oge McBryan O'Kelly of Coolerough, Donough McBryan O'Kelly of Cloondarra and Rory McDonnell O'Kelly of Cloonengly, gent. Errick, ½ qr, Cloondarah, ½ Qr, Clooningly ½ qr, Clooncahan ½ qr, Attiknockan ½ qr, Killevoney 1 cart, Correnaphalis ½ cart, the two islands of Correlan and coill, one third of ½ cart.....To Donnagh McColla O'Kelly, Pierce Dillon and Bryan McHugh (O'Kelly)of Cloonacleige, gent, Cloonacleige ½ qr..'. This patent shows that Brian Og O'Kelly is now living in Cloonruff with Rory McDonnell O'Kelly resident in Cluain na gCloidhe. Brian Og's brother Donnagh has possession of Attiknockan. Myles Cavanagh owns Cloonlaughnan and the tower-house at Cloghan. Cloonakilleg and the islands of Corlann and Coill are in the ownership of Donnagh McColla O'Kelly, Pierce Dillon and Bryan McHugh O'Kelly.

The Books of Survey and Distribution for Roscommon give a full list of the landowners in the area in 1641. The Survey is a fantastic source of information as it provides details on the amount of land owned, the quality of the land (pasture, bog, woodland etc) and the number of profitable and unprofitable acres in each holding. At this time Brian Og O'Kelly owned Cluain na gCloidhe and Cloonca, he also owned other lands in the parish of Tisrara including Cullawinna, Cloonashade, Carrickmore and parts of Attiknockan and Errick. Donnogh McBrien McLaughlin Kelly owned Cloondara and he also owned the townland of Cornapallis in the parish of Tisrara. Dundermot (Bushy Park) was owned by four O'Kelly families namely Donnogh McLaughlyn McDonogh O'Kelly, Laughlin McFeogh Kelly, Hugh McCollo Kelly and Turlogh McCollo Kelly. Cloonakilleg was owned by John McCollo Kelly, Donnogh McCollo Kelly and Hugh McBryen Kelly. Justice Donnellan of Cloghan Castle owned Cloonlaughnan and all the bogland in Cloonakilleg. Garrier was owned by John Kelly who also owned the neighbouring castles at Aughrane, Correbeg and Scrine. The Burkes of Clanricarde owned the townland of Srahaunnagort (now Thornfield), the leader of this family held the titles of the Earl of St Albans and the Earl of Clanricarde at this time.

Maps of County Roscommon were prepared in 1633 and these are attached to the Books of Survey and Distribution for Roscommon, they show the parish of Tisrara and the townlands that existed at

---

[17]Irish Patent Rolls of James I, Irish Manuscripts Commission, p162.

this time. In the Barony Maps there are two castles shown in the area, the first one is located in Cloonakilleg and the second castle is shown in Cloonlaughnan. The maps are not very accurate but the river Suck is plotted reasonably accurately and may be used to estimate the location of the featured townlands and structures shown on the maps.

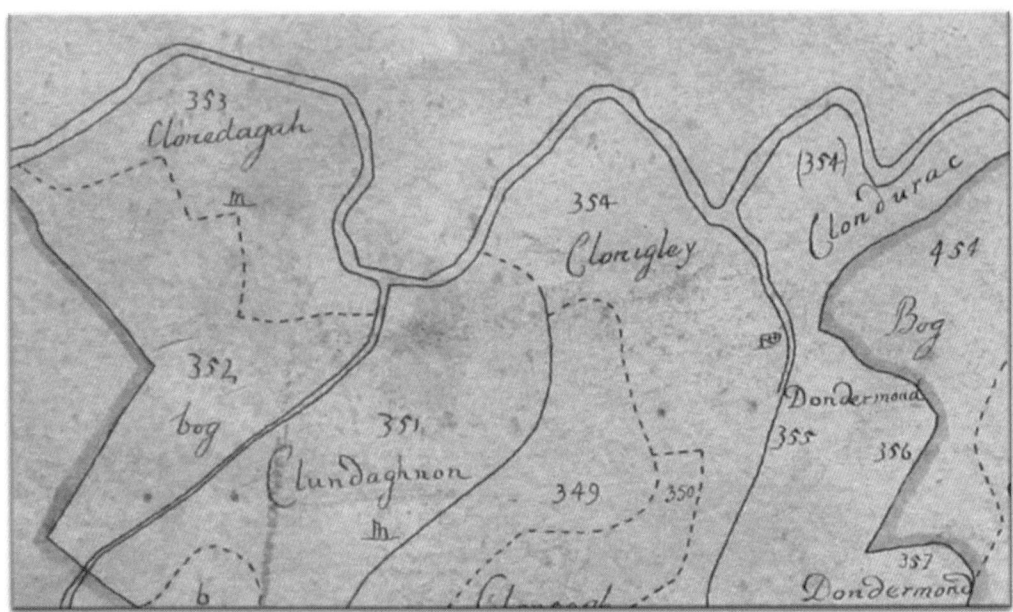

Down Survey Map of 1633 showing Cluain na gCloidhe (Clonigley) and adjacent townlands. A castle may be seen within the townland of Cloonakilleg (Cloneclagah) and another castle is shown in Cloonlaughnan (Clundaghnon)

The river Suck is shown as a double line in the top half of the map with the Clooneleen Stream and the Millrace Stream shown entering into the Suck from the south. The townlands referred to are Cloneclagah (Cloonakilleg), Clundaghnon (Cloonlaughnan), Clonigley (Cluain na gCloidhe), Clondarae (Cloondara) and Dondermond (Bushy Park). The castle in Cloonakilleg was located not surprisingly on the highest ground in the townland. Cloonlaughnan Castle seems to have been a bigger structure and this was located within or adjacent to the modern townland of Cartron.

A very interesting structure is shown on the map along the banks of the Clooneleen Stream. This structure was a water mill owned by Brian Og O'Kelly and it was used for grinding large amounts of corn. The survey maps only showed objects that added value to an area and a mill was a structure of immense importance in 17th century Ireland. The building was most likely constructed from stone and it was located on the Mount Talbot side of the stream a short distance upstream of the modern road (N63).

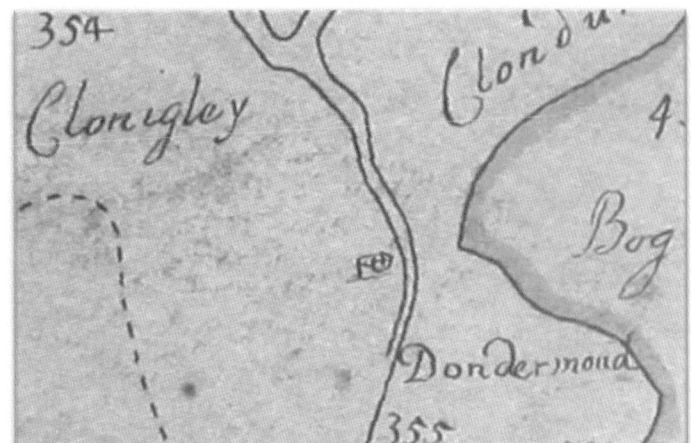

Water Mill at Clooneleen
from Down Survey Map.

Modern Photo of the stream at Clooneleen, the 17th Century Water Mill existed on the left bank of the stream.

Larger scale County Maps were also prepared at this time and they show the townlands of Cluain na gCloidhe and Cloonca being enclosed to the west by the river and east by bog and forest leaving only a narrow channel of high ground to the south to allow uninhibited access to the area. The County Maps for Co. Galway depict the area now known as Garrier as 'Carra'. The Gaelic name 'Carra' suggests that a causeway or stepping stones existed here and these must have been used to access the ford that existed across the river Suck at this time.

Down Survey County Maps – Showing Parish of Tisrara and parts of adjoining Parishes.

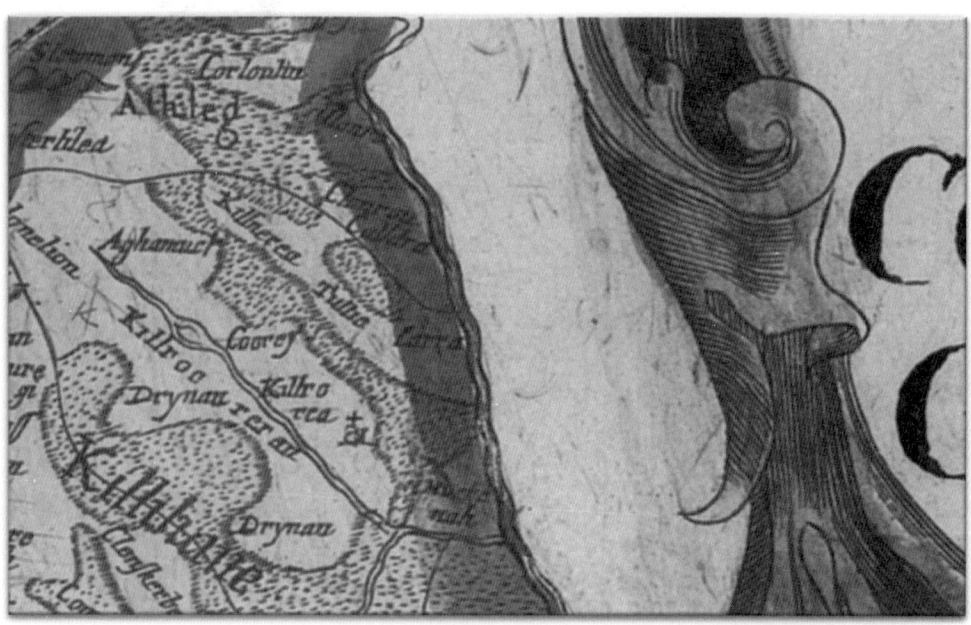

Down Survey County Maps – West of river Suck in Co. Galway. The ford crossing the River existed approximately where the map shows the word 'Carra' (meaning causeway or stepping stones).

The Cromwellian War and its Aftermath

The Gaelic and old English Catholic families that had survived the land confiscations of the Nine Years War had in the following decades been steadily displaced at the top of Irish society. The Irish Parliament constituencies had been altered over the years and by 1641 Catholics held just 70 out of 240 seats. The Irish rose in revolt in 1641, forced into action by the repressive anti catholic laws instigated by the Irish Parliament. The Irish still accepted Charles I of England as their monarch but wanted Catholics to be treated equally with full representation in Parliament. The first year of the rebellion developed into general disorder with terrible ethnic atrocities being committed particularly in the northern section of the Country.

In late 1641 a meeting or rendezvous took place at the 'ford of Garroure' (Garrier)[18], in attendance at this meeting were the Earl of Clanricarde, Sir Charles Coote and the President of Connacht, Lord Ranelagh, three of the most prominent and powerful men in the Country. Also in attendance were other local gentry from the barony of Athlone, all these men would have brought their armies to the meeting as tension was high and the area was in open rebellion. The purpose of the meeting was to try and reach agreement on what steps were necessary to counteract the rebellion. Clanricarde and Coote were very wary of each other and mistrust existed all through the early stages of the war primarily due to their conflicting political and religious views. During this volatile meeting one of Lord Ranelaghs soldiers named Thomas McEgan noticed two footmen *'upon a bog towards a wood'*, he believed these men were rebels and rode away from the meeting and followed the two footmen into the bog where he *'presented his carbine and gave fire'*[19]. The carbine musket jammed and before McEgan could reload the two rebels killed him and fled on foot towards the safety of the woodland. It is not clear where this bog and wood were located but they would not have been too far from the current bridge at Mount Talbot. The two footmen were believed to be soldiers attached to the Irish regiment of Conn O'Kelly of Cluain na gCloidhe (it is probable that this Conn O'Kelly was a son of Brian Og O'Kelly). The significance of this event is enormous as it gives a clear understanding of the volatility of the times and it also signifies the importance of the ford between Cluain na gCloidhe and Garrier. It also highlights the fact that the O'Kellys of Cluain na gCloidhe were one of the first families in Connacht to rise out with the rebels.

A government known as the Irish Catholic Confederation was formed by the disaffected Catholics in Kilkenny on the 24th of October 1642 and this brought more order to the rebellion. The Confederation was formed two months after the English Civil War began in August 1642 and Charles I needed as many soldiers as possible in England, he therefore took a less militant approach to the Irish Rebellion and a ceasefire was declared in September 1643. The war continued sporadically during the following years with more ceasefires declared and the subsequent engagements that took place generally involved the Irish against forces who had sided with the English parliamentarians.

In Connacht the Irish did not officially organise an army until late December 1641 when at a meeting held by the confederates in Ballintubber the aging Brian Og O'Kelly of Cluain na gCloidhe was appointed a Colonel of the Connacht forces. An attack was made in January 1643 on the castle at

---

[18] TCD, 1641 Depositions, MS 830, fols 108r-109v.
[19] Ibid, fols 110r-111v.

Castlecoote where 1,200 confederate soldiers were repelled by Sir Charles Coote the owner of the castle and a man possessed with an intense hatred of Catholicism. Coote was subsequently driven from Connacht by confederate forces in September 1643 and he went directly to London to try to convince the King to send more soldiers and provisions to fight the rebels. When the King refused Coote immediately declared for Parliament. He did not return to Ireland until May 1645 after being made parliamentary president of Connacht by Cromwell. Roscommon castle was taken by the confederates under General Preston in June 1646 five days after a major confederate victory at Benburb by General Owen Roe O'Neill. It is probable that Brian Og O'Kelly of Cluain na gCloidhe took no part in the direct fighting due to his advancing years but his brothers and his sons were active and may have taken part in the taking of Roscommon Castle.

John Kelly of Aughrane was a son of Colla O'Kelly and he was a close friend of Ulick Burke, who held the official titles of the 'Earl of Clanricarde' and the 'Earl of St Albans'[20]. Clanricarde was a Catholic but was loyal to the crown sitting as a member of the House of Lords in the 'Long Parliament' that commenced on 3rd Nov 1640. He was alarmed at the outbreak of the rebellion in 1641 and raised a regiment of foot to defend the city of Galway from the rebels. John Kelly of Aughrane was made colonel of infantry of his own raising and he subsequently stationed a garrison in Ballygar Castle on instruction from Clanricarde[21]. John also owned the castle and lands of Correbeg near Cluain na gCloidhe and the Earl of Clanricarde is recorded as staying at this castle as a guest of John Kelly in 1641.

As Clanricarde was a man of enormous political and financial power he came under immense pressure from his fellow Catholics to join the Confederation. Clanricarde was sympathetic to the cause of the Confederates and he managed to avoid direct confrontation with the Catholic armies. In the early years of the war he worked covertly with the Connacht Confederates but refused to openly declare his support. As the war progressed and the Parliamentarians were inflicting heavy losses on the Kings forces in England, Clanricarde began to seriously consider uniting with the Confederates. He wrote a letter to James Butler (Earl of Ormond and commander in chief of King Charles army in Ireland) in December 1644 requesting permission to temporarily hand over to the Confederates his castles at Athleague and Ballygar so *'that they may place a garrison there for preservation of the Country from spoil'*[22]. The confederates armies were under enormous pressure in south Roscommon and Clanricarde writes that they *'met with disaster in my town of Athleague'*, Clanricarde is concerned that if the only two passable fords in winter months are not secured then his lands west of the River Suck will be pillaged by the Parliamentarians. The two fords in question were at Athleague and Cluain na gCloidhe. He pleads with Ormond to allow him to hand over the castles *'which he conceives men of reason should not refuse to do'*. This letter confirms that Clanricarde is extremely concerned about his lands and within a year he is openly supporting the confederates. It is believed that in 1646 the confederate general Owen Roe O'Neill stayed for a night in Colonel John Kelly's castle at Scrine thus confirming that O'Kelly and Clanricarde were now fully behind the Irish Confederate cause.

---

[20] The family were stripped of the title 'Earl of St Albans' after the Cromwellian war.
[21] Ballygar Castle was owned at this time by the Earl of Clanricarde and it was a separate Castle to Aughrane, Ballygar Castle was not inhabited after the Cromwellian war and fell into disrepair. It is shown as a ruin in the first edition OS map from 1838.
[22] J Lowe, Ed., *Clanricarde Letter Book 1643-47*, p120 & 121.

In 1646 Parliamentarian Officer Major Ormsby was marching his regiment from Athleague towards the ford at Cluain na gCloidhe when his forces encountered Confederate soldiers. In a deposition taken after the war a Robert Clarke recalled that the event occurred '*at a little wood neer unto Bryan Kellys Mill*'[23]. This Mill belonging to Brian Og O'Kelly of Cluain na gCloidhe was located at Clooneleen, during the skirmish a Trumpeter attached to Ormsby's regiment was slain by Confederate soldiers. Hugh McGerraghty of Fuerty and Bryan McOwen Kelly of Athleague were named in the depositions as the men who killed the Trumpeter and they were part of a larger confederate army that was under the control of the O'Kellys of Cluain na gCloidhe.

In January 1649 the 'Second Ormond Peace' was declared and this secured an official alliance between the Confederates and the Royalists. Even though they generally shared the same religion this uniting of these forces did not improve the chances of an Irish victory due to the centuries old mistrust that existed between the Gaelic Irish and their Anglo-Irish neighbours. After the parliamentarians achieved victory in the English Civil war and the subsequent be-heading of Charles I, Oliver Cromwell arrived in Ireland on 15[th]August 1649 to quell the rebellion at the head of an army of 12,000 battle hardened soldiers and a large train of siege artillery. Cromwell's forces joined with Parliamentarian soldiers already stationed in Ireland and together they routed the Irish with a ferocious savagery that the Irish soldiers or the civilian population had never witnessed before and by late 1652 the entire country was in the hands of the Parliamentarians. Cromwell had returned to England prior to the assault on Connacht leaving his son and Sir Charles Coote to close out the war. It was Colonel John O'Kelly of Aughrane that surrendered the fort of Jamestown (near Carrick on Shannon) to the Parliamentarians. This strategically important fort had been held by the Irish since 1649 when it had been taken from the armies of Sir Charles Coote. It was one of the last Confederate garrisons to surrender to the Parliamentarians in the country. The surrender terms offered and accepted by Col. John Kelly were as follows:

1. That Jamestown be surrendered by three of the clock in the afternoon, with articles for all stores of ammunition and public stores of provision.
2. That the Governor, Officers and Soldiers shall have quarter for life, liberty to depart the town with their arms, colours flying, bullets in bouch, one barrel of powder, match and bullet proportional and six days provision, bag and baggage, with a safe convoy to any place desired.
3. That such of the inhabitants as desire to stay shall have protection, enjoy their goods and corn in ground, paying contribution according to their estates, and those who will remove shall have six weeks time to remove their goods.
4. That Colonel John Kelly, and such of his friends as shall submit to the state before the last of this month, shall enjoy their estates in lands, goods and chattels as freely as others of their condition, upon a general settlement and that such officers, soldiers, and others as desire the protection of the state shall be admitted there unto, provided they lay down arms before the end of this month, provided also they are not guilty of the massacres and robberies committed upon the English in the first year of the war, nor under protection, nor served the Parliament in their armies since the 9th of August 1649.

---

[23] TCD, 1641 Depositions, MS 830, fols 203r-203v.

5. That the said Colonel John Kelly shall have licence, at any time, for 4 months ensuing the date hereof, to depart this nation, if he shall desire the same and in the meantime four servants, with their horses, and arms, be allowed unto him in passing to and fro (for his security), in the Parliament quarters, where his occasions are, and that his wife and children shall enjoy the benefit of these articles in his absence.

6. That the said John Kelly shall have liberty to reside in the Castle of Aghrane or elsewhere upon his estate, free from molestation, with twelve musketeers for his defence, and that arrears of the contribution there to be not laid upon him for his estate lying in the half barony of Killian.

The surrender terms seem quite agreeable particularly item 6 allowing John to reside in his Castle at Aughrane. Item 4 clearly states that if he surrenders to the parliamentarians he will retain ownership of all the lands he had in his possession prior to the war. This seems however not to have been honoured as the total amount of land he actually possessed after the war was 1,000 acres[24], a reduction of 8,000 acres from what he had inherited from his father Colla prior to the rebellion. John subsequently re-gained possession of *'the manor, castles, towns and lands of Skryne'*[25], the townland of Cloonakilleg and a number of other townlands after the restoration of the monarchy under Charles II.

After the complete surrender of the Confederates the Cromwellian Parliament began the process of confiscating lands from the Catholic Irish. Connacht and County Clare were selected as areas to be used for the transplantation of dispossessed landowners from other parts of the country. Many of the existing landowners in Connacht also had their lands confiscated to make land available to the new settlers. The Parliament carried out testimonies or 'depositions' and local Irish families were accused of committing widespread murder of Protestants during the first year of the war. The O'Kellys of Cluain na gCloidhe, Cloondara and Dundermott were interrogated at hastily convened courts in Athleague throughout 1652 and 1653. The O'Kellys were in rebellion at an early stage in the conflict and losses they inflicted on enemy combatants during the first year of the war were classified as murders and not war casualties. As mentioned previously in this section soldiers under the command of Brian Og O'Kellys son Conn were accused of killing Thomas McEgan (soldier) at a wood near Cluain na gCloidhe in 1641[26]. In a separate deposition taken from a John Dodwill, Conn O'Kelly was accused of being involved in the killing of a trooper called Thomas Kiggan during a skirmish elsewhere in the parish of Tisrara, the other men involved were named as Callaugh O'Kelly of Funshinagh and Hugh O'Kelly of Turpane[27]. Daniel O'Kelly of Dundermot and Teige O'Kelly of Attiknockan were questioned at Athleague on the 20th of March 1652 about the killing of a 'Trumpeteer' in the army of Major Robert Ormsby of Athleague. Turlough McColla O'Kelly of Dundermot was separately questioned at Athleague about the killing of the Trumpeteer *'neere unto*

---

[24]Galway County Council Archives, Kelly Papers, G00/04 /124. Letter from Duke of Ormond to Lord Chancellor dated 26th of February 1661, this letter states 'Colonel John Kelly having upon the distribution of lands in Connacht by the late usurpers gotten 1,000 acres of land'. R.C Simington, *The Transplantation to Connacht 1654-58,* IMC 1970, p132 states that John Kelly of 'Corbeg' received 923 acres in the parishes of Tisrara and Killeroran (John Kelly of Aughrane owned the castle at Corbeg adjacent to Cloondara).
[25] Galway County Council Archives, Kelly Papers, G00/04/ 45
[26] TCD, 1641 Depositions, MS 830, fols 110r-111v.
[27] Ibid, fols 030r-031v.

the *Mill of Bryann oge Kellys in the parish of Tisserara*[28]. As mentioned previously in this section this event occurred at Clooneleen during a skirmish between the parliamentary forces under General Ormsby and the confederate forces under the O'Kellys. The Commonwealth Government were collecting all the information necessary to secure the convictions of the extended family of the O'Kellys of Cluain na gCloidhe to 'legitimise' the confiscation of their lands. As Brian Og O'Kelly was the leader of the O'Kelly armies in this area, special attention was given to his evidence. Robert Clark, one of the Commissioners for the Administration of Justice interrogated a Brian Kelly in late 1652. This 'examination' omits the address of the suspect but the contents of the document strongly suggest that the person named is Brian Og of Cluain na gCloidhe. Brian stood accused of killing a Robert Stanly at a location between Castlecoote and Athleague in 1641. Stanly was bringing provisions to the English army from Athleague to Castlecoote when he encountered Brian and his allies. Stanly was a parliamentarian soldier but the interrogator believed him to be unarmed which seems very unwise for the job in hand. The concluding line of this deposition shows the decision reached by Commissioner Clark: '*Bryen Kelly his examination about the murther Robertt Stanly and the said Bryan committed to the comon gaole*'. Brian O'Kelly who was by this time in his seventies was convicted of murder and was to spend the last years of his long and eventful life in Jail as a common criminal. The depositions do not give details of what happened to his brothers, sons and extended family who served with him during the rebellion but we do know that most of them disappear from written sources. Brian Og O'Kellys brother Teigh of Attiknockan had a son called Edmund who was killed fighting for the Confederates during the war. After the castle and lands of Attiknockan were confiscated, Edmunds widow Evelyn received land in Dysart and moved there with their son Teigh[29]. Descendants of this significant family still reside in the area today[30]. The fate of the other O'Kelly women and children are unknown. Transportation to the English colonies in Barbados is the fate that befell many families of Irish soldiers, to live as indentured labourers in the vast profit making estates that existed on these newly acquired islands. Prior to the war Laghlin O'Kelly owned a small amount of land in Dundermott[31] and after the land was confiscated he was transplanted to Rahara where he received 37 acres[32]. Besides Brian Og, no details exist of the fate of the O'Kelly soldiers from the area, the ones that did not end up in jail were probably transported out of the country where they joined other Catholic armies in Europe. It is believed that over 1,000 O'Kelly soldiers left the area after the war as part of the surrender terms imposed by the victorious Parliamentarian army.

Comparing the landowners listed in the Roscommon Books of Survey and Distribution from 1641 with the landowners listed after the Act of Settlement of 1652 we can see very clearly the vast amounts of lands lost by Brian Og and his immediate and extended family. The O'Kelly castles at Cloonakilleg and Cloonlaughnan were immediately knocked down by the Cromwellian Government, all 'superfluous' castles were removed in Roscommon by Sir Charles Coote to avoid possible

---

[28] Ibid, fols 204r-204v.
[29] R.C Simington, *The Transplantation to Connacht 1654-58*, IMC 1970, p238.
[30] R.C Simington ed, *Books of Survey and Distribution*, Roscommon, Dublin 1949, p107. 'Evellin and Teigue Kelly' are shown as owning 127 acres in feevaghmore, Dysart.
[31] The Roscommon Books of Survey and Distribution list a 'Laughlin McFeogh Kelly' as owning 61 acres of profitable land in 'Dondermot' in 1641, p113.
[32] R.C Simington, *The Transplantation to Connacht 1654-58*, IMC 1970, p240. To have received any land in the Act of Settlement Laghlin O'Kelly must have been a non-combatant in the Cromwellian War.

repossession by the conquered people. The castles at Scrine and Correbeg however seem to have lasted for a number of years after the Cromwellian War but they too were demolished before the end of the century. The courts at Loughrea and Athlone divided out the lands of Roscommon among transplanted landowners and the few remaining native landowners. The list of O'Kelly lands that were seized in the parish of Tisrara include: Cluain na gCloidhe, Cloondara, Cloonca, Derrinlerrig, Attiknockan, Cornapallis, Dundermott, Cullawinna, Erric and Cloonashade. Cromwell's transplantation to Connacht signalled a new chapter in the history of Cluain na gCloidhe and its environs with the arrival of an old Anglo Norman family, the Talbots of Templeogue, Co. Dublin.

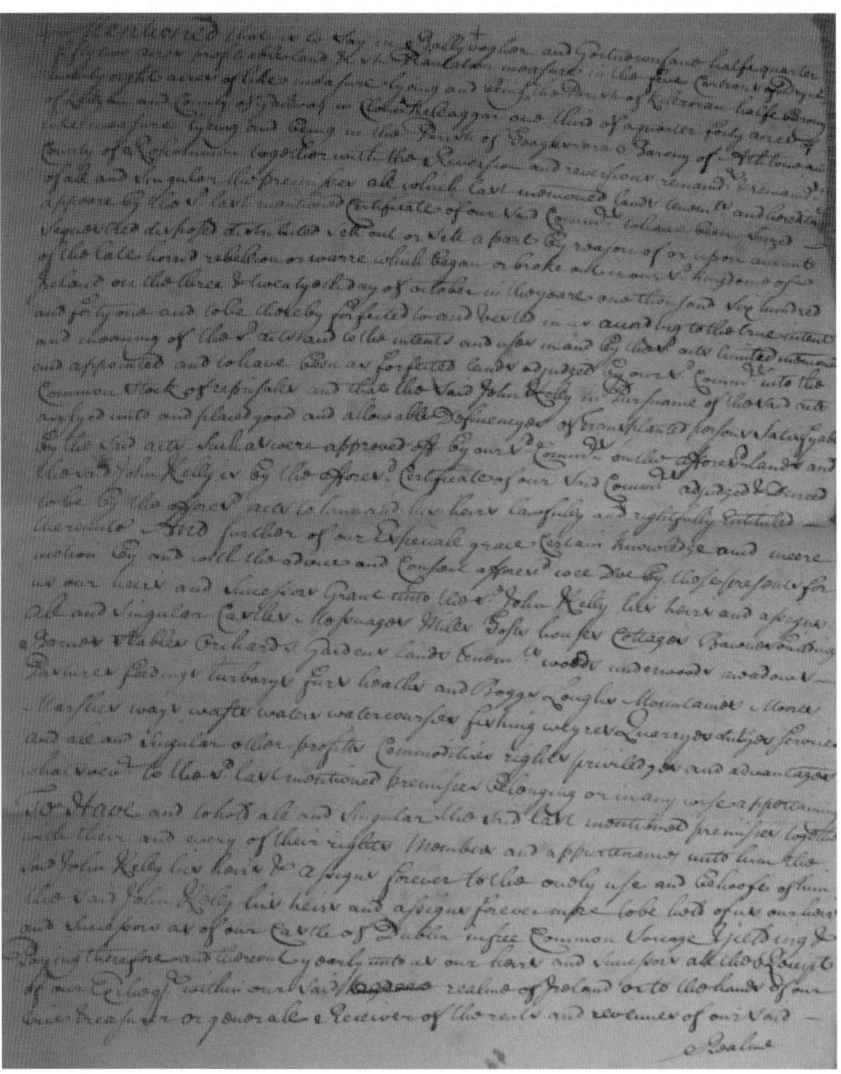

Deed dated the 15th of February 1676 confirming that Cloonakilleg and other townlands have been re-granted to John Kelly of Aughrane by King Charles II (see centre of fourth line of text). Galway County Council Archives, Kelly Papers, G00/04/88.

The Talbots

The Talbots were granted all the lands previously owned by Brian Og O'Kelly and they were also granted some other holdings that had belonged to the extended O'Kelly family. In total Sir Henry Talbot received 1,140 acres of land in the area[33], he was also granted 978 acres in the barony of Ballintober and 475 acres in the barony of Roscommon (parishes of Kilcoolagh and Shankill). Penders Census of 1659 shows Sir Henry Talbot living at Cloondara and owning most of the surrounding lands. Living with him in Cloondara at this time is Theobald Dillon who was 7th Viscount Dillon of Costello-Gallin, Theobald was married to Sir Henry's daughter Mary. Henry seems to have been a landowner of importance prior to and during the Cromwellian war, he was a direct descendent of the powerful Talbot family of Malahide. He married Margaret Talbot of Carton (Maynooth) and had eight children, James, Barbara, William, Elizabeth, Bridget, Mary, Alice and Ellen. It is difficult to ascertain the exact location of the Talbots residence within the townland of Cloondara, as mentioned previously in this chapter Cloondara contained a large double ringfort and it is probable that Sir Henry lived within the confines of these forts as it would have acted as a formidable defensive barrier to possible attack from the remaining dispossessed landowners. Modern aerial photos of the double ringfort in Cloondara reveals that one of the forts was not the regular circular shape (see aerial photo shown in chapter 2). It contained two corners on its north east side which suggest a shape more associated with an Anglo Norman site. The side of the fort nearest the river is curved suggesting the fort was originally circular but adapted later to suit the needs of the new inhabitants.

Throughout the 17th century the Talbots of Templeogue carried out many duties for the government including acting as Commissioner of the Muster and providing a mounted archer to the militia. They also had responsibility to the citizens of Dublin to look after the water course for which they were granted a tribute of corn paid by Mills drawing water power from the course. In 1627 Sir Henry inherited Templeogue and in 1635 he was returned as a Member of Parliament for Newcastle Lyons but was subsequently expelled for non-attendance. When the rebellion of 1641 commenced he played a non-active role and moved to County Kildare to live with his brother in law Sir John Dongon. However his loyalty to the crown was subsequently questioned by the Lord Justices and the Council who wrote to the Secretary of State, Sir Edward Nicholas in August 1642 complaining about the behaviour of Henry and his bother in-law, stating that *'Sir John Dongan, baronet, and Henry Talbot esqr., who have late, privately and without our licence and privity departed hence for England, have some commission or instructions from the rebels to negotiate for them in England'*, they ask the secretary to *'have on eye on them'* and suggest that they should be imprisoned *'as there may be cause'*[34]. It seems however that King Charles I believed that Henry Talbot may be of some use in his impending separate battle with parliament as he awarded Henry a knighthood. Sir Henry Talbot subsequently supported the King throughout the English Civil War, after the Parliamentarians under Oliver Cromwell gained overall victory, Sir Henry's loyalty to the King resulted in the loss of his castle and lands at Templeogue and he was forcibly transplanted to Cluain na gCloidhe. Ironically he had looked at the possibility of buying lands in this area prior to the rebellion that were offered for sale

---

[33] R.C Simington, *The Transplantation to Connacht 1654-58*, IMC 1970, p234.
[34] The Irish Manuscripts Commission, *Letters and Papers relating to The Irish Rebellion between 1642-46.* James Hogan (ed.) Dublin 1936, pp116-117.

to raise money for the Kings many wars by the then Lord Deputy Thomas Wentworth. After the restoration of the monarchy Sir Henry regained possession of the castle and lands of Templeogue and he also retained ownership of his lands at Cluain na gCloidhe.

The Books of Survey and Distribution for County Roscommon show Sir Henry Talbots son James Talbot having possession of Cluain na gCloidhe and all the surrounding lands in the 1680's and it was James that officially changed the name of Cluain na gCloidhe to Mount Talbot. Historical records from this time indicate that James Talbot was living in Mount Talbot and this confirms that the family had moved out of Cloondara and constructed a large house or small castle within the townland of Mount Talbot. The location of this first Talbot residence is unknown but it is probable that it existed at the same location as Mount Talbot House that was constructed in the following century. James Talbot had also inherited lands and properties around Dublin from his father including Templeogue Castle. James leased Templeogue out to a Sir Thomas Domvile and he seems to have resided permanently in Mount Talbot. James Talbot married Bridget Birmingham and they had two daughters, Mary and Bridget.

The Williamite War

The War of the two Kings or Williamite War began in 1689 and was fought between supporters of the Catholic King James II and the supporters of Protestant Prince William of Orange. James had lost the English throne to his son in law William a year earlier in the bloodless coup termed the Glorious Revolution. The Talbots of Mount Talbot had remained Catholic and were fearful of the consequences of the appointment of a Protestant King to the throne of England. James Talbot the son of Sir Henry Talbot joined the armies of King James II as did his brother-in-law Theobald Dillon. James Talbot's uncle, Richard Talbot, the Earl of Tyrconnell was King James II Lord Deputy in Ireland between 1687 and 1688 and was disliked by Irish Protestants as he placed Catholics in positions of control in the state and the militia. A Patriot Parliament was set up in Ireland by King James in 1689 with Viscount Theobald Dillon in the House of Lords and James Talbot an MP in the House of Commons[35]. It sat from the 7th of May to the 20th of July 1689 and it was the only Parliament assembled in Ireland under James II. The Parliament passed legislation affirming that no act of the English Parliament was binding on Ireland unless passed by the Irish Parliament. Legislation was also passed relating to the repeal of the Cromwellian Land Settlement of 1652 and the second Act of Settlement of 1662. It is interesting that James Talbot signed up to this as if carried out it would result in the Talbots losing Mount Talbot and the descendants of Brian Og O'Kelly being reinstated to their ancestral lands. The Patriot Parliament never got to implement its legislation as William landed on Irish soil in June 1690 and assembled an enormous army of 36,000 well trained and disciplined soldiers. King James had an army of 25,000 at his disposal and the two forces met at the River Boyne near Drogheda on the 1st of July 1690. The Irish forces were routed and King James fled the battlefield and immediately departed for France. On leaving the battlefield it is believed that King James met the wife of Richard Talbot (James Talbots uncle) saying '*the rascally Irish have run away from me*', Mrs Talbot replied '*it seems your majesty has won the race*'.

---

[35] T Davis, *The Patriot Parliament of 1689*, 3rd edition, Dublin, p156 & 162. James Talbot held a seat in the Patriot Parliament for the town of Athenry, Charles O'Kelly of Aughrane held the seat for Roscommon so James had to look elsewhere for a vacancy.

James Talbot had been given the rank of Colonel in the army of James II and spent much of the early months of the war involved in attempting to secure the province of Connacht. He was however heavily involved in the next major field battle of the war together with Lieutenant-Colonel Theobald Dillon at the ancient O'Kelly stronghold of Aughrim. On the 12th of July 1691, 45,000 soldiers from eight European countries took part in the battle of Aughrim and by nightfall 9,000 soldiers lay dead on the battlefield, the bloodiest battle in Irish history. Among the dead lay Colonel James Talbot and Lieutenant-Colonel Theobald Dillon.

Edward MacLysaghts in his book entitled 'Irish Life in the Seventeenth Century' gives a poignant account of the battlefield at Aughrim after the Irish defeat: *'After the battle the English did not tarry to bury any of the dead but their own, and left those of the enemy exposed to the fowls of the air, for the country was then so uninhabited that there were not hands to inter them. Many dogs resorted to this aceldama where for want of other food they fed on man's flesh, and thereby became so dangerous and fierce that a single person could not pass that way without manifest hazard'.*

Mary Talbot had accompanied her husband Theobald Dillon to Aughrim and watched the slaughter unfold from the safety of the Irish camp. She did not have much time to mourn the death of her husband or the death of her brother, she moved on with the Irish armies and eventually ending up in Limerick where the final and deciding engagement of the Williamite War was to take place. During the siege of Limerick, Mary was killed by a shell from the artillery barrage on the city by William's armies. The armies of King James II, under Patrick Sarsfield, eventually surrendered and sought terms which were granted in the Treaty of Limerick on the 3rd of October 1691.

James Talbot had been charged with high treason at Swords on the 20th of August 1689 and was outlawed and attainted at Kilmainham on the 6th of April 1691. On the 18th of May 1694, 3 years after his death on the battlefield at Aughrim, all the lands he had owned in Dublin prior to the war were seized by King William. Templeogue Castle and lands were lost together with additional lands at Clondalkin, Gallonstown, Newcastle, Uppercross, Sagard and a premises in Rathcoole[36]. However the Talbots managed to retain ownership of their lands in Roscommon. Colonel James Talbot had died without issue and the lands of Cluain na gCloidhe passed briefly to his brother William and then to his nephew Henry Talbot. James Talbots daughter Mary had married John Burke the 9th Earl of Clanricarde in October 1684 and his other daughter Bridget married Valentine Browne from Westport, Co. Mayo. Valentine Browne's father John Browne had gained the rank of Colonel in the Irish Army of King James II.

In 1690 prior to the conclusion of the war Arthur Dillon the son of Theobald Dillon and Mary Talbot left Ireland with 2,000 raw recruits and entered the French military under his father's 'Dillon Regiment' and as part of Lord Mountcashel's Brigade. The French King sent 6,000 experienced soldiers in their place. After the Treaty of Limerick the Dillon regiment remained in the service of the King of France and recruited many of the Wild Geese Irish exile community that poured into France after the Treaty of Limerick. Arthur later became Governor of Toulon and was created Knight of the Thistle in 1715. The Dillon regiment remained part of the French army and fought for the French

---

[36] Margaret C. Griffith, *Calendar of Inquisitions formerly in the office of the Chief Remembrance of the Exchequer prepared from MSS of the Irish Record Commission*, Dublin 1991, p422, 423.

expeditionary force in the American Revolutionary War, capturing Granada from the British in 1779. During the French Revolution the regiment had remained loyal to the King of France resulting in its dissolution and its last leader Colonel Arthur Dillon was guillotined in 1794 by French Republicans.

At the time of the Williamite War, Charles O'Kelly was the owner of Aughrane Castle and lands including the townlands of Cloonakilleg, Garrier and Srahaunnagort (Thornfield). Charles was a son of Colonel John Kelly and commenced studying in St Omer's College in northern France at the age of 12. He was an exceptional student becoming fluent in Latin and Greek and proficient in Flemish, Spanish, French and Italian, therefore together with Irish and English, Charles could converse in eight languages. When the Cromwellian War started the then twenty year old was summoned home where he gained command of a troop of horse under the Marquis of Ormond. After the overall defeat in the War he left Ireland with 2,000 fellow Irish soldiers and joined the army of the exiled King Charles II in France and later offered his services to the King of Spain. He moved to England on the restoration of the monarchy and returned home in the early 1670's. He lived for a time at Correbeg before moving to Aughrane on his father's death in 1674. He held a variety of political positions under James II including Knight of the Shire for County Roscommon, he was a Burgess for the town of Athlone and he sat as an MP in the Patriot Parliament of James II for the County of Roscommon. His brother John Kelly of Cloonlyon also sat in the Patriot Parliament as an MP for the Borough of Roscommon. Charles and John would have sat in the same chamber as James Talbot of Mount Talbot. When the Williamite War began Charles was commissioned by the King to raise a regiment of Infantry. He fought most of the early part of the war in Connacht and like his neighbour and political colleague Colonel James Talbot he played an active role in the Battle of Aughrim where his son Denis, who fought in Lord Galway's regiment had his horse shot from under him. After defeat at Aughrim, Charles marched on Galway where his brother Lieutenant-Colonel John Kelly was captured by the enemy and held as a hostage during negotiations of the armies surrender terms at the island of Inis Boffin. Charles and his son Denis fought at the Siege of Limerick and when the War ended Charles returned to his home at Aughrane. The Treaty of Limerick ended the war and the terms agreed between Patrick Sarsfield on the Irish side and Baron de Ginkel on the English side were quite favourable to the Irish Catholics. Charles O'Kelly was almost 70 years of age at the end of the war and when he returned to live at Aughrane he wrote two very detailed books about his wartime experience including the best known 'Marcarie Excidium' or 'The Destruction of Cyprus'. This book was written in Latin and all the war combatants and the place names were given pseudonyms. It is the only contemporary account of the Williamite War from the Irish perspective and it seems he wrote it in Latin and with fictional characters to avoid prosecution by the victors of the recent War.

Charles saw thousands of his comrades that had survived the War board ships at the southern ports that would take them to the armies of Europe. The Treaty of Limerick contained a specific clause ensuring all family members could depart with each soldier but the ships did not have capacity for everyone resulting in many of the wives and children being left on the shore. Some women and children drowned trying in vain to swim to the ships after they were ordered to set sail and likewise many soldiers died after leaping from the ships to reach their families left on the shore. In his book 'The Destruction of Cyprus' Charles gives a wrenching account of these Wild Geese sailing out of Limerick Harbour: *'and now, alas! The saddest day is come, that ever appeared above the horizon of Ireland. The sun was darkened, and covered with a black cloud, as if unwilling to behold such a woeful spectacle, there needed noe rain to bedew the earth, for the tears of the disconsolate Irish did* abundantly moisten their native soile to which they were that day, to bid the last farewell. Those who resolved to leave it never hoped to see it again, and those who made the unfortunate choise to continue therein, could at the same time have nothing in prospect but contempt and poverty, chains and imprisonment, and, in a word all the miserys that a conquered nation could nationally expect from power and malice of implacable Enemyes. Here might be seen the aged Father (whom Yeares and Infirmityes rendred unfit to travail,) giving the last embraces to his onely son, Brothers parting in Teers, and the dearest Comerades forcibly divorced by a cruell Destiny, which they could not avoid. But Nothing was more dismall than the sad Seperation of Man and Wife; for tho' the Husbands and Children, but also of a Maintenance to be established for them in France, yet when the ablest Men were once got on shipboard, the Women and Children were left on the shore, exposed to Hunger and Cold, without any Manner of Provision, and without any Shelter in that rigourous Season, but the Canopie of Heaven; and in such a miserable Condition, that it moved Pitty in some of their Enemyes. The lamentable cryes of this poor forlorn Troup (when the Fleet that carried away their Fathers and Husbands was under Sail and gon out of Sight) would beget Compassion in Wolves and Tygers, and even in Creatures that were insensible....'[37]. Charles never recovered from the disappointment of losing the war, he realised that after three major wars in the 17th century and three losses that Gaelic Ireland was in a perilous position. He saw the Treaty of Limerick thrown aside to be replaced by the penal laws. Charles O'Kelly died in 1695 a broken man and the final paragraph of his book gives a clear picture of his tortured mind prior to his death: '...the publick Calamity of my Countrymen, unfortunate Countrymen in generall, and the lamentable Condition of some particular Friends, added to the Incommodities of old Age, rendring me unable to pursue that Remnant of a wofull History, that requires Ink mixed with the Writer's Teares; and the Fountain of my weak Eyes hath been drained up already, by the too frequent Remembrance of the Slaughter at Aughrim, and the sad Seperation at Limerick'[38]. On the death of Colonel Charles O'Kelly the lands and castle of Aughrane passed to his son and army comrade Captain Denis Kelly.

Kilconnell Abbey – Captain Colla O'Kelly (Nine Years War) , his son Colonel John Kelly (Cromwellian War) and grandson Colonel Charles O'Kelly (Williamite War) are all buried at this location, the abbey was founded in the early 15th century by William O'Kelly, Chief of Hy-Many.

---

[37] Colonel C. O'Kelly, Macarie Excidium or The Destruction of Cyprus, Ed by J.C O'Callaghan, Dublin 1850, p 156 to 158.
[38] Ibid, p 159.

Agreement between Colonel John Kelly of Aughrane and Captain Nicholas Mahon dated 22nd January 1672 relating to the impending marriage of John Kelly Junior and Mary Mahon, this document confirms that Colonel Charles O'Kelly lived for a time at Correbeg near Mount Talbot when he returned home from exile in Europe (Galway County Council Archives, G00/04/49).

The Donnellans of Cloghan Castle also played an active part in the Williamite War. This family had been large landowners in the area since the early 17th century and owned the entire townland of Cloonlaughnan. The Donnellans were an ancient Gaelic family who originally came from Ross near present day Elphin and were Ollamhs of poetry for the O'Connor Kings of Connacht, they were also the hereditary keepers of arms for the O'Kelly Chiefs of Hy-many. The O'Kelly Chief always had in his retinue a champion fighting man to answer challenges that may arise to single combat, this honour was generally bestowed on a member of the O'Donnellan clan and they were rarely defeated. After the Anglo-Norman invasion of Ireland the Donnellans subsequently proved to be loyal servants to the Crown and they were rewarded by a grant of Cloghan Castle and a large amount of surrounding land including Cloonlaughnan by Sir Richard Bingham, President of Connacht. Myles Kavanagh was living in Cloghan castle and owned the surrounding lands prior to the arrival of the Donnellan's.

Sir James Donnellan owned Cloghan Castle and lands before and after the Cromwellian War. He was the third son of Nehemiah Donnellan who was Archbishop of Tuam. He entered Trinity College in 1607, graduating with a BA in 1610. He was subsequently elected a fellow of Trinity in 1612 and graduated with an MA in 1613. He entered Lincolns Inn in 1616 and was called to the bar in 1623. Sir James was appointed Chief Justice of Connacht in 1634, he was elected Treasurer of the Kings Inns in 1639 and acted as Justice of Assizes for the north-west circuit between 1637 and 1641. He was a close friend of the Earl of Clanricarde who called him *'his true and faithful friend'*. Sir James supported Clanricarde during the Cromwellian war and was sent by the King Charles I to Oxford to negotiate a truce with the confederates in 1644. He served in the House of Lords throughout the Cromwellian war and after the war ended he retained all of his lands in the parish of Tisrara and actually received some additional lands in the parish. Sir James became a faithful supporter of the new parliamentarian regime and even went so far as to persecute his former political allies. He served at the High Court of Justice in 1653 and returned to the Common Pleas in 1655 and became a

Commissioner in matters testamentary in 1656. After the restoration of the Monarchy in 1660 he was received back into royal favour and re-entered the House of Lords in 1661. Sir James Donnellan died in 1665 and was buried in Christ Church Cathedral in Dublin. Sir James resided prior to his death at Rathwire in County Westmeath and he owned an enormous amount of land and property throughout the country, in his will he left Cloghan Castle and lands to his son Edmund Donnellan. Jamestown village that is located between Four Roads and Ballyforan is named after Sir James Donnellan.

Edmund Donnellan served as High Sheriff of Roscommon in 1664 and 1679 and was High Sheriff of Galway in 1666. He married twice, first to Hannah Gilbert of Kilminchy, County Laois who died in 1666, they had two sons James Donnellan of Cloghan and Gilbert Donnellan of Streamstown in County Westmeath. His second wife was Anne Coffy of Lynally in County Westmeath and they had two sons and five daughters. Edmund died in 1694 leaving his estate to his son James. James Donnellan of Cloghan married Anne Wentworth who was a sister of Lord Strafford, Anne had been a maid of honour to Queen Anne of England[39]. James was a Captain in the Army of King James II during the Williamite War and played an active role in the battle of Aughrim, his involvement on the side of King James suggests that this branch of the family had reverted back to the Catholic faith[40]. The Donnellans had their own army consisting of 600 local men including infantry and a mounted cavalry and they made all their own weapons at their foundry at Teach Shane. The Donnellan army together with their spouses marched to the battlefield of Aughrim by crossing the River Suck by ferry at Muckloon near Ballyforan. Local oral history believes that none of the people that arrived at Aughrim ever returned with many having been slain in battle. It is also believed that some of the Donnellan retinue that survived the battle subsequently settled in the area around Aughrim. Captain James Donnellan survived the war but he was in serious financial difficulties. A bill was presented to the Houses of Parliament in 1711 with the title: *'A bill for enabling James Donelan of Cloghan in County Roscommon, esquire, to sell or mortgage certain lands or tenements for payments of his debts, and for securing a jointure for his wife'*. The bill received Royal Assent on the 9th of November 1711, the bill was now an Act of Parliament and it seems James Donnellan subsequently sold and mortgaged some of his lands. James became a Member of Parliament for Roscommon in 1713 but was unseated by petition, possibly because of his religious background. The financial and political power of this branch of the Donnellan's was decimated and the great tower house at Cloghan began to fall into disrepair.

Gilbert Donnellan of Streamstown in County Westmeath had remained Protestant and had managed to retain much of his wealth after the war, his son Edmund took control of Cloghan after the death of his uncle James but died in 1738 at the young age of 37. Edmunds son Gilbert was born in 1733 and he gained possession of Cloghan when he reached the required age. He attended Eton public school in England between the years 1748 and 1751 and entered Trinity College Dublin in October 1751. Gilbert died without issue in 1778 and his will made reference to his preferred resting place: *'that I may be buried in the same place with my father in the Church of Tassara in the County of Roscommon afs. And I do hereby direct my trustees hereinafter named to lay out one hundred*

---

[39] Murray, J. (1824) *Letters to and from Henrietta, Countess of Suffolk and her second husband the Hon. George Berkeley from 1712 to 1767, Volume 1*, London, p98.

[40] Captain James Donellan's father wrote in his will that he would bequeath land to his grandsons *'if they are Protestants'*, this suggests that their father James was a catholic. Will taken from www.ballyd.com.

pounds according to the value of money in Ireland in erecting a monument and repairing said church in such manner as my uncle the Rev. Wm. Donnellan shall think proper'. This monument was erected by Gilberts family as requested in Tisrara old cemetery at Carrowntemple and parts of it still exist today. Gilbert had died in Middlesex, England where he had been living and he seems to have left all his lands in Ireland to his cousin William Rochford on condition that he adopted the Donnellan name. This William Rochford Donnellan is recorded as owning lands in Cloghan and elsewhere in Tisrara in the Tithe Applotment Books from 1838. The Donnellan estate reduced in size at the onset of the 19th century and by the 1830's the McGann family owned parts of the lands. By the early 1850's the estate was in the possession of the Reverend Edmond Riley and John Owen. The owners later suffered financial difficulties and advertised the estate for sale in the Encumbered Estates Court with the petitioner being Catherine Edwards Donnellan. By the late 1850s the estate was owned by the Reverend James McIvor and Percy Magan.

The Williamite War left a lasting impression on Mount Talbot and the surrounding areas with all the major landowners in the locality playing an active part in the battles, particularly the Battle of Aughrim. Many local people were slain in battle and many more were left without land and without the means of supporting themselves. An interesting fact about this time was the arrival in the area of families from other counties and in some cases from other countries. The battle of Aughrim in particular resulted in many people settling in the area, the late John Collins of Garrier believed that the Collins family came to Cloonakilleg at this time after taking part in the battle of Aughrim, *'they came from Limerick, a place called Mount Collins[41]'*.

---

[41] Taken from transcript of conversation between John Collins and Tommy Connolly at John's house in Garrier in the mid 1980's.

Chapter 4 - The 18ᵗʰ Century

The introduction of the Penal Laws in Ireland in the late 17ᵗʰ and early 18ᵗʰ Centuries resulted in many of the remaining Catholic Landowners converting to Protestantism. The Popery Act of 1703 stipulated that Catholic inheritances of land were to be equally subdivided between all of the landowners sons resulting in the dilution of the landholding, however if the eldest son converted he would become the sole inheritor of the entire estate. Catholics were prohibited from possessing arms, owning a horse worth more than £5, holding political positions, practising law, receiving an education and were not allowed to be members of a grand jury. The Talbots and the O'Kellys had spent the 18ᵗʰ century fighting for their rights but as the 19ᵗʰ century dawned they had no realistic chance of retaining ownership of their lands if they remained Catholic. The Talbots changed religion very soon after the conclusion of the Williamite War. Henry Talbot inherited Mount Talbot after the death of his father William in 1692, William had held the lands briefly after the death of his brother James at the battle of Aughrim. Henry Talbot married Isabella Forward and they had two sons, William Talbot and Reverend John Talbot. Henry held the office of High Sheriff for the county of Roscommon in 1713. When Henry died the lands passed to his son William who began building a large house in Mount Talbot during the 1730's, this house may have encompassed an earlier smaller structure built by Colonel James Talbot in the previous century. Herman Molls Map of Ireland from 1714 shows Mount Talbot as a crossing point for two important routes, mid and north County Galway to Dublin and Galway city and county to Roscommon. This map also shows the existence of a bridge crossing the river at Mount Talbot. It seems this bridge was constructed in the latter part of the 17ᵗʰ or the early 18ᵗʰ century as a ford was still the only means of crossing the river at the time of the Cromwellian War. The bridge must have been of poor construction as it was replaced with a new twelve arch stone bridge between the years 1750 and 1770. This bridge is still in existence and it is now part of the Galway to Roscommon National Primary Road (N63).

The village of Mount Talbot in the early and mid 18ᵗʰ century was entirely located on the Galway side of the River Suck with Talbots house being the only residence in existence on the Roscommon side. A newspaper report from the 24ᵗʰ of May 1743 gives details of the existence of an Inn and Spa at Mount Talbot. The report states: *'William Egan who kept new Inn near Mount Talbot Roscommon has moved to big house where William Rigney lately kept an Inn, he will provide lodgers with food. There is a Spa there, he will build a Ballroom in a pleasant grove over the Suck'*. The Inn was located on the banks of the river suck adjacent to the bridge within the townland of Garrier. It is unknown if William Egan ever got to build his Ballroom in a pleasant grove over the Suck. This report confirms that the construction of Mount Talbot house was completed by the early 1740's, most commentators have dated the house to 1749-50. Mount Talbot House was constructed in the Palladian Revival style that had become the most fashionable architecture of the early to mid-eighteenth century. The house contained two separate wings that were connected to it with high curved and arched walls with ornate urns on the parapets. Outbuildings were constructed to the east of the house enclosing a large yard and the back of one of the aforementioned wings formed the south western corner of the yard. The entrance to the avenue leading to the house was located directly across from the present day Cloonca road. In the years following the completion of Mount Talbot House a new twelve arch stone bridge over the river Suck and a single arch bridge over the Clooneleen Stream were constructed resulting in an impressive approach to the new house from the main roads.

William Talbot, constructed Mount Talbot House in the 1730's. He married Sarah Rose, on the 30th of May 1739 (courtesy of Donald Cameron).

Photo from the late 19th Century showing one of the impressive archways or arcades that connected Mount Talbot House to the outer wings. These arcades date to the construction of Mount Talbot House in the 1730's, The two men in the photo are Alex Eustace and Walter Tigue (courtesy of Emmy Eustace).

The Census of Elphin

The 1749 Elphin Census gives excellent details of the population of Mount Talbot and its environs. The census was authorised by the Protestant Bishop of Elphin, Edward Synge and the purpose of the census was to ascertain the ratio of Catholics to Protestants in the diocese. For the first time names other than the major landowners are made available together with their occupations and religion. The head of the house is named together with the amount of children that are under the age of 14 and also the amount of children over the age of 14. The survey also gives details on the amount of servants working for the various families in each townland. William Talbot owned Mount Talbot House at this time and he is shown in the census as having 3 children under the age of 14. Living in the house with him at this time were Miss Jane Rose Talbot, Miss Talbot and a Miss Southwell who was probably a visitor or may have been a governess to the children. Mount Talbot house had 16 servants carrying out various tasks, 14 of these servants were Catholic and 2 were Protestant[42]. As stated previously in this chapter no other house existed in Mount Talbot on the Roscommon side of the river at this time but 11 houses are listed in the village on the Galway side in the townlands of Garrier and Thornfield[43]. 47 people lived in these houses including a shopkeeper, a tailor, 7 labourers and 1 farmer. The surnames of the residents were: Walsh, Rigney, Morrisy, Stephens, Kennedy, Fallon, McDermott, Mannian, Kelly and Keogh.

A large settlement containing 32 houses existed in 1749 on the north eastern extremity of the townland of Mount Talbot in an area known as Clooneleen. This settlement seems to have developed around a Watermill and contained people with a variety of different occupations and trades. Among the occupants of the houses were a miller, a periwig maker, a constable, a nailor, a weaver, a gardener, a cowherd, a smith, a merchant, a butcher, a shoemaker, a joiner, 2 pumpmakers, 3 ale-sellers, 3 masons and 5 labourers. Many of these tradesmen may have worked on the building of Mount Talbot House together with its outbuildings and demesne walls. The population of Clooneleen village at this time was approximately 142 people making it considerably larger than the village of Mount Talbot [44]. Some of the occupations mentioned in the census suggest that the village also served as a meeting place for social and retail activities by people living outside the village in the surrounding areas. There were three 'ale-sellers' and these seem to have been busy establishments as nine people were shown as working in them. Interestingly two of them were owned by Catholics, Hugh Keogh and Denis Derham and one was owned by a Protestant called Widow Egan.

The Mill was in the possession of a William Kelly and this must also have been a hive of activity as 4 people are shown as working in the Mill. Andrew Tute had a butcher shop and he employed 3 people and a labourer called Richard Dillon had 2 employees. This mill was constructed by Brian Og O'Kelly in the early 17th Century and a skirmish occurred near here during the Cromwellian war. The surnames of all the residents of the village of Clooneleen in the mid 18th century were: Cuthburt, Conboy, Garman, Birn, Bodkin, Field, Walsh, Delany, Kelly, Pettit, White, Brenan, Hoey, Derham,

---

[42] Legg M.L, *The Census of Elphin 1749*, IMC 1968, p204.

[43] Ibid, p294, 295.

[44] An estimate for the total population of this village may be obtained by adding up the heads of each family, the children and servants and also adding spouses for each of the people listed that have children, this gives a figure of 142 people.

Lians, Egan, Keogh, Turner, Dillon, Graddy, Tute, Ward, Lawlor and Lians. None of the surnames in this census are preceded by 'O' and this suggests that the people had intentionally removed it from their surnames or it was purposely omitted by the authorities when writing up the survey.

It is difficult to ascertain when Clooneleen was established but looking at the amount of houses and businesses it seems this village was in existence for some time prior to the Elphin Census of 1749. There are a large number of medieval ringforts shown in early maps on the opposite side of the Clooneleen stream and the occupants of these forts may have been the people that commenced building the village in the centuries after the ringforts were no longer used as a place of habitation in the area. A settlement definitely existed in the mid 17th century as a mill is shown on the map attached to the Books of Survey and Distribution from the mid 1600's. Penders Census of 1659 show 13 people living in 'Clooneingly', this 'Clooneingly' is a mis-spelling of Cluain na gCloidhe (Mount Talbot) but we know that there were no houses other than the big house in the townland of Mount Talbot in the census of 1749 as all the houses were in the townland of Garrier. This suggests that the 13 people listed in the earlier census actually lived at Clooneleen but still within the townland of Cluain na gCloidhe.

It is also difficult to ascertain when Clooneleen ceased to exist as a place of habitation, it seems however that the centre of population shifted from here to Mount Talbot shortly after the Elphin census was carried out. Tisrara old cemetery at Carrowntemple contains a gravestone inscription for the Keogh Family dated July 1755. Hugh Keogh is listed as living in Clooneleen in 1749 but the gravestone inscription erected 6 years later states that Hugh Keogh was living at Mount Talbot: *'This monument was erected Ye 3rd of July 1755 by Mr Hugh Keogh of Mountalbot for his wife Jane Keogh for their posterity'*[45]. This change of address suggests that Hugh Keogh moved from Clooneleen to Mount Talbot sometime between the years 1749 and 1755. Oral history recalls that the village of Clooneleen was levelled by the local landlord not long after 1749. It seems the landlord needed to use this area for a 'sheepwalk' and the occupants of the houses were the unfortunate victims of his planned expansion into sheep farming. However eight houses remained in place and these were located at the eastern extremity of the village, these eight houses were later collectively called 'Churchborough' and they were in use until the mid 19th century when they also succumbed to 'progress' and were levelled by the landlord.

Another reason for the demise Clooneleen may be due to the occupations of the residents, none of the occupants are listed as farmers or tenants and they all worked at various trades that experienced a reduction in numbers in the latter half of the 18th century. With the Big House completed and landlordism firmly in place the occupations of the people living in the community changed from trades people or labourers to tenants, this trend is replicated nationwide at this time as landlords needed tenants to pay rent. None of the buildings that were located in Clooneleen village exist today but some evidence of habitation is still evident. Loose building materials are strewn along the site with a large volume of building stone scattered throughout the forest that now exists in the area.

---

[45] Higgins, J. *The Tisrara Medieval Church, Carrowntemple, Four Roads, Co. Roscommon, Its Archaeology and History*, Tisrara Heritage and Graveyard Restoration Committee, 1995, p135.

Modern photo showing evidence of former buildings at Clooneleen (P.Connolly, March 2014).

A large building stone used in one of the houses or businesses at Clooneleen is still visible along the edge of the modern forest road that leads through this area (P.Connolly, March 2014).

In the Elphin Census the townland of Cloondara contained 6 houses including the house inhabited by the local Vicar, Reverend William Digby[46]. Reverend Digby had two children aged over 14 years and had 6 servants, 2 protestant and 4 catholic. The other houses were occupied by Widow Bannon, Bryan Ceasey, William Kelly, Widow Lanis and Patrick Conboy, these families were all Catholics and had 11 children between them, no servants were employed in any of these houses.

Cloonlaughnan contained 30 houses including the house occupied by the local Catholic Priest Father Frank Hanley[47]. The names of the other occupants of this townland were Daniel Ward, Andrew Tute, William Kelly, Henry Lawler, James Lians, Patrick Dowel, Widow Box, Widow Walsh, Roger Killen, Patrick Tooll, Michael Egan, Hugh Conner, Denis Ward, Bryan Geraghty, Owen Daily, John Paine, Widow Bryan, John Fallon, Thomas Fallon, Luke Kelly, Thomas Cormick, Roger Kenedy, Mathias Treasey, Redmond Dillon, William Greely, Hugh Clogher, Augustine Clogher, John Dolan and Partick Concannon (the last 5 families lived in Cartron). All the families were Catholic with the exception of John Paine and his family. The townland included 2 joiners, 2 butchers, 9 labourers, 1 farmer, 2 tailors, 1 pumpmaker, 1 nailor and 2 tenants, there was 62 children living within the townland and 10 servants.

Cloonca contained 4 houses and these were occupied by Edward Giltenane, Roger Mullon, Bryan Mullon and Morgan Kenedy. These 4 families had 19 children between them and none of the families had any servants.

Lismaha contained 14 families with a total of 30 children, 2 servants were employed in this townland, all the inhabitants were Catholic with the exception of 1 family. The names of the inhabitants of this townland were Darby Finan, Barth. Connolly, William Mulry, Roger Kellaghan, James Butler, John Butler, Widow Kelly, Michael Fallon, Widow Mulry, Miles Queeny, Mark Madden, Patt. Courale, Widow Goldrick and Widow Goldricks daughter occupied the last house. The inhabitants included a shepherd, a blacksmith, a weaver and 6 labourers.

Cloonakilleg contained 12 families and these families had 29 children between them. The surnames of the inhabitants were Mr. Daniel Fallon, Francis Heally, Laurence Clerk, Stephne Collon, John Lenon, Peter Healy, Carbary Healy, Laurence Mullon, Conner Mannen, Laughlin Kelly, David Collins and Charles Collins. At the time of the Elphin Census this townland was owned by John Kelly of Aughrane who leased half of the lands to Daniel Fallon and the other half to eleven separate tenants. This is the only townland in the area that contained only farmers and tenants, all the other townlands contained mostly trades people with tenants usually making up a small proportion of the population. Daniel Fallon was Catholic and although he did not own the lands he farmed in Cloonakilleg (it was illegal for a Catholic to own land) he seems to have been a man of considerable wealth living in a large house with 4 servants.

---

[46] William Digby was born at Mote and was a son of Bishop Simon Digby who was Bishop of Elphin from 1690 to 1720. He was educated by the Rev. Michael Griffin at Elphin and was admitted to TCD in 1712 aged 18. He graduated with a BA in 1716.
[47] Father Francis Hanley was pastor for the parish of Tisrara and was also prebendary of the parish of Killian. He died in 1761 and is buried in the old cemetery at Carrowntemple where Francis Finglass erected a memorial in his memory.

The Kellys of Aughrane (Castle Kelly) in the 18th Century

Denis Kelly owned Aughrane Castle and estate at the turn of the century, he was the only son of Colonel Charles O'Kelly and both these men had taken an active part in the Williamite War. Denis seems to have remained Catholic until his death in 1740. He married Lady Mary Bellew in 1702 and they had three children, a boy and two girls. His son Thomas died at five years of age and both girls also died young resulting in Denis outliving all of his children. On the 30th of July 1722 Denis was charged with high treason and sent to the Tower of London on suspicion of being involved in the Atterbury Plot[48]. This coup was instigated by the remaining Irish and English jacobites who attempted to restore the house of Stuart to the throne during the reign of George I. Denis was admitted to bail on May 26th 1723 by order of the Privy Council and was finally acquitted six months later[49]. He settled back to life as an Irish landowner and accumulated vast estates throughout the country. Denis rarely stayed at Aughrane and spent most of his time in Dublin or on his other estates in counties Louth and Meath leasing out his lands in Roscommon and east Galway to other landowners. He had possession of the townlands of Cloonakilleg, Garrier, Srahaunnagort, Cartron and in 1727 purchased the townland of Araghty (adjacent to Cloondara) from Lord Clanricarde. He was also in possession of the townland of Leanamalla in the parish of Tisrara.

When Denis died in 1740 the estate passed to his cousin John Kelly of Cloonlyon who subsequently moved to the Castle of Aughrane becoming the 11th Lord of the Manor of Screen. An interesting item listed in the will of Denis Kelly relates to the tenants of Cloonakilleg stating that they are to have '*a half years rent remitted*,' this suggests that the people of Cloonakilleg were particularly favoured by Denis[50]. In 1750 John Kelly leased the lands of Araghty and Correbeg to Robert Walker at a yearly rent of £147 and a map attached to this lease dated 20th February 1722 shows the townlands in question together with the neighbouring townlands of Cloondara and Lismaha[51]. John Kelly married Lady Honoria Burke in 1729, she was a daughter of the Earl of Clanricarde thus binding in marriage the centuries old friendship that existed between these two families. Interestingly Lady Honoria Burkes mother was Mary Talbot of Mount Talbot, Mary Talbots father was Colonel James Talbot who had died fighting for King James II in the battle of Aughrim. John Kelly was the first of the Kellys of Aughrane to convert to the established church[52]. He died in 1748 leaving his entire estate to his son Denis. Denis Kelly married Anne Armstrong of Gallen in 1750 and they had seven sons who all went on to lead eventful lives. Five of them joined the British Army including Major John Kelly, Lieutenant Denis Kelly, Captain Charles Kelly, Lieutenant William Kelly (who died while on active duty with Lord McCartney in China) and Major Robert Kelly (who was killed during the siege of San Sebastian[53]). Denis Kelly died at Worcester in 1794 and left his estate to his son Rev. Andrew Armstrong Kelly. From the mid 18th Century onwards Aughrane Castle was also known as Castle Kelly.

---

[48]This plot was named after the most prominent conspirator Francis Atterbury, Bishop of Rochester and it is also known as the Rochester Plot.
[49]John T. Gilbert (ed), *A Contempory history of affairs in Ireland, from 1641 to 1652 for the Irish Archaeological and Celtic Society*, Dublin 1880. Details and dates of Denis Kelly's incarceration and also details of his family life appear under section xviii 'memoir of Colonel Charles O'Kelly'.
[50] Galway County Council Archives, Kelly Papers, G00/04/165.
[51] Ibid G00/04/46.
[52] Ibid G00/04/288, this document gives the date of John Kelly's conversion as 1724.
[53] The Siege of San Sebastian in northern Spain occurred between the 7th of July and the 8th of August 1813 during the peninsular war, Allied forces under Wellington eventually took the town from the French.

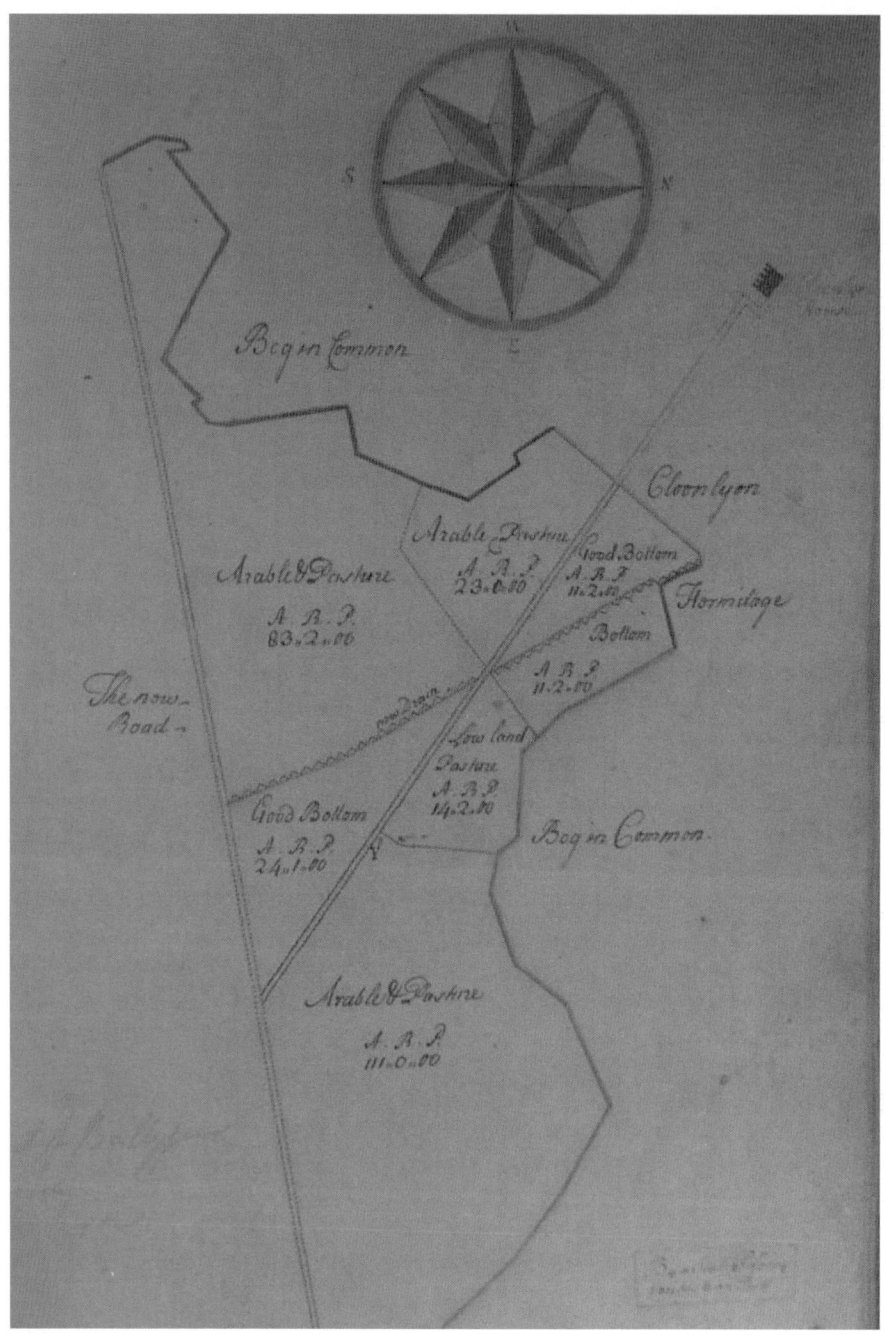

Map from the 1740's showing Cloonlyon House. John Kelly moved the short distance from Cloonlyon House to Aughrane Castle after inheriting the castle and lands from his cousin Denis Kelly (courtesy of the National Library of Ireland, Ms 14,310).

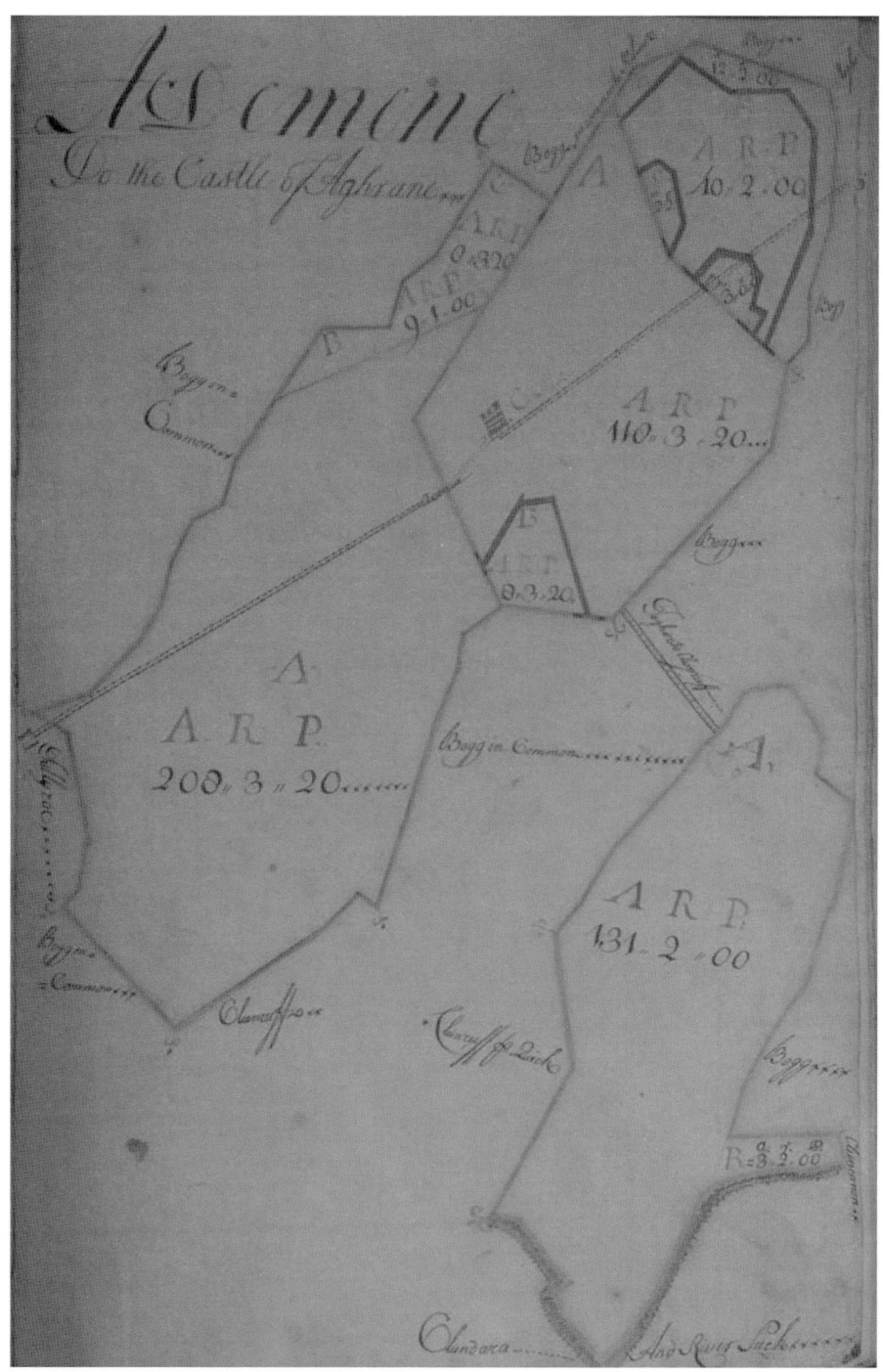

Map from the 1740's showing Aughrane Castle and surrounding lands. A 'togher' or bog-road was used at this time to gain access to the townland of Cloonruff (courtesy of the National Library of Ireland, Ms 14,310).

The Expansion of Mount Talbot

A Statute passed in the Irish Houses of Parliament in 1765 shows that a large village had by this time emerged in Mount Talbot and this signifies that Mount Talbot had replaced Clooneleen as the centre of population in the area. The statute refers to the *'Town of Mount Talbot'* and it was passed to allow the upgrading of the road from Athlone to Mount Talbot. Mount Talbot must have been a substantial settlement to have been referred to as a town although the 18th century definition of a town is somewhat different to what it is defined as in later centuries. It seems from surnames listed in later surveys that some of the residents of Clooneleen moved to Mount Talbot and others moved to the townlands of Lismaha and Cloondara.

William Talbot was the owner of Mount Talbot House and lands in the mid 18th Century. He married Sarah Rose, daughter of Rt. Hon. Henry Rose on the 30th of May 1739. They had four children, Henry Rose (died 29th Dec 1759), William John (also known as William who inherited the house and lands), Bridget and Jane. The popular English dramatist Richard Cumberland spent some time at Mount Talbot house in the late 1760's and wrote some scenes from his most famous play 'The West Indian' during his visit. William Talbot provided Cumberland with a quiet and secluded building within the demesne allowing the author write his scenes free from interruption. Cumberland described his stay at Mount Talbot as follows: *'During an excursion of a few days upon a visit to Mr. Talbot of Mount Talbot, a very respectable gentleman in those parts, I found a kind of hermitage in his pleasure grounds, where I wrote some few scenes, and my amiable host was afterwards pleased to honour the author of the West Indian with an inscription, affixed to that building, commemorating the use that had been made of it, a piece of elegant flattery very elegantly expressed'*[54]. The West Indian was first staged at the Drury Lane Theatre in 1771 and it was a great success with 28 performances staged in its original run making it Cumberland's most popular comic work. It is unknown where the 'hermitage' used by Cumberland was located within the demesne and the plaque made to commemorate his visit is lost but later maps show a feature near the house called 'Cumberlands cave' suggesting the hermitage was located in this part of the estate.

A Protestant Church was built one mile north of the village in 1766 on lands donated by William Talbot. £415/7s/8.5p of the cost of construction was covered by the 'board of first fruits' with an unknown private subscription covering the remaining cost[55]. It is probable that the private subscriber was William Talbot. Landscape Draughtsman Gabriel Beranger gave the following description of the building: *'one of the prettiest country Churches I have ever seen, being finished in the Gothic style, somewhat in the manner of the chapels at Westminster Abbey, the seats and organ elegant and the whole adorned with nice stucco ornaments, the ground of which being coloured differently, makes said ornaments more conspicuous. The very pulpit is adorned with raised stucco and when the east window is finished (which is stained glass) it will certainly be a curiosity worth visiting by travellers*[56]'. It seems from this description that the church was not fully completed by 1779. The Vicar that held the first services at Mount Talbot church was Rev William Digby. The last service was held here in the 1960's and the church subsequently fell in to disrepair. The Church still

---

[54] William Mudford, *The life of Richard Cumberland*, Esq., pp 191, 192.
[55] The Parliamentary Gazetteer of Ireland, 1844-45, Volume III, Dublin, London & Edinburgh, 1846.
[56] Sir William Wilde, M.D, *Memoir of Gabriel Beranger, and his labours in the cause of Irish Art and Antiquities from 1760 to 1780.*

exists today and is currently being renovated. A cemetery was developed within the church grounds and although it was initially used for deceased members of the Protestant community, Catholics have been interred here for the last 100 years. After completion of the church the 8 remaining houses that were once part of the village of Clooneleen were renamed 'Churchborough' presumably because of their proximity to the new church.

The surveyors Taylor and Skinner produced the first accurate maps of the roads of Ireland in 1778 and the road from Athleague to Mount Talbot is shown on these maps. Mount Talbot is depicted as a substantial settlement with a line of houses existing on both sides of the road over a distance of approximately half a mile from the present day Cloonca road to beyond the bend in the road at Garrier. Mount Talbot House, the Protestant Church and Castle Kelly are also shown on the maps. The surveyors plotted the main roads and associated settlements reasonably accurately but they did not have enough time or funding to get accurate details of the locations of roads, rivers or houses that existed outside the main thoroughfares. Castle Kelly is shown over a mile south west of its actual location and the river Suck is not drawn accurately but the surveyors would have spent sufficient time recording Mount Talbot village as it was located on a main road.

Taylor and Skinners map from 1778 showing Mount Talbot Village and surrounding areas.

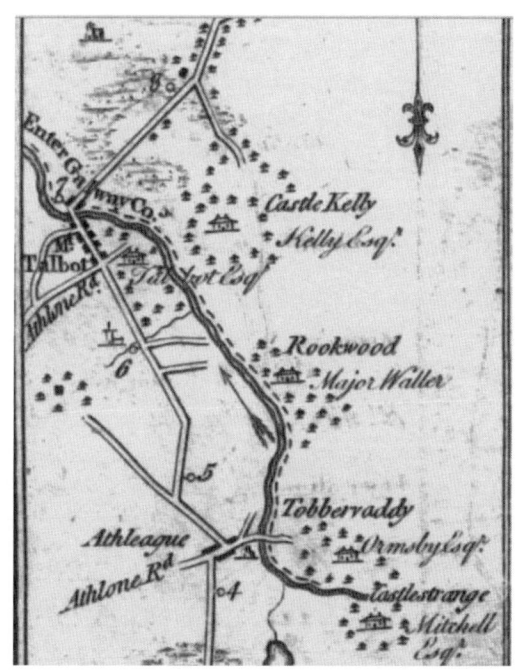

Landscape Draughtsman Gabriel Berenger and his associate Angelo Maria Bigari visited Mount Talbot in 1779 during their 'sketching tour of Connacht'. They stayed at Mount Talbot house and were lavishly entertained by the Talbots and the Kellys of Castle Kelly. The following description of their stay taken from Berenger's diary vividly depicts the wealth and opulence that existed within the demesne walls of Mount Talbot House: *'arrived at Mount Talbot, the seat of William Talbot, Esq. Met in the avenue Mr. Talbot, Jun., with Denis Kelly of Castle Kelly, County Galway, Esq., which last gentleman invited us at dinner at his house for the Sunday following, with the family of Mount Talbot. We were introduced by Mr. Talbot, Jun., to Lady Anne Talbot, his lady, and to Lady Theodosia,*

and Lady Arabella Crosbie, her sisters, to Mr. Talbot, Sen., and other gentlemen and ladies then residing there on a visit. After refreshing ourselves for some time, we went with Mr. Talbot, Sen., to see the concerns, which are a continued wood, and occupying near 800 acres, through which are walks adorned with rural seats, temples, and hermitages, and vistas are cut through the wood, all terminated by the river Suck, which meanders through the estate, and separates the counties of Roscommon and Galway. If these concerns were situated on unequal ground, and not on a level as they are, they might be ranked amongst the finest in the Kingdom. The town of Mount Talbot is yet in its infancy, and may in time become a decent town. We dined with the family and visitors in a rural temple on the banks of the river Suck, and in the evening walked to another, in which we drank tea. Towards 9 o'clock we all embarked in a barge and went home by water. August 7th, got up at six o'clock, worked at our drawings, I went after breakfast with Mr. Talbot, Junior, on horseback, to Castle Kelly, returning by 12 o'clock, found at Mount Talbot, Captain Sandy's, formerly of the Carabineers (an old acquaintance), who took up there his quarters, went in the evening with the company to walk, came home before dark, and were treated by the ladies with a concert before supper. August 8th, worked until 3 o'clock, set out with the family and visitors (two coaches, our chaise, and gentlemen and servants on horseback, forming a large caravan), for Castle Kelly, Co. Galway, distance two miles from Mount Talbot, arrived, and were elegantly entertained at dinner, being thirty in number. I left the gentlemen at their bottle, and escaped to the ladies, but was soon after joined by them all at tea, after which Mr. Bigari (an excellent dancer) danced with Miss Kelly and some other ladies. Returned home at 10, and found supper ready. August 9th, Mr. Talbot, Junior, obliged to go abroad, left the company to the care of Lady Anne. Worked at our drawings, walked about, paid a visit to Castle Kelly, and got a concert before supper'. This description of life at 'the big house' vividly portrays the wealth and excess that existed among the landed gentry at this time. The exact location of the two 'rural temples' mentioned in the text are unknown.

William John Talbot (left) of Mount Talbot and his second wife Lady Anne Crosbie (right), William and Lady Anne entertained Gabriel Berenger at Mount Talbot during his stay in 1779 (courtesy of Donald Cameron)..

The 'New' Road

A new road was constructed from Mount Talbot to Four Roads in the late 18th Century as part of a larger road scheme that involved installing a toll road or turnpike road between Athlone and Mount Talbot and from Athlone to Ballyforan. As mentioned previously in this chapter a Statute was brought before the Irish Houses of parliament in 1765, this statute was listed as: *'An Act for making a Turnpike Road from the Town of Athlone in the County of Roscommon to the Bridge of Ballyforan on the River Suck, and from Athlone to the town of Mount Talbot in the County of Roscommon'*[57]. The bill was approved by the Irish Privy Council and submitted to the English Privy Council on the 3rd of April 1766 where it received approval 15 days later. The bill received 'Royal Accent' on the 7th of June 1766. The condition of the existing road dictated what sections of road needed to be upgraded and what sections needed to be entirely replaced. The cost of replacing the entire length of these roads would have been excessive but it seems the section of road between Four Roads and Mount Talbot was in very poor condition and needed complete replacement, a new route for the road was selected a short distance south of the existing road. The act refers to the installation of 'turnpikes' and 'toll gates' along the new road and a 'toll house' was approved within the village of Mount Talbot to allow tolls to be collected, this toll money was to be used to cover the cost of maintaining the road. A 'turnpike' generally consisted of a gate across the road and this gate would only be opened when the approaching road user paid the appropriate toll. The costs of tolls varied depending on the size or quantity of the item passing through, for example a carriage drawn by six horses was charged 1 shilling and 6 pence to pass through the turnpike[58]. Tolls were also paid for groups of farm animals that needed to be moved to lands or to markets on the opposite side of the turnpike. This must have caused much anguish to the people of Cloonlaughnan, Corrocot and Cloonakilleg who were attending fairs at Mount Talbot. Any landowners adjacent to the turnpike that allowed passage through their lands to road users trying to avoid the tolls would be fined 15 shillings[59], an enormous amount of money at this time.

The 'Taylor and Skinner' map from 1778 shown previously in this chapter depict the old road entering Mount Talbot from Four Roads. These maps date to 13 years after the Act of Parliament of 1765 and the depiction of the old road confirms that the new road had not been completed by this time. Both the Athlone to Mount Talbot and Athlone to Ballyforan Roads were to be constructed simultaneously and these roads would have taken a considerable length of time to complete due to the labour and materials available at this time. The works would have started at Athlone and continued at a relatively slow rate towards the end points at Mount Talbot and Ballyforan. It is probable that immediately after the statute was approved turnpikes and toll houses were installed along the existing road and the monies gathered over a number of years were used to help pay for the construction of the new road. It is also probable that the Toll House at Mount Talbot was constructed soon after the Act was passed and this building was used to collect and process all the tolls collected at the turnpikes along the last section of the route.

---

[57] Statutes Passed in the Parliaments Held in Ireland Vol. V. *From the Fifth Year of George III.A.D 1761 to the Eleventh and Twelfth Years of George III. A.D 1771-2 inclusive*, Dublin 1795, p262.
[58] Ibid, p263.
[59] Ibid, p264.

An Act for making a Turnpike Road from the Town of Athlone in the County of Roscommon to the Bridge of Ballisoran on the River Suck, and from Athlone to the Town of Mount Talbot in the County of Roscommon.

WHEREAS the high road leading from the bridge of Ballyforan on the river Suck, which divides the county of Galway from the county of Roscommon to the town of Athlone, and from the town of Mount Talbot to the said town of Athlone, are the great roads, through which the inhabitants of the towns of Galway, Tuam, and of the counties of Galway and Mayo, usually travel to the city of Dublin, and the same are greatly out of repair, and dangerous for travellers, and cannot in a considerable space of time be amended by the ordinary course appointed by the laws for the repair of highways: wherefore, that the said roads may be amended with convenient speed, be it enacted by the King's most excellent Majesty by and with the advice and consent of the lords spiritual and temporal and commons in this present Parliament assembled, and by the authority of the same, That the most reverend lord archbishop of Tuam, the right honourable earl Lowth, the right honourable lord Mounteagle, the honourable Peter Kelly Browne esquire, John French esquire of French Park, Thomas Mahon esquire, Robert French of Monivae esquire, William Talbot esquire, John Blakeney esquire, John Bingham esquire, Henry Bingham esquire, Luke Dillon esquire, Arthur French esquire, sir Richard St. George, Dennis Kelly esquire, reverend Dean Ryder, reverend Dudley Ryder, Robert Waller junior esquire, Ross Mahon junior esquire, John Mahon esquire, Daniel Kelly esquire, Samuel Simpson esquire, reverend William Digby, Edmund Nettervil esquire, reverend Jeremy Marsh, Francis Marsh, esquire, John Blake esquire, Anthony French esquire, Gregory French esquire, reverend Alexander Seaton, Charles Blakeney, gentleman, Dominick Blake esquire, Christopher Bellew gentleman, Thomas Coleman gentleman, Martin Darcy, gentleman, Andrew French gentleman, Simon Blakeney esquire, Peter Kelly gentleman, John Farrell gentleman, Thomas Lister Grange esquire, Mark Browne esquire, Darcy French esquire, Frederick French gentleman, Bernard Rochfort gentleman, Dominick Bellew gentleman, Michael Bellew gentleman, Pierce Lynch gentleman, may be, and they are hereby, nominated and appointed trustees of the said roads, and the survivors of them.

II. And

II. And be it enacted by the authority aforesaid, That they or any five or more of them, or such person or persons as they or any five or more of them shall authorize and appoint, shall and may erect or cause to be erected one or more gate or gates, turnpike or turnpikes, in, upon, or across any part or parts of the said roads, and also a toll house or toll houses, and there shall receive and take the tolls and duties following, before any horse, mare, mule, gelding, cattle, coach, berlin, chariot, calash, chaise, chair, waggon, cart, carr, or other carriage, shall be permitted to pass through the same (that is to say) for every coach, chariot, berlin, calash, chaise, or chair, drawn by six horses, geldings, or mares, one shilling and sixpence; for every coach, chariot, berlin, calash, chaise, or chair, drawn by a lesser number of horses, mares, or geldings, than six, and more than two, one shilling; for every coach, chariot, berlin, chaise, or chair, drawn with two horses, mares, or geldings, six pence; for every waggon, wain, or cart, with four wheels, five shillings; for every waggon, wain, or cart, with two wheels, drawn by more than two horses, mares, geldings, mules, or oxen, three shillings; for every cart, waggon, or carr, drawn with two horses, mares, geldings, mules, or oxen, two shillings; for every carriage called a chair or chaise, drawn by one horse, mare, or gelding, three pence; for every cart or other carriage drawn by one horse, the wheels of which car are three inches broad, two pence; but if the wheels be a lesser gauge, four pence; for every other horse, mare, gelding, mule, or ass, laden or unladen, one penny; for every drove of oxen, cows, or neat cattle, the sum of ten pence *per* score, and so in proportion for any greater or lesser number; for every drove of hogs, calves, sheep, or lambs, the sum of five pence *per* score, and so in proportion for any greater or lesser number; which said respective sum or sums shall be demanded and taken in the name of or as a toll or duty; and the money, so to be raised as aforesaid, is and shall hereby be vested in the said trustees, and shall be applied and disposed of for the uses, intents, and purposes herein after mentioned; and the said trustees or any five or more of them are hereby impowered by themselves, or any person or persons by them or any five or more of them under their hands and seals thereunto authorized, to levy the toll or duty hereby required to be paid upon any person or persons, who shall after demand made thereof neglect or refuse to pay the same.

The first two pages of the Statute passed in the Irish Houses of Parliament in 1765 relating to the upgrading of the road from Athlone to Mount Talbot and from Athlone to Ballyforan.

The location of the Toll House in Mount Talbot is unknown but it seems that it would not have been located anywhere along the main Roscommon to Galway road through the village of Mount Talbot as this road was not a part of the toll road. It is therefore probable that the Toll House was located a short distance down the Mount Talbot to Four Roads road.

The Statute from 1865 stated that tolls were to be charged along the Athlone to Mount Talbot road until 1827 and as this statute was never amended during the intervening period it seems that tolls were not collected after the initial charge period ended and the road subsequently reverted back to a public road. Nationally all toll roads were abolished in 1858 due to their excessive cost and also due to corruption among the trustees appointed to manage these roads.

The old road from Four Roads had existed for many centuries and it was part of an ancient pilgrim route that was used during the Medieval Period to transport the bodies of deceased Gaelic leaders from central and southern Connacht to Clonmacnoise for burial. The road went through Mount Talbot, Cartron, Cloonca, Cloonlaughnan, Carroward and passed by the ancient hostelry at Carrowntemple where the bearers of the bodies of deceased leaders rested for a night prior to continuing their journey to Clonmacnoise. As may be seen in the Taylor and Skinner map the old road entered Mount Talbot at two locations, the first location was across the road from the present day ball-alley and this was used by people to access the village and to continue over the bridge into County Galway. The other road entered the village close to the present day Cloonca road and it seems this road was used to access Mount Talbot House and was used by people that needed to continue towards Athleague. Unfortunately Taylor and Skinner did not survey and draw the remainder of the road leading from Mount Talbot to Four Roads, an accurate depiction of this road would have shown the exact route that the 'old road' took through the townlands mentioned above. The Statute from 1865 stated that Mount Talbot was positioned along a *'great road, through which the inhabitants of the towns of Galway, Tuam and the Counties of Galway and Mayo usually travel to the City of Dublin'* and this confirms that the old road through Mount Talbot was a busy thoroughfare. It is possible to trace the route of this old road by examining the first edition Ordnance Survey maps from 1837. This map was drawn approximately 60 years after the new road was completed but many parts of the old road still exist at this time. However these sections were now used in most instances to access land and houses. To prevent road users avoiding the payment of tolls the builders of the new road blocked off access to Mount Talbot through Cartron and Cloonca but this route was re-opened in the decades after the road was made public.

The location of the old road was still known by some local people up to the mid 20th century after being handed down through the generations. In the 1960's an elderly man from Cloonakilleg when cycling to Naughton's Shop in Mount Talbot used to dismount from his bicycle at the sand-drain bridge and enter the 'chapel field' at this point carrying his bicycle. When questioned why he entered the village this way he was known to say that he was 'taking the old road'. A grassed walkway existed at this time through this field and it seems the walkway was located along the line of the old road.

Chapter 5 - The 19th Century

Mount Talbot had by the start of the 19th century developed into a picturesque village with many shops, businesses and trades. Two licensed premises existed in the village and both were on the Galway side of the bridge. It is possible one of these may be the 'Inn' at Mount Talbot that is mentioned in a local newspaper report from 1743 (see previous chapter).

Number of Retail Spirit Licenses now in force; Number held by Persons who are Grocers; and		
	Total Number of Retail Spirit Licenses now in force.	Number of such Licenses held by Persons who are Grocers.	Number of Persons holding such Licenses as Occupiers of Premises under the value of £. 10 per Annum.
Town of Creggs -	4	–	4
Clifden -	19	–	19
Clarencebridge	6	–	6
Dunmore	25	–	24
Eyrecourt	14	–	12
Gort -	36	–	29
Headford	16	–	16
Kinvara	15	–	15
Loughrea	64	–	54
Mount Bellew	14	–	13
Mount Talbot	2	–	2
Outerard	10	–	10
Portumna	12	–	8
Tuam -	58	–	37
In other Places -	244	–	243
County of GALWAY	708	–	585

Extract from British Parliamentary Papers from 1836 showing existence of 2 Licensed Premises at Mount Talbot (in Garrier, County Galway)

Mount Talbot was an important post town and records from 1815 show a Mrs M. Robinson running the post office. British Parliamentary records from 1817 show that the Deputy Postmaster at Mount Talbot earned £36 16s and 1p per annum. The mail was dispatched to Mount Talbot from Roscommon by horse at 10.35am every morning after arriving from Athlone at 10am, the mail addressed to the Talbots arrived at Mount Talbot Post Office in its own separate leather bag. The post office was initially located adjacent to the present day ball-alley in Mount Talbot. A Petty Session Court existed in Mount Talbot until the early 1850's when it was moved to Coolderry near Four Roads. These Courts dealt with the vast bulk of lesser legal cases both civil and criminal. The court was presided over by two or more unpaid Justices of the Peace (JP) or by a single paid magistrate. The integrity of the Court was often compromised as the position of JP was often held by the local landlord, as was the case in Mount Talbot in the early part of the 19th century. The Court had a clerk who kept the registers and collected fees from those involved in cases. The Petty Session Courts were replaced by the present day District Courts in 1924.

Mount Talbot House provided employment to local people within the house, in the yards and outbuildings and through seasonal work, particularly at harvest time and during the turf cutting season. The owner of Mount Talbot house for the entire first half of the 19th century was William Talbot who was born in 1766. William was a son of William John Talbot and Lady Anne Crosbie and commenced his third level education at Christ Church, Oxford on the 21st of June 1794. He entered the Irish House of Commons as a member for Kilkenny city on a vacancy in March 1799 and was chosen by lot to continue as MP in 1801 but resigned his seat shortly after the Parliament reconvened. He married Susannah Kemmis on the 20th of December 1802. Susannah came from a very wealthy family and the marriage settlement entered into by both families included a payment of £18,000 to William Talbot[60]. William held the office of Justice of the Peace (J.P) for County Roscommon and was High Sheriff of the County in 1819. William's younger brother Charles entered the British military and was killed in action at the battle of Walcheren in 1809. William and Susannah carried out a major expansion of the big house in 1820 transforming it into a Tudor Revival mansion. Some parts of the previous palladian house were incorporated into the new design by the architect Richard Richards from Roscommon Town. The two wings that existed on either side of the main house were retained together with the arcades that connected them to the house. The architect was a specialist in the design of churches and he incorporated many features associated with ecclesiastical buildings into his design of Mount Talbot House such as Gothic arches, large towers, pinnacles and pointed windows many of which contained stained glass. The entrance to the avenue leading to the castle was changed from its location across from the Cloonca road to a location nearer the village and a very impressive classical arch was constructed at the new entrance with rusticated piers and four urns on its entablature. This arched entrance became known as the 'Grand Gate' and it still exists today but it is now located nearer the Protestant Church after being moved to its present location in the late 19[th]century. The gatehouse was located across the road from the Grand Gate and this building still exists today and is owned by the Flynn family.

Earliest known photo of Mount Talbot House from 1865 showing the impressive remodeling that took place in 1820 (courtesy of the National Architectural Archive).

---

[60] From a conversation between Tommy Connolly NT and the late John Collins of Garrier. John also revealed that when Susannah died her brother was overheard saying at her grave: *'there you lie with your £18,000'*.

Photo from 1865 showing the original location of the 'Grand Gate' at Mount Talbot. The gatehouse shown in the background still exists today and is the residence of the Flynn family (Courtesy of the National Architectural Archive)

Modern photo taken from the same location as above showing the 'Wicket Gate' that replaced the 'Grand Gate' after the latter was moved to its present location in the early 1880's (P. Connolly, June 2014)

Two well known writers of the early 19th century visited Mount Talbot and wrote very positive reports about the village and the big house. The first writer was Isaac Weld who wrote his report in 1832: *'Mount Talbot, upon the river suck, might be mentioned as perhaps holding one of the first places: of late years the house has been enlarged and castellated, under the direction of Mr. Richards, of Roscommon, and the effect which has been produced is very pleasing. The towers are square and massive, and diversified, without being broken, as so often seen, into those minute and insignificant parts which are utterly destructive of grandeur and dignity. An arcade, extended from one side of the house, or rather castle, with open arches, through which a view is discovered of the garden and pleasure grounds in the distance, has a happy effect. The building stands upon an elevated bank over the Suck, with a slope in front shelving down to the water, but so much covered with trees as to impede the view, neither is the house visible at a distance, owing to the woods which surround it, although, if opened, it could not fail of affording a fine feature in the landscape. Trees grow with great luxuriance here, and the ilex was amongst the most flourishing in the plantation, though no one has yet attained a large growth. Immediately below the house, the Suck is traversed by a rather lofty bridge of twelve arches, across a water way of about eighty yards. A small village extends down to the bridge, along the slope of the Roscommon side, the houses of which, though good, are by no means so well built or so pleasing as some that are scattered along the road side on the upper bank. I was informed, that the wishes of the proprietor rather militated against the increase of this place, so near his residence, otherwise, probably, a town would soon arise. The fine trees and hedges bordering upon the road, the breadth and excellence of the road itself, and the neat cottages scattered along it, render the approach to Mount Talbot peculiarly agreeable, from whatever side the traveler arrives, for its improved aspect affords a striking contrast to the bareness and openness of the districts in its neighborhood'*. Samuel Lewis wrote a similar positive description of the village when he visited in 1837.

The first edition Ordnance Survey maps from 1838 give the first accurate depiction of the layout of the village and also of Mount Talbot House. A line of buildings are shown on the western side of the main road from the present day ball-alley to the village pump and the post office is shown within this line of houses. An RIC Barracks was located at the 90 degree bend on the road at Garrier and a Catholic chapel was located in a field directly across from the present day ball-alley. The chapel was located along the edge of the 'old road' suggesting that the building may have been in existence prior to the construction of the modern road in the late 18th century, however it is probable that the building had a different function prior to its use as a chapel as Catholic emancipation did not occur until 1829. Local tradition recalls that this chapel was never completed as the Landlord objected to its location within viewing distance of his recently re-modeled house. However some historical sources seem to indicate that this small church was completed. The Parliamentary Gazetteer from 1846 states that Mount Talbot *'has a post-office, a church and a Roman Catholic chapel'*, this suggests that the chapel was a complete building at this time. The OS maps from 1838 also depict this chapel as being completed, the dimensions of the chapel depicted on the maps suggest that this was quite a substantial building. Later editions of the ordnance survey maps from the 19th Century show the chapel as a ruin indicating that it was in existence for a short period of time, there are no records of this church ever functioning as a place of worship. The field where this chapel was located is still called the 'Chapel Field'.

The first edition OS maps show a school a short distance down the Four Roads road and a Nursery is depicted in the centre of the village. The local Catholic priest lived within the townland of

Cloonlaughnan at this time, his house was located approximately midway between Mount Talbot and Four Roads and his residence was known as 'the Cottage' and later as 'Woodbine Cottage'. The local vicar lived at Thornfield House in the early 19th century but later moved to a house in Corrocot. This house still exists today and is currently being renovated by its owners the Cunniffe family who reside in a modern house next door.

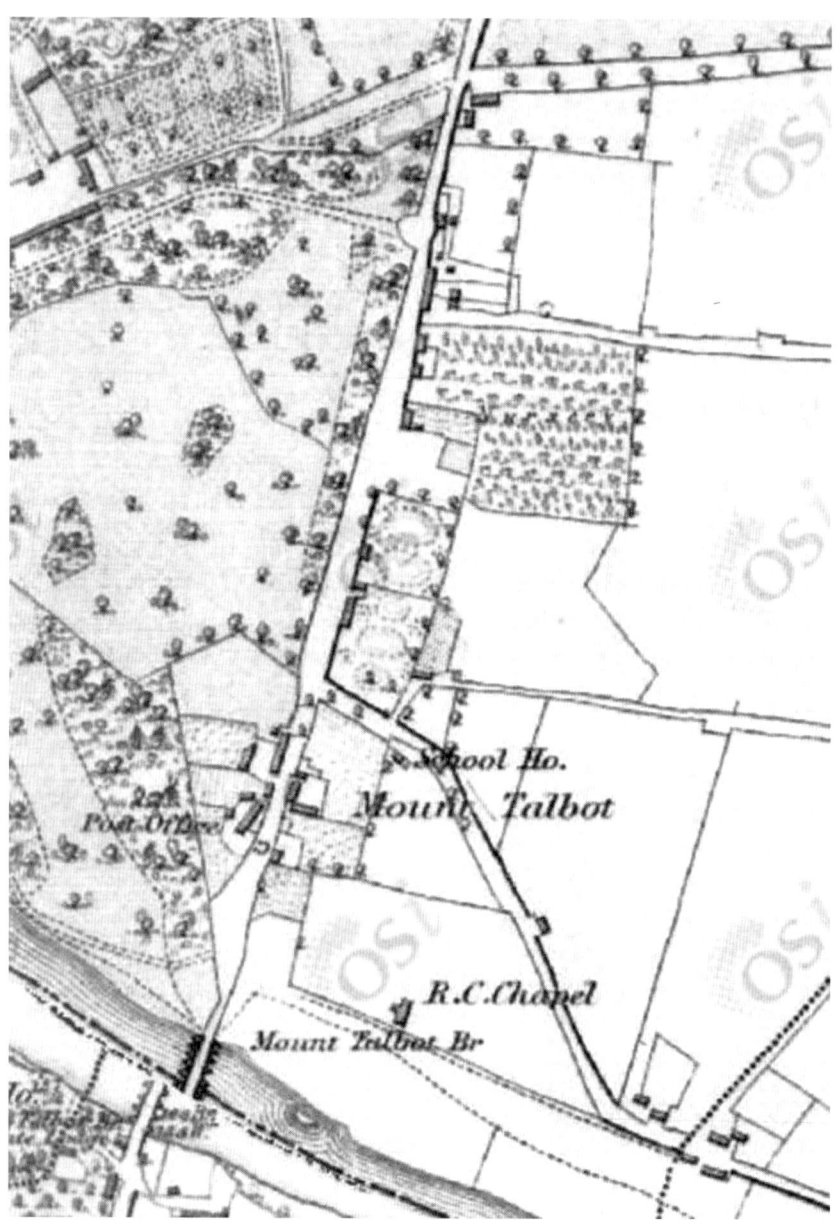

Mount Talbot in 1838, from the first edition Ordnance Survey Maps (OSI, Licence number 2010/15CCMA/Galway County Council).

The Tithe Applotment Books

The 'Composition Act' was passed by the British Government in 1823 making it compulsory for all occupiers of land over one acre in Ireland to pay tithes (taxes) to the established church. The Protestant Church was the established church in Ireland from the reign of Henry VIII until its disestablishment in 1871. The Tithe Applotment Books were compiled between 1823 and 1837 in order to determine the amount of money payable by each household and tithes were payable by all occupiers of land irrespective of their religion. The books give the names of the occupiers of the land, the amount of land held and the sums to be paid in tithes. Mount Talbot and its environs were surveyed in 1836. Most of the heads of the households were still Irish speakers and it seems the Commissioner that recorded the names spent very little time writing the correct spelling in English. The surnames shown below are taken directly from the tithe applotment books, some of the surnames are spelled differently to their modern equivalent but in most cases it is possible to ascertain the modern surname from the original source.

The Tithe Applotment books show that Mount Talbot townland contained 20 houses including Mount Talbot House. The townland contained 253 acres 1 perch & 35 roods of taxable land and paid a collective Tithe of £9 17 shillings and 2 ½ pence of which the local vicar received 3/5 and the Incorporated Society 2/5. The heads of the houses in Mount Talbot at this time were: William Galvin, Bernard Lyons, Edward Cor, Robert Little, William Talbot esq, Rev. Peter Kirwin, Martin Finaughty, James Loghan, James Lilo, Pat O'Mealy, Andrew Kelly, John McDermot, William Lyons, Edward Carty, Ronan Kelly, William Fallon, Elenor Clogher, Pat Murphy, Pat Kelly and Henry Lawlor. The largest occupier of land is unsurprisingly the landlord William Talbot with 201 acres and this land was used directly by the landlord and not leased out to tenants. It is probable that a large portion of the 201 acres surrounded the big house and was part of the impressive gardens and woodland planted by the Talbots throughout the previous century. The person with the second largest holding was James Loghan with over 9 acres. The third largest holding contained over 8 acres and this was used as a nursery by William Galvin. The smallest holding amounted to 1 rood and 30 perches and this occupier had to pay 5 pence in tithes even though the Act clearly stated that only occupiers of land of one acre or over were required to make a payment.

In the Tithe Applotment Books the townland of Lismaha is also called 'Boherbee' a name that was commonly used by local people throughout the 19th and even into the 20th centuries. The name written in the books is an attempt to spell the Gaelic word 'Bothar Buí' (the yellow road) and this road is now part of the modern 'Bushy Park Road'[61]. A field located mid-way along the Bushy Park road is still called Bother Buí. The surnames in Lismaha at this time were: Clougher, Conboy, Doogan, McCon, Mylane, Cooney, Staunton, Quirk, Healy, Keogh, Mullane, McDermott, Hannon, Branaly, Queeny, Lennon, Murray, Fallon, Mailey, Moran, Reilly, Cor, Harison and Mooney. The total amount of land in Lismaha was 121 acres and 2 roods with tithes amounting to £3, 3shillings and 7 ½ p.

---

[61] Bothar Bui or yellow road received its name from the colour of the road surface along a short section of the Bushy Park road. An underground spring occasionally caused flooding on this section of the road resulting in yellowish clay or 'maulia' seeping upwards from underground giving the road a distinctive yellow colour (from a conversation with Mickey McConn of Bushy Park).

The townland of Cloondara contained 19 families and their surnames were: Boughly, Minton, Mylon, Lyons, Moran, Flanagan, Butler, Queeny, Conboy, Healy and Connor. The acreage amounted to 49 acres, 0 rood and 20 perches with a total tithe payable of 19 shillings and ½ pence.

Cloonlaughnan is shown as 'Corricot or Cloonloughnan' and this signifies that the village of Corrocot had become a large settlement within the townland of Cloonlaughnan. The family surnames are: Dolan, Gilmor, Murray, Dealy, Kelly, Burns, Connolly, Gaffy, Mannion, Flanagan, McGanne, McDermot, Lyons, Healy, Grealy, Carrol, Fallon, Field, Mannion, Ferto, Mullen, Moran, Lyman, Fallon, Logan, Connor, Timolty, Lyons, Farrell, Ready, Plunket, Burke, McKelly, Smyth, Little, Cormican, Mulvahon, Walsh, Birne, Carty, Cruse and Bodkin. The acreage amounted to 189 acres 2 rood and 39 perches with a total tithe payable of £6, 4 shillings and 3½ pence. The landlord that owned all the lands in this townland was McGann who resided in County Westmeath. The McGanns later moved permanently to the area after building Correal House near the present day village of Four Roads. The hill located on the road between Four Roads and Correal House is still known as 'McGanns hill'. A large corn mill and kiln existed in Cloonlaughnan at this time and this mill dated back to the previous century. The stream that drove the mill-wheel became known as 'the mill-race' and this stream still enters the river Suck in the townland of Cloonakilleg in an area know locally as 'the Planks'. This name came from a narrow pedestrian timber bridge that once existed over the stream at this point.

This stone trough was used by the blacksmith Jiminy Smith of Corrocot to cool iron in his forge during the late 18th and early 19th centuries. Jiminy is listed as living in Corrocot in the Tithe Applotment Books under the name James Smyth and he was known to be a man of enormous physical strength. This trough remains a treasured possession of Jiminy's great grand-son Marty Smith.

The area known as Churchborough was located adjacent to Mount Talbot Protestant Church and contained 8 houses. These houses were previously part of the village of Clooneleen that existed in the mid 18th century. The families surnames were : Dealy, Fallon, Dougherty and 5 Conboy families lived here. The total amount of taxable land was 24 acres, 1 rood and 28 perches and the tithe payable was 17 shillings and 2 pence.

The townland of Cartron is shown as 'Cartron Kelly' and it contained 9 houses. Rev. Armstrong Kelly of Aughrane Castle owned this townland. The surnames of the inhabitants of Cartron were: Dolan, Coonaly, Grealy and Clougher. The total amount of taxable land was 72 acres and 3 roods and the tithe payable was £2, 6 shillings and 9½ pence.

Cloonakilleg contained 24 families and Rev. Armstrong Kelly of Aughrane Castle owned the land. The surnames in Cloonakilleg at this time were: Coonaly, Lennon, Mannien, Ward, Smyth, Collins, Kelly, Cormican, Divine, McLaughlin, Tansey, Turley and Dolan. The total amount of taxable land was 238 acres and 39 perches and the tithe payable was £7, 12 shillings and 11¼ pence.

Cloonca contained 8 families and the land was owned by William Talbot, 139 acres of Cloonca was farmed directly by William Talbot and was not leased out to tenants . The surnames of the tenants that farmed the remaining land were: Flanagan, Kelly, Kennedy and Murray. The total amount of taxable land including the land farmed by Talbot was 185 acres 1 rood and 10 perches and the tithe payable was £4, 16 shillings and 7½ pence.

The townland of Lisgillilea was known by this time as Bushy Park, named after the large house built within the townland in the 18th century. Six families resided in Bushy Park and the entire townland was leased to John Barlow by the owner William Talbot. The family's surnames were: Barlow, Kelly, Lenan, Logan and Queeny with a total acreage of 102 acres 1 rood and 25 perches. The tithe payable amounted to £2, 14 shillings and 5 ¾ pence.

Garrier contained 69 acres and paid a tithe of £3, 13s 5p, the surnames of the people leasing the land were: Dignan, Fallon, Plunket, Kelly, Mannion, Burns, Kennedy, Cunningham, Pitch, Lyons, Crofton and Brennan. Thornfield contained 44 acres and paid £1 16s 8p in tithe's. The surnames of the occupants of this townland were McHugh, Burns and Crofton. Thornfield house was inhabited by Reverend Henry Marcus Crofton and he farmed 43 acres and 1 rood in Thornfield and 1 acre in Garrier, the house and lands were leased from Rev. Armstrong Kelly of Castle Kelly[62]. Reverend Crofton was to have a very disturbing end to his life. He refused to sign a document that accepted the Catholic Emancipation Act of 1829 stating that he would *'burn his hand to his shoulder before he'd sign it'*[63]. When he was pressurised into signing, he took his own life after entering the river Suck near the present day metal bridge in an area known locally as 'Linn na nÉan'.

The Tithe Applotment Books give an excellent insight into the people living in the village of Mount Talbot and its environs in the first half of the 19th Century. The people that gave the required information to the Commissioners were undoubtedly unhappy with the purpose of the survey but they inadvertently have left a lasting record of their lives that is invaluable to the modern researcher.

---

[62] Born in Mote Park, Roscommon, entered Trinity College Dublin in June 1802, completed BA in 1805, ordained Jan 22 1806.
[63] From an interview with the late John Collins in Garrier by Tommy Connolly NT in the mid 1980's.

The Great Hunger

Famine was unfortunately something that was a constant worry for the people of Mount Talbot throughout the 18th and 19th Centuries. A famine occurred throughout Ireland in 1740 caused by a winter of very severe frost that decimated the crops. Almost 38% of the Irish population died from starvation and hypothermia as a direct result of this frost. The well-being of the community was entirely dependent on a good harvest as the stable diet of the inhabitants of Mount Talbot and its environs mainly consisted of cereal crops and vegetables, particularly potatoes. Documents that exist relating to the sick and impoverished in the parish of Tisrara for the year 1822 show that fever and other sickness were common throughout the area particularly in the townlands that relied entirely on miniscule plots of land to provide food for the household. Accounts showing expenditure on food, medical and pharmaceutical supplies indicate that extreme levels of poverty and hunger existed in the area at this time. The local Vicar, Rev. Henry Marcus Crofton sent a letter to the General Board of Health pleading for financial assistance for the impoverished people of Tisrara[64]. Dr Francis Barker, Secretary of the Board subsequently wrote a letter to the Under Secretary of Ireland stating that no aid was forthcoming as the board *'have closed their accounts and have ceased to recommend to the Lord Lieutenant the issue of any further grants for the relief of the distressed poor'*. The people had to carry on with no medical or food aid and some people died from malnutrition and disease. An equitable loan fund was established in Mount Talbot in 1834 with capital of £400[65], for the benefit of the industrious poor but it done little to alleviate the suffering of the people. It was very difficult to be 'industrious' when no opportunities existed for the people to reach a higher standard of living.

AND REGULATIONS OF LOAN FUNDS. 7

COUNTY OF ROSCOMMON.

No.	Name of Loan Fund.	Place where Office is held.	No.	Name of Loan Fund.	Place where Office is held.
1	Boyle - -	Boyle.	13	Kiltoome - -	Kiltoome.
2	Roscommon -	Roscommon.	14	Frenchpark -	Frenchpark.
3	Western District	Roscommon.	15	Donamore -	Donamore.
4	Ballymurry -	Roscommon.	16	Croghan - -	Croghan.
5	Elphin - -	Elphin.	17	Fuerty - -	Fuerty.
6	Strokestown -	Strokestown.	18	Ballygar - -	Ballygar.
7	Ballymoe - -	Ballymoe.	19	Castlerea · -	Castlerea.
8	Knockcroghery	Knockcroghery.	20	Kilkevin - -	Castlerea.
9	Woodfield -	Woodfield.	21	Athlone - -	Athlone.
10	Ardcarn - -	Ardcarn.	22	Derrenwillan -	Derrenwillan.
11	Kilmore - -	Kilmore.	23	Corderry - -	Corderry.
12	Mounttalbott -	Mounttalbott.	24	Kiltrustan -	Kiltrustan.

John Morow, Deputy Clerk of the Peace.

Extract from British Parliamentary Papers from 1836 showing existence of Loan Fund office at Mount Talbot.

---

[64] National Archives of Ireland (NAI), CSO/RP/1822/2625.
[65] S Lewis, *A Topographical Dictionary of Ireland*, 1837, p347.

The 1841 census gives details of the standard of house that the people were living in together with their occupations and general health. The population of the parish of Tisrara in 1841 was 3,356 with the total number of houses listed as 627. The majority of people lived in very poor accommodation as 318 lived in 4th class houses and 217 lived in 3rd class houses. 769 males and 33 females are classified as being in need of food with 80 males and 63 females in need of clothing, 54 males are in need of lodgings, 869 males and 1,106 females (over the age of five) could not read or write. These figures give startling evidence of the poverty in the area with 802 people admitting to being in need of food. Nothing however can compare to the horrors that occurred after blight was detected in the Irish potato crop in early September 1845. By October 50% of the crop was destroyed and by February 1846 the people of Mount Talbot were in a high state of distress. The famine lasted for seven years and decimated the local population. The British Government response was late and inadequate. In October 1845 British Prime Minister Sir Robert Peel stated that *'there is such a tendency to exaggeration and inaccuracy in Irish reports that delay on acting on them is always desirable'*. Local Relief Committees were eventually established in Tisrara (based in Mount Talbot), Killian and Killeroran (based in Ballygar) in early 1846. These Committees were voluntary organizations and were made up of local dignitaries, local officials, poor law guardians and clergy. The secretary of Tisrara Relief Committee was the local Vicar, Rev. William McClelland who lived in Corrocot in the townland of Cloonlaughnan. A number of documents exist written by McClelland to the Famine Relief Commission and these documents include letters requesting Indian corn and labour tickets for the starving of the Parish[66]. The letters are very critical of the behavior of the local landlords, McClelland complained to the Commission that most of the landlords are not resident in the area and are not providing enough relief to the starving people.

Roscommon Workhouse was inundated with people trying to gain access and soon had 1,100 starving people within its walls. However many more people were in great need of help and in January 1848 2,000 people were recorded in one day as being outside the workhouse begging for admission[67]. The people arriving at the workhouse were described as being *'creatures almost dead or dying. Eight, nine and ten could be seen on carts given for the purpose, affected by contagious fever the young and old were huddling together'*. In 1849 a famine relief grant was put in place by the Board of Guardians to repair bridges and walls from Athlone bridge to Mount Talbot bridge with each person employed being 'paid' with one bowl of maize meal per day. The people of Corrocot were struggling to survive and on Christmas Day 1849 their world came crashing down around them. Many were out in their gardens frantically searching for small potatoes and edible roots to provide food for their Christmas dinner when they were interrupted by the arrival of the local landlord together with his land agents and bailiffs and all the families in the village were subsequently evicted from their homes[68]. Every single house was demolished by the battering ram and the 26 families were now homeless as well as starving. The first edition OS maps show the location of these houses with most being located on the main road and some in the village of Corrocot. OS maps drawn post famine show none of these houses in existence confirming that the appalling act of land 'clearance' was carried out in the vicinity of Mount Talbot. It is worth noting that Percy Magan who was a

---

[66] National Archives of Ireland (NAI), Famine Relief Commission (RLFC), 3/1/2714, 3/1/2858 & 3/1/4340.
[67] Roscommon Journal, 29th January 1848.
[68] Tisrara Heritage Society, *A History of the Parish of Tisrara*, 1997, p85.

landlord that owned land in Four Roads and a relatively small portion of the townland of Cloonlaughnan treated his tenantry with decency and kindness but this was not replicated by many of the other landlords in the area.

A comparison of the census populations of each townland for the years 1841 and 1851 gives a clear indication of the devastation caused by the famine. The population of Cloonlaughnan fell from 582 to 298 with the number of houses falling from 102 to 52. This is an enormous drop in population and it is probable that many of these people starved to death or died from disease caused by hunger. The evictions at Corrocot also contribute to this fall in population together with large scale emigration to America. The population of Mount Talbot fell from 144 in 1841 to 115 in 1851 and the number of houses fell from 27 to 21. The population of Cartron fell from 74 to 66, Cloonakilleg from 262 to 201, Cloonca from 57 to 41, Cloondara from 93 to 68, Lisgillalea (Bushy Park) from 75 to 66 and Lismaha from 221 to 157.

Nationally the population of Ireland fell by 20 to 25% with an estimated 1 million people dying from hunger and another 1 million people emigrating, many of these emigrants never actually made it to their destination after dying on board the 'coffin ships', a fate that is certain to have befallen many of the local people who had to take this perilous journey.

Letter to the Freemans Journal dated 8th February 1848 from Rev Michael Walker PP of Tisrara outlining contribution made to the parish by local landlord Percy Magan.

THE LANDLORDS AND THE PRIESTS
TO THE EDITOR OF THE FREEMAN
Cottage, Mount Talbot
Mr Editor—May I request that you will afford space in your valuable paper to the following communications which I have received from Percy Magan, Esq., one of the landed proprietors of this parish
I have the honour to be, Mr. Editor, your humble servant, MICHAEL WALKER, P.P , Tisara.
Glass-house, Portarlington January 5, 1849
My Dear Sir—Some time since, and after mature deliberation, I came to the conclusion that EVERY LAND-LORD was in duty bound to contribute according to his means, to the support of the Parish Priest of his tenantry, consequently I now request that you as the Parish Priest of my tenantry will be pleased to accept the enclosed ten pounds as my dues for the past year.
I shall, as a matter of course feel called upon to pay you a similar sum every Christmas.
That you may live to see many a happy Christmas is the sincere wish and prayer of, my dear Sir yours very sincerely, PERCY MAGAN.
To the Rev Michael Walker, P.P , Tisara.
On my acknowledging the receipt of Mr. Magan's esteemed favour, he sent me the following letter —
Glass-house, Portarlington, January 10, 1848
My Dear Sir—In sending you the sum acknowledged in your letter of the 7th instant, I did merely what I considered to be my duty as a landlord, and I am confident that, if others were to act similarly and to consult and associate more than they do with your body—the people and the country would not be in the r present unnatural state Now, a word as to law and justice —
The law compels us to pay a body of clergymen with whom our tenantry hold no communion either temporal or spiritual from the day of their birth to the hour of their death. Surely, then, justice requires that we should contribute to the support of your body, to whom our tenants daily run, as a matter of course, for temporal as well as spiritual advice, in sickness and health, in poverty and in prosperity, by night and by day, from their birth to their death Believe me, my dear Sir, yours very sincerely, PERCY MAGAN.
To the Rev Michael Walker, P P., Tisara.

The landlord at Mount Talbot House during the famine was William Talbot and he seems to have made a dismal effort to alleviate the suffering of his tenants. A list of people who gave financial contributions to the famine relief committee confirms that William Talbot provided no financial assistance to help alleviate the enormous suffering occurring within his lands. Oral history recalls that he evicted families at 'Bothar Bui' (Bushy Park) during the famine and this event very nearly resulted in his death. A disgruntled tenant farmer who had been evicted waited one evening in Finnerty's cow-house adjacent to the present day national school for William Talbot to return from Thornfield House. Talbot visited Mahon's at Thornfield most evenings and always returned home alone at dusk, the tenant farmer was armed with a shot-gun with the intention of shooting William Talbot but luckily for the landlord he delayed longer than usual at Mahon's resulting in the potential assassin falling asleep. The opportunity was missed by the evicted tenant farmer and William Talbot was blissfully unaware that his extra glass of sherry at Thornfield House had saved his life.

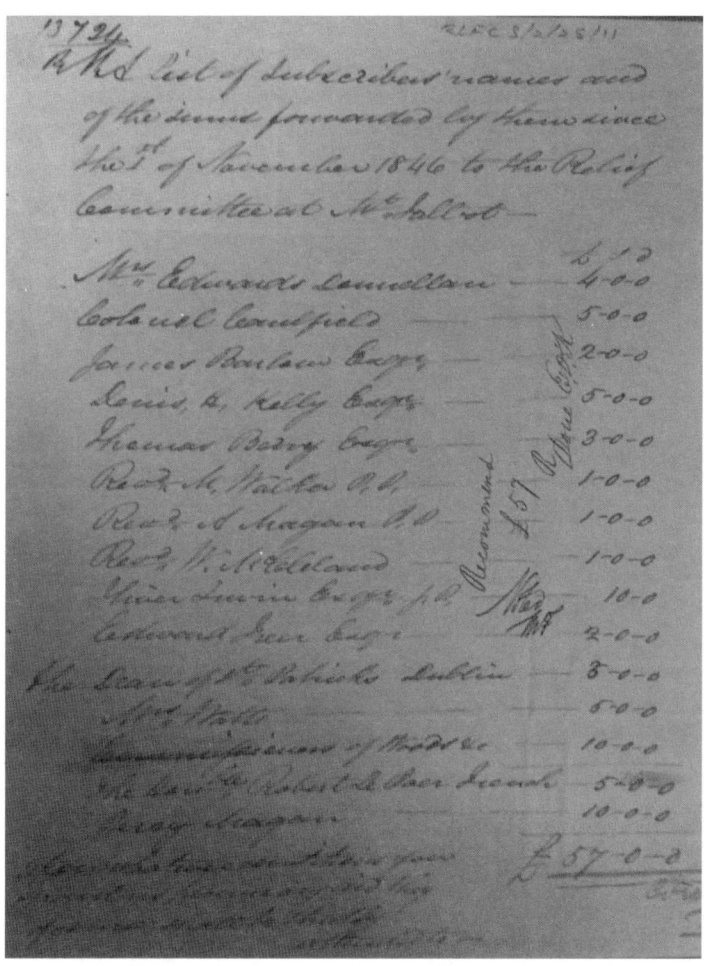

List of Subscribers to the Tisrara Famine Relief Committee (based at Mount Talbot), dated November 1846. William Talbot is not recorded as giving any financial contribution to the Relief Committee, (National Archives of Ireland (NAI), Famine Relief Commission (RLFC), 3/2/25/11).

Denis Kelly of Aughrane was heavily involved in the Killian and Killeroran Relief Committee's, many letters exist in the National Archives of Ireland written by Denis to the Famine Relief Commission including letters requesting food and labour tickets for the people in his area. He sent a letter to the Commission in 1846 predicting the failure of the potato crop for the following season and warning that if the crop fails again *we shall have a sore time of it'*. Denis Kelly also organized large drainage schemes in the area that were funded by loans received from the British Governments Relief Schemes Programme. Many local people were employed carrying out these drainage works but they received little more than food in payment and many men in the area were simply not strong enough to take part in the scheme due to weakness from starvation. Despite Denis Kellys effort, people in the townlands around Mount Talbot that were owned by him suffered enormously during the famine. The population of Cloonakilleg was greatly reduced and Garrier and Thornfield were practically uninhabited after the famine. Cartron however did not see a large population reduction but Araghty seems to have suffered large scale depopulation. Denis Kelly was however accused of using the horrors of the famine to entice the predominantly Catholic local population to convert to Protestantism prior to providing food or other relief items. He also carried out evictions on parts of his estates during the worst year of the famine in 1847[69].

SCHEDULE REFERRED TO IN THE FOREGOING AWARD, AND FORMING PART OF SAME.

Name of Proprietor.	Lands Charged.	Barony in which Lands are situate.	County in which Lands are situate.
Denis H. Kelly of Castle Kelly in the County of Galway Esquire)	Townlands of Srahaunnagort, Tully and Garrier	Killian	Galway

Document giving approval to the carrying out of drainage works at Garrier, Srahaunnagort (Thornfield) and Tully as part of a famine Relief Scheme instigated by Denis Kelly (Galway County Council Archives, Kelly Papers, G00/04/209).

The Famine ended in 1852 having caused terrible suffering to the people of Mount Talbot and the neighbouring townlands. It took many decades before its devastating effects dissipated and the people slowly lifted themselves from this disaster and began to rebuild their lives. The famine was subsequently rarely spoken about in the locality. When people gathered around the fire on a winter's night and the older members of the community recounted past tales to a spell bounded audience the one topic that was rarely discussed was the great hunger. It seems even talking about it was difficult and this tells its own story about what effects the famine had on the locality.

---

[69] This issue and other details relating to Denis Kelly during the famine are examined in more detail later in this chapter under the heading 'Castle Kelly in the 19th Century'.

The house shown in the photo on the left is located in the townland of Cloondara. Derelict houses like this were very common throughout the area during and after the famine. The poem on the lower left was written by Noelle Davies of Bushy Park. Although written in the following century this poem perfectly encapsulates the sadness of this time.

Everyone was affected by the famines devastation but the people that endured it protected their children from ever hearing of the most horrendous single incident ever to befall the local population. There are however some positive and enlightening stories that emerged after the forced emigration that occurred in the area at this time. A starving family had been evicted from their miniscule plot of land by the local landlord in the nearby townland of Funchinagh. The family stayed for a while with their relatives in the village of Corrocot before they were left with no option but to set sail for America. This penniless family arrived on the shores of America owning nothing but the ragged clothes on their backs but within two generations they had achieved the American dream. A grand-son of a member of this family was one of the three men aboard Apollo 11 that took part in one of the most significant events in world history, the lunar landing. On July 20th 1969, Michael Collins piloted the command spacecraft alone in lunar orbit to allow his colleagues Armstrong and Aldrin to set foot on the moon. Collins later received the NASA Distinguished Service Medal, Air Force Distinguished Flying Cross, Air Force Command Pilot Astronaut Wings, Presidential Medal of Freedom and Congressional Gold Medal. Together with Armstrong and Aldrin he received the Collier Trophy, the Hubbard Medal and the Langley Gold Medal. He has had an asteroid and a lunar crater named after him. This family had gone from sitting huddled together and starving under a wall in Corrocot to being part of one of the greatest achievements in human history. A rare bright beacon of light among the darkness of famine times in Mount Talbot.

Scandal

On the 29th of July 1856 a divorce that had been granted in the Irish High Court was ratified by an Act of Parliament bringing to an end a bitter and lengthy divorce case that caused great sensation among the landed gentry in Ireland and in England. The divorce case involved John and Marianne Talbot of Mount Talbot. John Talbot was born John Crosbie at Ardfert, Co. Kerry on 4th of October 1818. His father Reverend John Crosbie, was a brother of William Talbot who owned Mount Talbot house and lands, Reverend John had changed his name by Royal licence from Talbot to Crosbie after inheriting the lands of Ardfert from his uncle, John Crosbie, the last Earl of Glandore. John Crosbie (son of Rev. John Crosbie) married Marianne McCausland on the 2nd of January 1845 in Co. Derry and their daughter Marianne Jane Theodosia was born the following year. In 1847 they moved to Summer Hill in Co. Cork where they remained until October 1850. They then moved to Eden Hill in Co. Cork and in June 1851 they moved to Mount Talbot after the death of John's uncle the previous month. John Crosbie took over the Talbot estate and obtained a royal licence to take the name Talbot in September 1851[70]. William Talbot had left Mount Talbot house and lands to John but his will specifically stated that the ownership was for John's lifetime only and complete possession could only be achieved by having male issue (a son).

The only staff member that the Talbots had brought with them from their former home in County Cork was a groom named William Mullen. In May 1852 the world of Marianne Talbot came crashing down around her. On the 17th of May a butler working for the Talbot's called Michael Halloran went to John Talbot and informed him that Marianne was having an affair with the groom William Mullen. Two other servants at the house made the same allegation on the same day. On the 19th of May John Talbot and a number of employees went to confront Marianne and found her in Mullens room with the door bolted, they broke open the door and found Marianne and Mullen together in the room. Mullen was found standing by the fire and the Talbot's child was also in the room in her mother's arms. Marianne and Mullen were ordered into the yard where John Talbot took the child away from Marianne. John and his daughter went directly to John Barlow's house (his land agent) and spent the night there leaving his wife in the care of two male servants. Marianne spent the night at Mount Talbot house and allegations were subsequently made that one of the servants assaulted Marianne during the night. The next morning the local vicar Rev. McClelland brought Marianne to Dublin in a state of distress and she was very emotional. When she arrived in Dublin Rev. McClelland stated that she attempted to throw herself out of a window and she also tried to take poison, she mistook a grown woman to be her daughter obviously heartbroken after their sad separation. It is believed that William Mullen came to Dublin to try and see Marianne but was refused entry to her lodgings by Rev. McClelland. Marianne was declared insane and was sent to England under a false name. Prior to her departure and after she was declared insane it is alleged that she admitted guilt of having an affair to Rev McClelland. John Talbot filed for divorce and the case was heard in the Consistory Court in Dublin where a divorce was granted. Marianne's family and legal team challenged the ruling as they believed that she was innocent of any wrong doing. The case was subsequently referred to the High Court of Delegates in Dublin where it was heard in May 1855 and again the divorce was granted. A motion was subsequently brought before the House of Commons

---

[70] NLI, Ms. 152, pp.128-31, *'copy of royal licence to John Talbot Crosbie of Mount Talbot in Co. Roscommon to take the name and bear the arms of Talbot'*.

in London by J.G Phillimore MP on the 28th of February 1856. The motion was seconded by J.C Ewart MP but after a lengthy discussion in the chamber the motion failed to carry. The case went before the House of Lords under a petition of *'John Talbot of Mount Talbot in the County of Roscommon, Esquire, praying that he may have leave to bring a bill for dissolving his Marriage with Marianne Talbot, and to enable him to marry again'*, the Bill was subsequently simply called the *'Talbot Divorce Bill'* and it was read to the house on two occasions with the second reading taking place on the 11th of March 1856. After a lengthy hearing the divorce bill was enacted by the House of Lords on the 29th July 1856 and this decision closed the avenues of appeal available to the defence at that time. Marianne Talbot could not attend any of the Court or Parliament proceedings as she was 'officially' declared insane prior to their commencement.

It had taken four years but John Talbot had obtained his divorce. The text from the High Court case and the House of Commons debate are particularly interesting and both sides make convincing arguments throughout the proceedings. In the high court Michael Halloran's evidence is taken on board by the Judge even though he describes Halloran as *'a loathsome and detestable wretch, a scandal to his species, not worthy of being believed in a court of justice'*. The Judge was also aware that Halloran had allegedly assaulted Marianne on the night her husband had left Mount Talbot with their daughter. Two other servants at Mount Talbot house and two servants from their previous house in County Cork also gave evidence that they observed Marianne and Mullen together on a number of occasions. However it seems that the judge made his decision largely on the evidence that came from Rev McClelland of Mount Talbot. It is worth noting that Rev. McClelland had been very critical of the Talbots for their lack of assistance during the famine and this shows he was not under any sort of control or had no fear of the owners of Mount Talbot House. It was to McClelland that Marianne is alleged to have admitted to adultery and he also stated that Marianne had come to him years before the first allegation was made to inform him that she intended to elope with Mullen. Rev. McClelland contacted her father at that time asking him to intervene and attempt to change his daughter's mind. Mr McCausland wrote to Marianne asking her to call to see him but it seems Marianne decided to stay at Mount Talbot.

Marianne's solicitor believed that his client was a victim of a vile conspiracy and was completely innocent of any wrongdoing. They believed that John Talbot knew that Marianne could not have any more children and concocted the whole affair to ensure the inheritance of the Mount Talbot estate. It was alleged that Talbot treated Marianne terribly and never gave her any money for the running of the household or for her own needs. She even had to borrow £5 from a servant to pay for essential items and she subsequently paid the servant back in 3 instalments over a long period. Her solicitors alleged that on the morning of the 19th of May 1852 her husband had arranged for two of his servants to go to Mullen and inform him that Marianne needed to speak with him. When Mullen and Marianne subsequently met in Mullen's room they broke down the door even though it was unlocked and accused Marianne of adultery. When Marianne was brought to Dublin and from there to London her husband told none of Marianne's family where she was staying (she stayed for the first few days at Coffey's Hotel). Marianne was given a false name to ensure that none of her family could make contact with her. Her ill father had attempted to see his daughter when she was in Dublin but was refused access. Marianne's sister and husband (Mr and Mrs Paget) eventually found her in England in a house owned by a Mrs Trueman (who had also been given a false name) and they removed Marianne from this house and brought her back to their family home in London. Marianne was examined by four independent physicians and they all agreed that *'there is no more common cause of this delusion and self accusation being entertained and persisted in than that of a person of pure and unblemished reputation being suddenly assailed with a vile charge of this description which at the time was perfectly unfounded'*, it seems that all four men deemed her innocent. As Marianne was unable to attend court due to her illness and the fact that she had no witnesses or friends resident at Mount Talbot house that could testify on her behalf gave John Talbot an enormous advantage throughout the proceedings. Her husband could call on five staff members and a number of clergymen of the established church to testify on his behalf. The divorce case caused an enormous scandal and the public sensation resulting from its outcome took many years to dissipate. The lives of all the participants were changed forever but they were changed in very different ways:

Michael Halloran – the butler at Mount Talbot house that made the first allegation to John Talbot was retained as an employee on the Talbot estate. Halloran received a £10 increase in his yearly pay immediately after the first court case effectively doubling his wages. He never stood trial for the alleged assault on Marianne.

Reverend McClelland – returned to live at his house in Corrocot and continued to administer his duties as vicar. He died in January 1882 and is buried in Mount Talbot cemetery.

Marianne Talbot – stayed with her sister and her family in London but they could not give her the proper treatment needed to help her deal with her mental illness and she ended up in care in England. She was described by J.G Phillimore MP as follows *'she was unable to appreciate the noble, generous and heroic exertions of those who had surmounted so many obstacles in her behalf. For her there was no conversation, no joyful sympathy of tried friends, no voice of children, no fathers careful counsel, nothing but complete oblivion and endless darkness'*. The date of her death and her place of burial are unknown.

Marianne Jane Theodosia Talbot – John and Marianne's only child was ten years old when her parents officially divorced. She had gone to school in England at six years of age and letters sent to her at school by her father are available to view at the National Library of Ireland. The letters were written during the bitterest part of the divorce proceedings, however the letters do not contain any mention of the case and it seems John Talbot was eager to protect his daughter from the reality of the situation at home. Whether this protection was borne out of care and affection for his daughter or out of his feeling of guilt for destroying her mother we will never know. It is worth noting that in these letters John called his daughter 'Theo' (from Theodosia, her third name) and never called her by her first name 'Marianne'. She had been called Marianne in her early years but after the divorce she was always referred to as Theodosia Talbot, it seems any connection to her mother even through her name was not acceptable. She married Arthur Rickard Lloyd of Beechmount, County Limerick on 21st of October 1869. She died on 3rd January 1894 and is buried in Mount Talbot cemetery, ironically her burial plot is located adjacent to Rev. McClelland's.

John Talbot – John Talbot remained at Mount Talbot House and went on to carry out large scale drainage works on the land. He married Gertrude Caroline Bayley of Ballyarthur, County Wicklow on the 15th of October 1858 and they had a son William John Talbot, born on the 1st of July 1859. John

Talbot died just two weeks after the birth of his son having fulfilled his objective, securing the Mount Talbot estate for his family.

William Crosbie and his brother John Crosbie as young boys in Ardfert, Co. Kerry, John later inherited Mount Talbot from his uncle William Talbot and changed his name by Royal Licence to Talbot, he was later involved in a scandalous divorce case. The portrait on the right is of John's mother, Jane Lloyd of Beechmount, Limerick, wife of Rev. John Crosbie (courtesy of Donald Cameron).

Headstone of Theodosia Lloyd (nee Talbot) in Mount Talbot cemetery. She died at the young age of 48 in 1894 having endured a torrid and unsettling childhood (P.Connolly, March 2014).

Griffiths Valuation

Irelands Valuation Office carried out the first full survey of property ownership in Ireland between the years 1848 and 1864. The survey is now known as 'Griffiths Valuation' named after Richard Griffith who was the Director of the Valuation Office at that time. The valuation was carried out in order to determine the amount of money each person should pay towards the support of people in financial difficulties within each Poor Law Union. The survey shows the names of occupiers of land and buildings, the names of persons from whom the properties were leased and the amount and value of the property held. The village of Mount Talbot in 1857 at the time of Griffiths Valuation contained 16 houses (including the big house). The head of the family in each house were: John Talbot (landlord), Mary Field, Joseph A. Holmes, James Galvin, Patrick Kelly, Robert Little, Patrick Lalor, Andrew Feenerty, Michael Lennon, Charles Lyons, Patrick Killian and William Cinnmon. Patrick Killian collected the tolls and customs of the fairs. John Talbot owned all the houses and lands in the village and the Church and graveyard were owned by the Protestant Ecclesiastical Commissioners. Charles Lyons operated a forge that was located a short distance from the village on the Four Roads road.

Extract from British Parliamentary Papers showing rates charged for selling items at Mount Talbot Fair. Daniel Killian is mentioned as the toll collector in Griffiths Valuation.

The most striking information provided relates to the fact that the houses that were located at the present day ball alley had been removed by this time. The first edition Ordinance Survey maps from 20 years previously were used by the Valuation Office to map the location of each house. The houses that were subsequently removed are still shown on the map but no reference letters exist adjacent to them confirming that they had been demolished prior to the valuation taking place. Local oral history recalls that the houses were removed by the Landlord as he was concerned that they hindered the view from his mansion. The Post Office had been located here and this was moved to a location beside the present day national school. The Talbots built up the demesne wall during the demolition of the houses and he incorporated the front walls of the houses into the fabric of the new wall, the doors and the spaces between the gables of the houses are still visible in this wall today.

The eight houses located at Churchborough have also been removed by this time. It is unknown where the occupants of the houses at Churchborough or at the ball alley ended up but it seems unlikely that they were provided with alternative accommodation. The Famine occurred 10 years prior to Griffith's valuation and this may also have resulted in the depopulation of the area. The maps attached to Griffiths valuation show six dwelling houses adjacent to the Grand Gate that was located within the village at this time. No trace of these six houses are visible today and it seems they were demolished when the gate was moved to its current location later in the 19th century.

Modern Photographs showing the outline of doorways from the houses that were removed at the ball alley. The front walls of the houses were incorporated into the construction of the new demesne wall.

The total amount of rateable land in Mount Talbot was 657 acres and 25 perches with a total annual valuation of rateable property of £453 and 5 pence.

Cloonca contained 2 houses and one of these was a herd's house that was owned by the landlord John Talbot but it seems to have been uninhabited. The other house was inhabited by John Fallon. James Barlow of Bushy Park House was leasing 5 acres and 3 roods of land from John Talbot and Joseph A. Holmes was leasing just over 140 acres.

Cloondara contained 13 houses and the inhabitants of the townland were: John Butler, Roger Conboy, Bryan Flanagan, William Butler, Thomas Lyons, Edward Casey, James Boghly, Anne Raveney, John Heath, Martin Healy, James Queeny, Laurence Queeny and Patrick Conboy.

Cartron was owned at this time by Denis Kelly of Castle Kelly and the townland contained 7 houses. The inhabitants of the houses were: Matthew Connolly, Roger Clogher, Columbus Clogher, Thomas Clogher, Patrick Clogher, Patrick Boland and one house was vacant.

Cloonakilleg was also owned by Denis Kelly and this townland contained 26 houses. The houses were inhabited by: Patrick Connolly, John Lennon, Michael Comboy, John Ward, Owen Collins, Peter Collins, Michael Collins, Bryan Lennon, John Cormakan, Timothy Cormakan, Michael Cormakan, Thomas Collins, Patrick Collins, Winifred Lennon, Owen Divine, Patrick Devine, Hugh Devine, Patrick McLoughnan, Patrick Manion, John Collins, Patrick Tansy, Mary Dolan, Michael Turly, Thomas Turly and Andrew Turly.

Cloonlaughnan was owned by 4 different landlords, William G. Du Bedat, Col. John Caulfield, Percy Magan and the reps of Rev. Michael Walker PP. The people living in Cloonlaughnan were: James Smith, Thomas Little, John Cunniffe, John Hughes, Rev. William McCleland, Ellen Mulvehil, William Burke, James Kelly, John Carroll, Patrick Lennon, Hugh Byrne, Timothy Carroll, Honoria Burke, John Walsh, James Flanagan, John Dolan, Patrick Healy, Thomas McDonnell, James Lynn, Patrick Gannon, Margaret Dowling, William Galvin, John Galvin, William Healy, Bartholomew Healy, Patrick Kelly, Michael Tracy, James Moran, Matthew Manion, Michael Moore and Nicholas Daly (lived in a 'herds house') Francis Madden and James Daly had land leased in Cloonlaughnan but lived elsewhere. Mount Talbot national school was located at this time at the 'sand drain', the school had an exemption and did not have to pay the tax.

At the time of Griffiths Valuation the townlands of Garrier and Thornfield contained only one family, the Mahons of Thornfield House. John Mahon was farming over 164 acres in Garrier and 116 acres in Thornfied and the house and lands were leased from Denis Kelly of Castle Kelly. John Mahon began living at Thornfield and farming the surrounding land in 1838. The famine had a devastating effect on the inhabitants of Garrier and Thornfield as a sizable population lived here at the time of the Tithe Applotment Survey in 1828.

Castle Kelly (Aughrane) in the 19th Century

Reverend Armstrong Kelly was in possession of the Castle Kelly estate for the first half of the 19th century. He married Leonora Salvador of Twickenham, England in 1796 and they had 2 children, a daughter called Leonora who married John Mahon and a son called Denis Henry Kelly. Rev Armstrong Kelly died in 1849 and left the Castle Kelly estate to his son Denis. Denis H. Kelly married

Mary Moseley of Shropshire, England and they had 2 daughters, Leonora Mary and Mary Frances. Mary Moseley died at a relatively young age in 1830 and Denis later married for a second time, his new bride was Elizabeth Diana Cator of Kent, England and they had 3 daughters, Elizabeth, Charlotte and Lucy Anne.

Pencil Sketch of Castle Kelly from 1831. This drawing depicts the back of the castle and a 'reek' of turf may be seen in the foreground. The tall part of the castle to the left was originally a 13th century towerhouse (Courtesy of Tommy Kenny).

Part of a rental book from 1828 relating to lands in Co. Roscommon owned by Rev Armstrong Kelly of Castle Kelly, this page includes names of some of the tenants that lived in Cloonakilleg at this time, yearly rent from the Roscommon estates alone amounted to £702 11s 6 ½ p (Courtesy of Galway County Council Archives, G00/04/164).

Throughout his life Denis Kelly held a variety of political positions, he was Deputy Lieutenant for both the Counties of Galway and Roscommon and he also held the office of Justice of the Peace for both Counties, he served as a Magistrate for both Counties at the same time. He became a Member of Parliament for County Roscommon in 1820 at the young age of 23 and sat as an MP until 1821.

Denis had a keen interest in Irish literature, particularly ancient Irish texts recounting sagas, tales and legends. He seems to have been very proud of his Irish ancestry and wrote extensively on the ancient kingdom of Hy-Many. Irish Antiquarian John O'Donovan stayed at Aughrane in 1837 during his time collecting topographical and historical information for the Ordnance Survey of Ireland. Denis introduced O'Donovan to the local people and brought him on a tour of the locality stopping at various locations to examine some of the local antiquities. Denis also allowed O'Donovan to consult the extensive family collection of papers and manuscripts. This marked the beginning of a long friendship and in the early 1840's Denis assisted O'Donovan in the preparation of his book entitled 'The tribes and customs of Hy-Many commonly called O'Kelly country'. Denis also collaborated with Irish Scholar Eugene O'Curry who was a founding member with O'Donovan of the Irish Archaeological Society. It seems through his association with two of the founding members that Denis became a member of the Irish Archaeological Society. Denis was a member of the Royal Irish Academy and he published a number of articles in the 'Proceedings of the Royal Irish Academy'. His articles primarily concentrated on the local history and archaeology of the counties of Roscommon and Galway. Denis was heavily involved in translating ancient Irish texts into English including the first translation of the 'Annals of Inisfallen'. He collected an enormous amount of old manuscripts including the Hanrahan collection of Fenian Tales. The library at Castle Kelly was one of the finest in the country containing over 15,000 books and a very large collection of Irish manuscripts.

Denis Kelly was elected a life member of the Royal Dublin Society (RDS) in 1832. He resided during his visits to Dublin at his house at 51 Upper Mount Street and also at 9 Herbert Street. Denis served on the governing council of the Royal Dublin Society between 1866 and 1877, on the agriculture committee from 1866 to 1869 and he was on the committee of the first Horse Show in 1868.

Lithograph of
Castle Kelly
from 1863.

Denis Kelly the landlord is remembered very differently to Denis Kelly the historian. Oral history handed down through the generations recall his tyrannical behaviour towards the Catholic tenantry. As may be seen earlier in this chapter Denis seems to have been heavily involved in progressing relief schemes during the famine to help alleviate the suffering of his tenantry, however oral history paints a very different picture of his general behaviour during the famine. It is alleged that Denis brought two Protestant clergymen to the area to force the Catholic peasantry to convert prior to being allowed any relief aid. It seems some people converted rather than starve and these people were despised in the local community and were often referred to as 'soupers'. There is a small field in Cloonakilleg called 'Larrys Garden' named after Larry Clarke a local man who worked for Denis Kelly, he was one of the people that converted to Protestantism during the famine. Larry immigrated to Bristol in 1852 after he was shunned by the local community for being 'a souper'. Denis Kelly carried out some evictions during the famine in parts of his estate but there is no written evidence of this happening in the townlands he owned in the vicinity of Mount Talbot[71]. The townlands of Garrier and Araghty suffered enormous depopulation during the famine and in the subsequent decades but it seems this was caused by the general effects of the famine rather than evictions. Denis had introduced a Reproductive Loan Fund office on main street, Ballygar in 1835. This was a non profit making organisation giving an opportunity for tenants to access money during difficult times and in 1844, £1,000 of the loan fund was in circulation in the locality.

As mentioned earlier in this chapter (in the section that deals with the famine) Denis Kelly was heavily involved in the Killian and Killeroran Relief Committee's and carried out extensive drainage, road building and other relief works throughout his estate. It may be argued that drainage works on land were carried out for personal gain as it improved his holdings but all the money paid by the British Government for these works had to be paid back with interest. The drainage works approved at Garrier, Thornfield and Tully alone cost £88, 13s and 6p with repayments to be made on the 5th of April and the 10th of October each year. He carried out many more drainage works throughout the estate and received loans of over £755 to allow these works to be completed. This resulted in large repayments having to be made for many years after the famine ended. Denis employed many local people on his estate during the famine and regularly pleaded with the famine relief commission for aid yet he has no hesitation in evicting starving penniless families from their homes for non-payment of rent, this contradiction in his personality persists throughout his entire life.

In the years after the famine the Castle Kelly estate was in dire financial difficulties. The cause of this seems to have been a combination of the repaying of famine relief grants, overspending on the construction of unnecessary follies[72], large mortgages, an extension to Castle Kelly, historical debt and the decimation of the rent paying tenantry. Denis had also spent large sums of money building a new town called Ballygar on a green field site adjacent to the entrance to Castle Kelly. It seems that this venture did not produce the return on investment that he had envisaged. Creditors that were owed money began to instigate court proceedings and by the early 1860's the situation became untenable and the estate was practically insolvent. In May 1863, Castle Kelly together with 13,154 acres of land in County Galway and 1,709 acres in County Roscommon (including the lands of Garrier

---

[71] Galway County Council Archives, G00-04-210, 213, 217, 225, 238, 260, 290, these documents confirm that Denis Kelly carried out evictions or 'ejectments' prior to and during the famine.
[72] Denis spent £1,000 on the construction of a bridge within his demesne and he constructed an enormous round tower at the Kelly burial ground of Killeroran.

and Thornfield) were put up for sale by the Landed Estates Court (also known as the Encumbered Estates Court)[73]. The entire estate together with a substantial portion of the town of Ballygar was purchased by Christopher Neville Bagott for £105,000. The townland of Cloonakilleg however seems to have been sold separately to Thomas Kelly Mahon of Thornfield, a nephew of Denis Kelly prior to the main auction. The Mahons had been leasing Cloonakilleg from the Kellys from the early 19th century. The Mahons subsequently purchased Ballybaun House and lands near Newbridge at the auction but they continued to live at Thornfield House. William John Talbot of Mount Talbot later purchased Thornfield House and lands from Christopher Neville Bagott and continued leasing the house and lands to the Mahons[74]. From this time onwards Denis Kelly lived primarily at his house in Upper Mount Street, Dublin but he did retain ownership of Araghty House near Mount Talbot and 576 acres of surrounding land, he lived at Araghty occasionally throughout the year particularly during the summer months and kept permanent staff employed on the estate.

Castle Kelly in the latter part of the 19th century (courtesy of the Irish Architectural Archive).

[73] In 1861 Denis Kelly and John Mahon had signed a document whereby Mahon agreed to 'surrender to Denis Henry Kelly all his interest in the leases', this ensured that the land and house at Thornfield and lands of Garrier were available to sell without any complications. John Mahon was a bother in-law of Denis Kelly and they were good friends but legally this 'surrender' document was necessary to allow the sale to proceed. Galway Co. Council Archives, Kelly Papers, G00/04/153.
[74] The exact chronology of ownership of Thornfield House and lands is confusing as conflicting information exists in the available sources. However the house and lands were leased by the Mahons throughout all this time.

Denis Henry Kelly died on 7th May 1877 and is buried in Killeroran graveyard. Part of the text on his tombstone reads: *'he was chief of the branch of the O'Kelly's of Scrine and candidate for the Kingship of Hy Many'*, it seems even in death Denis wanted to inform future generations of his Irish ancestry. In his will Denis Kelly leaves most of his wealth to his daughters and their families, he also leaves a sizable sum to his nephews the Mahons of Thornfield House. He also leaves money to various people from the locality involved in the running of the Protestant Church and it is worth noting that he leaves £100 to the *'good old Irish Society, 16 Upper Sackville Street, Dublin for promoting the education of Irish Roman Catholics in the Irish Tongue'*[75]. He also leaves various sums of money to all of the people employed in his houses at Araghty and at 51 Upper Mount Street, Dublin. This does not seem to be the actions of an alleged sectarian bigot with a hatred of his tenantry and the Catholic working classes. Denis Kelly's very important collection of books, translations and original early Irish manuscripts had been sold in 1875 to James Ludovic Lindsey, 26th Earl of Crawford in 67 lots at a cost of £203 4s 6d. Mrs Enriqueta Rylands subsequently purchased the entire collection for the John Ryland's library in Manchester where they remain to this day.

Letter from 1853 that highlights the fact that the Castle Kelly estate was in dire financial difficulties in the years after the famine. The executors of the will of William Talbot of Mount Talbot were calling in all mortgages and it seems the Kellys were struggling to pay off the mortgage that was in place with the Talbots as they had debts amounting to over £40,000 (Galway County Council Archive G00/04/278).

---

[75] Galway County Council Archives, Kelly Papers, G00/04/164, approved draft will of Denis Kelly.

Araghty House in the 1970's, this house was inhabited by Denis Kelly after the forced sale of Aughrane in 1863. After the death of Denis the house was purchased by John Bourns who owned a shop in Ballygar and a farm in Castlefrench. This house has since been demolished and no trace of it exists today (from the Cronin collection).

The Tower at Killeroran built by Denis Kelly

Tombstone of Denis Kelly also at Killeroran

Denis Henry Kelly remains something of an enigma and his legacy in the area is best described by the late Tim Cronin of Mount Talbot: *'People saw Denis Kelly in various posses, to one he was an ogre, to another a scholar, to another a missioner, to another a womaniser, to another a builder, to another a liar, to another a tyrant'*[76].

COUNTY OF GALWAY.

IMPORTANT EXECUTORS' SALE
BY AUCTION
AT
A R A G H T Y G R A N G E,
1 mile from Athleague, 3 from Ballygar, and 4
from Roscommon,
On TUESDAY, the 26th of June, 1877,
Commencing at 12 o'clock noon.

THE Representatives of the late Denis H.
Kelly, Esq., have confided to us the conduct of the
SALE BY AUCTION,
as above, of the entire
F U R N I T U R E
of that fully furnished house, comprising every article
in every branch of a gentleman's residence—Drawing-
room, diningroom, hall, lobby, bedrooms, pantry, dairy
and culinary—the enumeration of which surpasses all
ordinary bounds of an advertisement, but may be stated
as modern and substantial. Also, the
CATTLE, SHEEP, HORSES,
Vehicles, Harness,
Farming Implements, Garden Tools, &c., &c.

The Cattle and Sheep comprise two year old heifers
and yearling ditto ; bullocks, cows, and calves; Kerry
springer, a purely-bred short-horn bull, 2 years old, by
Light of Dunraven (21670), &c, &c ; hogget long-woolled
sheep, &c.
The Horses are—A pair of carriage horses, brood
mare and foal ; two-year-old and yearling fillies,
highly bred ; one jennet, and, by permission, a pair of
steel grey ponies, three years old, untrained, 14 hands 2
inches high (detached property).
A number of garden plants, a quantity of oaten straw,
and a large quantity of prime hay in rick ; also 50 Irish
acres of pasture land, to 30th October next, with meadows and other crops. Private proposals will be received
in the meantime for the hay and grazing.
THE COACH-HOUSE AND STABLE-YARD
Comprise—
Phaeton and harness, family car and harness, cab-
carriage, made to order, with pole and shafts ; single
and double harness, bridles, saddles, and horse clothing,
and all et ceteras.
☞ We respectfully submit that the bounds of an
advertisement could not contain details of this property,
and we request our friends to estimate the in and out-
door establishments as those of a complete concern. Indoor : modern, replete, and full. Out-door : in stable
and farm yards, not wanting in any of the usual luxuries
of the former, nor of the improved modern necessaries
of the latter.
N.B.—Punctual attendance is requested, as it is intended to do all in one day for public convenience.
Terms —Cash.
Purchasers to pay 5 per cent. auction fees.

GANLY, SONS, AND CO.,
AUCTIONEERS.   11325

Newspaper advertisement for the auction of Denis Kelly's house at Araghty together with livestock and the contents of the house and out-houses, June 1877.

[76]Killian-Killeroran Historical Society (1982), *Newbridge, Ballygar, Toghergar News*, p33.

William John Talbot

William John Talbot inherited Mount Talbot House and the entire estate from his father John who died in 1859 but William John was only 2 weeks old when his father died and could not take ownership of the estate until he reached the required age. William John's widowed mother Gertrude married Capt. Hon. Francis George Crofton RN (Royal Navy) on the 18th of August 1864, a daughter was born on Christmas Day 1867 whom they named Gertrude Catherine Georgiana Crofton. Francis Crofton was the fourth son of Sir Edward Crofton, 2nd Baron Crofton of Mote Park, Co. Roscommon and he was a grand-nephew of Rev. Hon Henry Crofton of Thornfield House, who had been vicar at Mount Talbot in the earlier part of the 19th century.

REJOICINGS AT MOUNT TALBOT.

On Thursday evening last the happy tenantry, farm labourers, &c., on the extensive property of Mount Talbot were sumptuously entertained on the occasion of the return of the Hon. Francis Crofton and his beautiful and accomplished bride. Amongst the toasts drank during the evening were—The Queen, Prince and Princess of Wales, and all the Royal Family—the Hon. Francis and Mrs Crofton, their happy union, that God may bless and protect them—Master Talbot, the young heir to-to the Mount Talbot property—Lord and Lady Crofton and family—Colonel and Mrs Bayley and family—all of which were received with rapturous applause. Dancing commenced at an early hour and was kept up, with great spirit, all night; and the joyful assembly separated in the morning fervently blessing the "happy couple," and wishing them every health and happiness.

Newspaper article from the Roscommon Journal dated 1st of October 1864 outlining details of a party held at Mount Talbot House to celebrate the marriage of John Talbots widow Gertrude and the Hon. Francis Crofton of Mote Park.

The Croftons lived at Mount Talbot House after their marriage but Gertrude died at a relatively young age on the 19th of August 1869. William John was only 10 years old at this time and he was now an orphan as both his parents were dead. Francis Crofton seems to have vacated Mount Talbot House after the death of his wife but he continued to look after his step son. Francis married Emily Caulfield in February 1878 but by this time William John was 19 years old and nearing adulthood. The extended Crofton and Bayley families continued to make regular visits to Mount Talbot until William John came of age and inherited the estate. Francis George Crofton died at Harbour House, Kingston, County Dublin at the age of 62 on the 30th of September 1900. Francis was a brother of Augusta Caroline Crofton who was awarded an OBE in 1920 for her work as an amateur photographer. She had married Luke Gerald Dillon of Clonbrock near Ahascragh in 1866 and was one of the leading photographers in the country at this time. She had a photograph house built on the grounds of Clonbrock to develop her photographs which amounted to 3,000 by the time of her death. Many of the earlier photos of Mount Talbot House that exist today were taken by Augusta Dillon nee Crofton. William John Talbot later constructed a photograph gallery at Mount Talbot where many of Augusta Crofton's photographs were displayed.

Photo of Captain Francis George Crofton (left), step-father of William John Talbot. Newspaper report from 1866 (right) giving details of auction to be held at Mount Talbot House prior to the departure of F.G Crofton on active service with the Royal Navy.

Rent Book from the Mount Talbot estate showing the rental of Francis George Crofton for lands on his step-sons estate. The lands are 'surrendered and relet' in 1869, the same year as Francis Crofton's wife and William John Talbots mother Gertrude died, this suggests that Francis moved away from Mount Talbot after the death of his wife (rent book courtesy of John English).

William John Talbot attended public school at Eton College near Windsor, England between the years 1872 and 1876, in the house of Rev. Francis Edward Durnford. Two years after graduating from Eton, Johnnie enrolled at Jesus College, Cambridge University and was admitted to Magdalene College, Cambridge on 19th September 1879.

After the departure of Francis Crofton from Mount Talbot, William John's cousins the Talbot Crosbies of Ardfert moved into Mount Talbot House to run the estate until he came of age. The lands of Mount Talbot amounted to 6,026 acres at this time[77]. The Talbot Crosbies supervised the construction of a new Land Steward's House in 1871, this house was designed and constructed by Michael O'Farrell from Roscommon town and cost £278 to complete[78]. It seems that when William John returned from Cambridge University ready to take full possession of his inheritance the Talbot Crosbies were reluctant to vacate the house and hand over the estate to their cousin. Both parties reached a compromise and WJ Talbot built a beautiful new house for the Talbot Crosbies across the road from Mount Talbot house and he also gave them some land in the vicinity of the new house[79]. This new house was called 'Cloonca House' and it was built in the early 1880's.

The grounds of Mount Talbot House in 1865, in this photo are the young William John Talbot with his governess, Francis George Crofton and Gertrude Crofton (W.J Talbots mother) may be seen in the background (courtesy of the Irish Architectural Archive).

---

[77] House of Commons, Paper No:412, *Owners of land (Ireland)* , HMSO, 1876, this document states that 'Talbot, Reps of John' had an estate of 6,026 acres with an annual valuation of £2,633. In the '*Return of owners of land in Ireland of one acre and upwards*', Dublin 1876, William John Talbot is shown as 'a minor' owning over 3,500 acres with John Talbot (his late father) still owning over 2,416 acres.
[78] Irish Builder, Volume 13, 1 July 1871, p175. This house became Flanagans Post Office in the mid 20th century.
[79] House of Commons, Paper No:412, *Owners of land (Ireland)* , HMSO, 1876, this document states that 'Talbot, Crosbie' had an estate of 1,560 acres.

Photo of the Grand Gate at Mount Talbot from 1865, the boy in this photo is 6 year old William John Talbot. The Grand Gate was located in Mount Talbot village at this time (courtesy of the Irish Architectural Archive).

Photo taken at the front entrance to Mount Talbot House in 1890, standing (left to right): Lord Crofton of Mote Park, Gertrude Crofton (Johnnie Talbots half sister), unknown person, Mrs. Dillon, Hon. Charles Crofton. The people seated are (l to r): Di Crofton, Mrs. Bayley, May Crofton (courtesy of the Irish Architectural Archive).

William John Talbot was known by his friends and the local people as 'Johnnie' and he always preferred to be called this name. In the late 1870's or early 1880's Johnnie Talbot made some alterations and additions to Mount Talbot house, he also moved the Grand Gate from the village to its present location. It may not be a coincidence that these gates were positioned directly across the road from the entrance to the recently constructed Cloonca house that was inhabited by his cousins the Talbot Crosbies. The front door and main entrance of Mount Talbot house were moved to the north eastern corner of the building and it was approached by a new avenue leading from the repositioned entrance gates. After this time the back of the house faced the village of Mount Talbot and the front faced the river suck to the North West. A large open entrance porch was constructed to incorporate the new front door and stone steps were installed with side walls resulting in an impressive new entrance to the house.

Photo from the late 19th century showing Mount Talbot House after the remodeling that took place in the early 1880's, the repositioned front entrance is shown to the right of the house and this is approached by a new avenue leading from the 'Grand Gate' (courtesy of Donald Cameron).

The original front door was now used to gain access to a large new terraced area and to the lawns and tennis courts that existed on the village side of the house. The steps leading up to the original front door were removed and new steps were installed leading from the new terrace to the gardens. A small extension or annex was constructed at the point where the large tower intersected the centre block of the house and this extension included three new windows that looked out onto the terrace. After the remodeling was completed the upper floor of the house contained 9 bedrooms for family and guests with 1 of these rooms located in the turret located in the centre of the house, this floor also contained 5 bedrooms for the house servants. The master bedroom was lavishly decorated and this room also included a dressing room and bathroom. The ground floor contained Johnnie Talbot's bedroom, a large library, the grand hall, dining room, drawing room, billiard room and the kitchens and laundry were also located on the ground floor. The large cellars contained the Talbots large and varied collection of fine wines and rare spirits from around the world. Family portraits hung on the walls of the dining room. These portraits included all the descendants of the Talbot family including Sir Henry Talbot who was the first of this family to live in the area.

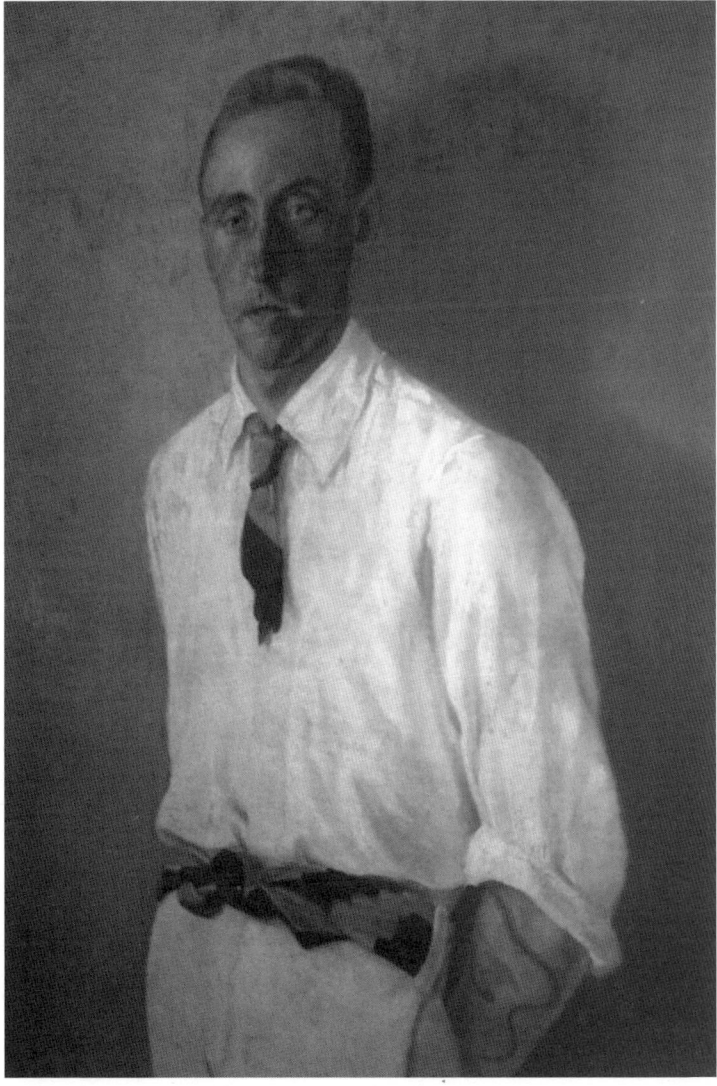

Portrait of a young Johnnie Talbot of Mount Talbot House, circa 1879 (courtesy of Donald Cameron).

The front of Mount Talbot House prior to its re-modeling in the 1880's. The front door of the house was located centrally and an avenue led from the Grand Gate to the front door, the Grand Gate was located in the village at this time (courtesy of Donald Cameron).

The front of Mount Talbot House after the re-modeling that was carried out by Johnnie Talbot. The front door of the house was now located at the opposite side of the house, the avenue was replaced by a footpath and the new terraced area is visible in the foreground (courtesy of Emmy Eustace).

The re-modeling of the house and the changing of the entrance gates and avenues allowed the visitor to see more of the impressive gardens and rare trees that existed within the demesne when approaching the house. Johnnie Talbot travelled extensively throughout Europe, Africa and America and he collected an enormous amount of rare trees and plants on his travels, making the grounds of Mount Talbot House one of the most impressive in the country. The original avenue leading to the house was changed to a walkway and a new pedestrian gate with impressive stone pillars was constructed where the original entrance gates stood. This new pedestrian gate was subsequently known as *'the wicket gate'* and this was used by workers on the Talbot estate to gain access to the big house, gardens or demesne lands.

Johnnie Talbot was well thought of in the local community and he seems to have treated his staff and tenants with respect. He generally left the running of the estate in the hands of his senior staff as he spent a lot of time away from Mount Talbot. Johnnie suffered from ill health for most of his life and had particular problems with asthma and bronchitis. He did not however allow his ill health to impact on his many interests. He was a good equestrian and visited the United States on a number of occasions to study horses and his fine bred horses won many prizes at the Dublin Horse Show in Ballsbridge. Hunts at Mount Talbot became an annual event and it was one of the most eagerly anticipated meetings for members of the Roscommon Hunt.

Hunt at Mount Talbot House, circa 1885.

THE STAGHOUNDS

THE staghounds, under the mastership of Mr. W. J. Talbot, of Mount Talbot, opened the season with a meet at Tulsk on Thursday last. Although the weather was unfavourable, the attendance was large, and a hearty welcome was given to the new master. The hounds were in splendid condition, indeed good judges consider them the finest pack in Ireland, and the whole turn-out of the hunt is very creditable. A good stag gave a run of about 12 miles, which was quite enough at this early part of the season when horses are not quite fit for a long spin over a heavy country.

The Roscommon Journal reports on a hunt that occurred in Tulsk during October 1892 under the mastership of Johnnie Talbot.

Guests relax at a party held at Mount Talbot House in the late 19th century; Johnnie Talbot is shown on the extreme right (courtesy of the National Library of Ireland).

Johnnie Talbot had a keen interest in botany and added many rare and exotic plants and flowers to the already impressive collection within the demesne that had been accumulated by his father. He was commended in the Irish Times for his 'splendid basket of Lord Palmerston peach' displayed at the Royal Horticultural Society's annual winter exhibition in Dublin in 1900. Johnnie also read extensively on a variety of subjects adding many books to the existing collection at the Library of Mount Talbot House. He occasionally wrote poetry and studied the classical languages of Greek and Latin. He also had an interest in music and was known to entertain guests at Mount Talbot on the piano and organ. He later purchased a grand organ and placed it in the large hall in Mount Talbot

House[80]. Like his forbears Johnnie entered the British Military and gained the rank of Captain in the 7th Brigade, South Irish Division of the Royal Artillery but it seems he did not see active service. He later joined the Wicklow Militia. His mother was originally from Ballyarthur, County Wicklow and Johnnie probably spent some time with her family, the Baleys, on occasions during this time. He also followed his forebears into politics becoming High Sherriff of County Roscommon in 1886. He also held the position of Deputy Lieutenant and Justice of the Peace for County Roscommon and was later Deputy Lieutenant for County Galway and for County Armagh. He was a candidate for the Conservative Party in the 1885 general election but only received 338 votes comparing dismally to the 6,033 votes received by the Nationalist Party candidate.

Johnnie Talbot married Julia Elizabeth Mary Molyneux of Castledillon, County Armagh on the 14th of August 1897 in Kent, England. He was 38 years old when he got married and his bride was 33 which would have been considered old at that time. Julia was the only daughter of the large landowner Sir Capel Molyneux, 7th Baron Molyneux who had died in 1879. Julia had inherited most of her father's estate making her one of the most independently wealthy ladies in the country. With the combining of their lands and wealth Johnnie and Julia Talbot entered the 20th Century in the upper echelons of Irish society.

The Wicklow Militia with Johnnie Talbot shown standing to the right with both hands on his sword (courtesy of Emmy Eustace).

---

[80]This Grand Organ is now located in the Catholic Church in Ballygar.

The entrance gates shown above are located at Northbrook near Aughrim in County Galway (left) and at Lissadorn near Carrick on Shannon (right). Both these entrance gates are exactly the same as the 'Grand Gate' at Mount Talbot (below) and this suggests all three structures share the same designer and mason.

Mount Talbot House in the late 19th century (courtesy of Emmy Eustace).

The dining room at Mount Talbot House, late 19th century (courtesy of the Irish Architectural Archive).

Mount Talbot National School

In 1892 a new national school was built in Mount Talbot providing local children with a dry, clean and modern building. The building of the new school was one of the most significant developments in the history of Mount Talbot and something that helped enormously in securing a better future for the children in the area.

Education of the Irish Catholic population had been prohibited under the penal laws thus denying the majority of the population access to essential learning. Throughout the 19th century records show large levels of illiteracy among the tenantry because of the unavailability of a proper education. The first schools in the locality were known as 'Hedge Schools' and these provided basic education to the local children but were not funded in any way by the Government. Parents of scholars provided any funding that they could afford for payment of the schoolteacher and provided fuel and other essential items to the school. Hedge schools were initially located in isolated hidden areas out of the watchful eye of the local government officials but when the penal laws became less severe many schools moved into small one room buildings. In the early to mid 19th century hedge schools were recorded in Lismaha and Mount Talbot village. Lismaha School was located along the Bushy Park road and it was described at the time as being 'a poor cabin'. The teacher of Lismaha School was called Luke Clogher who is recorded as earning £14 to £16 per year. Mount Talbot school was also of poor construction and was described as being a 'common cabin'. The teacher was called

George Carberry and he earned £10 per year[81]. The first edition OS maps show this school in Mount Talbot and it was located a short distance down the Four Roads road on the right hand side. Oral history recalls another hedge school in the area located in the townland of Cloonlaughnan and the teachers name was Mike Collins. Many children from Cloonakilleg, Cloonlaughnan and Corrocot attended this school and it seems the students received a good education with most achieving an excellent standard of literacy.

A state supported primary school system was initiated by the British Government in 1831 and from this time the schools are no longer referred to as 'Hedge Schools' as they were officially recognized by the state. Records exist of the local Catholic clergyman making an application to the commissioners for aid in 1847, requesting funding for a national school in Mount Talbot. The school was subsequently inspected and the attendance on the day of the inspection was 29 boys and 16 girls. The teacher at this time was called Mike Lennon and he was 22 years old. It is possible that this school at Mount Talbot was located in the same building as the hedge school from the previous decade but with more funding available schools often moved to more suitable accommodation. It seems this school did not stay open for long as records do not exist after 1847 and the demise of the school was probably due to the devastation that occurred in the area during the famine. The next school in Mount Talbot was known as the Sand Drain School and it was located at the western extremity of Cloonlaughnan townland close to the village of Mount Talbot. The Parish Priest of Tisrara made an application for aid to the commissioners in 1858 to cover the cost of employing the teacher Maria Carty who was only 19 years old. This school was inspected by the commissioners and it was described as being in a 'pretty fair' state with an earthen floor and plastered walls. It was a long one roomed thatched building with sliding windows and a small playground existed on the site. £1 10s per year was paid in rent to Martin Smith, the owner of the land on which the school was built. A Mrs. Collins also taught at this school, she had only one arm but was known to have been an adept knitter. By 1872 the school had a principal teacher called Maria Moore and a monitress called Miss Galvin was also employed[82]. However by 1889 the school was no longer fit for purpose and was described by the district inspector as being *'unsuitable in every respect'*. Another visit by an inspector three years later described the building as *'a wretched structure which is poorly finished and altogether unfit for teaching purposes'* but he also added in his report that a new school was nearing completion.

The new school at Mount Talbot was completed in 1892 to a very high standard by the main contractor William Beattie of Lismaha and the building stone used in the structure came from Tibarney quarry. The teachers and children closed the door of the old sand drain school for the last time in the autumn of 1892 and walked the short distance to their new school. They were escorted on this momentous journey by Johnnie Healy of Lismaha playing the fiddle and one can only imagine the excitement and anticipation of the school children as they turned the corner at the village pump and viewed their large, modern and dry new school with a slated roof, timber floor, toilet facilities and a large playground. 1892 also saw the introduction of legislation making attendance at school compulsory and the opening of the new school at Mount Talbot ensured that all the children in the area received excellent primary education. Many Protestant children living in the area attended the

---

[81]All references to these schools come from the *'Reports of the Commissioners of the Board of Education of Ireland, 1825-1827'*, National Archives of Ireland.
[82] A Monitress is a female student who helps keep order or assists a teacher in a school.

school particularly children of workers at Mount Talbot House. 32 Protestant and 2 Presbyterian children enrolled in Mount Talbot national school between the years 1873 and 1904. Father Bernard Dervin of Kilnagralta described how the children intermingled and played together without any difficulty, '*not once can I recall any differences between us and them. There were five or six from the Cole family, Robert Bruce from Cloondray – son of the gamekeeper, two girls from Crosbies, one boy from Blackwoods. We played the same games, had the same rough and tumble. One thing different though, they were better dressed than practically all of us. Their parents could afford the cost of clothes and shoes, ours could not*'[83].

A small Protestant school existed in Mount Talbot village from 1867 and Johnnie Talbot became patron of the school later in the century. This school was located across the road from the original entrance gate to Mount Talbot House. Johnnie Talbot applied to the Commissioners for aid in 1880 and the school was subsequently inspected. The inspector described the school as '*a one-roomed stone building with a slated roof and tiled floor*' and the average attendance was noted as 19. The teacher was called Thomas McCormack and he was 28 years old and untrained. The district inspector reported that he believed that this school was unnecessary in Mount Talbot but the school survived until June 1919 mainly due to continued private funding from Johnnie Talbot. It seems unusual that all the Protestant children in the area did not attend this school and this reflects well on the standard of education available in Mount Talbot national school.

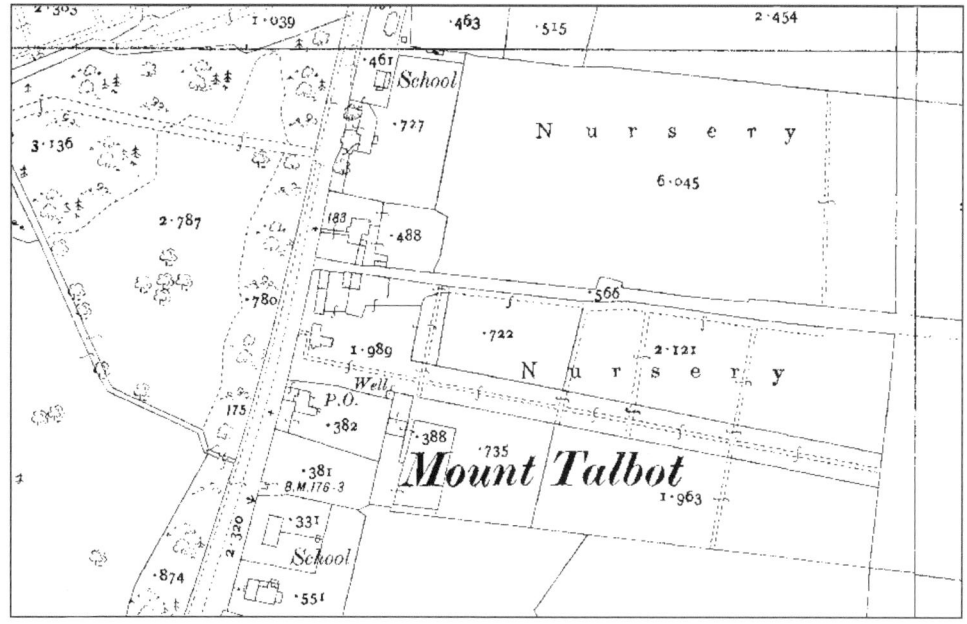

Map from the early 20th century showing the location of the schools in Mount Talbot. The National school constructed in 1892 is shown in the lower part of the map and the Protestant school constructed in 1867 is shown in the upper part of the map (OSI, Licence number 2010/15CCMA/Galway County Council).

---

[83] Mount Talbot School Board of Management, *Mount Talbot School - a window on the past*, 1992, p30.

The quality of the materials and workmanship of Mount Talbot national school has withstood the test of time and now over 120 years later this building is still used to educate the children of Mount Talbot and its environs.

Mount Talbot National School and Teachers Residence in the late 1970's. The School at this time had not undergone any external structural changes since its completion in 1892 (from the Cronin Collection).

Children

Oh, we were young, so gaily young
We deemed the world a garden
Where only roses met the birds,
And love was gentle warden.
We laughed because the breeze blew high,
We held our heads together,
And your own curls they danced with mine,
My dear, in that Spring weather.
Oh, we were young, so foolish young
That surely we were olden
And far from wise that wisdom is,
Let all her thoughts be golden.
Then take my hand and we'll go back
And hold our heads together,
And your own curls will dance with mine
My dear, in that lost weather.

This poem was written by the author and poet Patrick Kelly who was born in Mount Talbot in 1879 but moved soon after his birth to Cashel in Connemara, Co. Galway. He was the eldest son of Joseph Donnellan Kelly and Mary Anne Galvin of Mount Talbot who were both national school teachers. Patrick or 'Paddy' wrote many articles for the national press and also wrote a play called the 'Journeyman Cobbler' that was shown at the Abbey Theatre. He also published a book of poems entitled 'The Sally Ring' and it is believed that he wrote the famous Irish poem and ballad 'the Rocks of Bawn'. Patrick Kelly died in 1940.

An Gorta Beag

Famine reappeared in Ireland in 1879 and caused widespread suffering to the local population. This famine was known as 'an Gorta Beag' but unlike the Great Famine (an Gorta Mor) it caused hunger rather than mass death. The British Government responded quickly and adequately in contrast to the serious misjudged response to the Great Famine. The severity of the famine was also curtailed because of changes in farming practices and the structure of land holdings. Money sent back to Ireland by emigrants abroad particularly from the United States helped the local population to sustain themselves during this crisis. The parish of Tisrara is recorded as having 900 people in distress on March 1st 1880 and their condition was described by the Relief Committee as follows: *'Distress likely to last till next August, even should baronial works be commenced, the people will not get wages sufficient to support them, they must still look for outside help'*. Seven payments were made by the government to the people of Tisrara amounting to a total of £210. The people in the neighbouring districts of Taghboy and Dysart seem to have suffered enormously during this crisis. 1,450 people were recorded as being 'in distress' and their condition was described by the Relief Committee as follows: *'In very great distress, half naked, very little or no bed covering, children in rags'*. The authorities reacted quickly to the crisis and relief aid was provided in sufficient quantities to alleviate the suffering and by 1881 the crisis had abated[84].

Galvin Nurseries

By the end of the century more employment opportunities had become available to the people in the area providing households with a welcome additional source of income. Catholic Emancipation, compulsory education, the formation of Catholic Universities and the Government Land Acts earlier in the century resulted in a Catholic middle class emerging in Irish society. A number of businesses existed in Mount Talbot at this time and one of the largest of these was 'Galvin Nurseries'. This nursery was one of the most successful horticultural businesses in the country with a client base that extended into all parts of Ireland. Galvin Nurseries advertised in all of the well known national newspapers of the time and produced an annual catalogue containing a list of stock and prices for all their produce. The Galvins were members of the Irish Parliamentary Party and were strong supporters of Charles Stewart Parnell, they continued to support him after the split that occurred within the party over Parnell's affair with Katherine (Kitty) O'Shea. John and James Galvin represented Mount Talbot at a Nationalist Meeting in Ballygar on 15th June 1891 where *'resolutions were passed reiterating confidence in the leadership of Mr. Parnell and pledging themselves to return*

---

[84]The Irish Crisis of 1879-80, Proceedings of the Dublin Mansion House Relief Committee 1880, Dublin 1881, p285, 293, 303.

at the next election only supporters of the Independent Irish Party led by Mr. Parnell'[85]. Parnell did not survive the political repercussions of his private life and his political party moved on without him however the Galvins remained strong Parnellites.

Galvin Nurseries continued to be operational well into the 20th century but in the early 1920's Seamus Galvin moved the centre of their business to Mount Avon, Rathdrum in County Wexford. He did however continue to operate Mount Talbot nurseries for a number of years after moving to Wexford. Tom Flynn of Derrinlerrig was the last person employed in Galvins nurseries in Mount Talbot. It is worth noting that Seamus Galvin's brother John purchased 'Avondale House', the former home of Charles Stewart Parnell in County Wicklow.

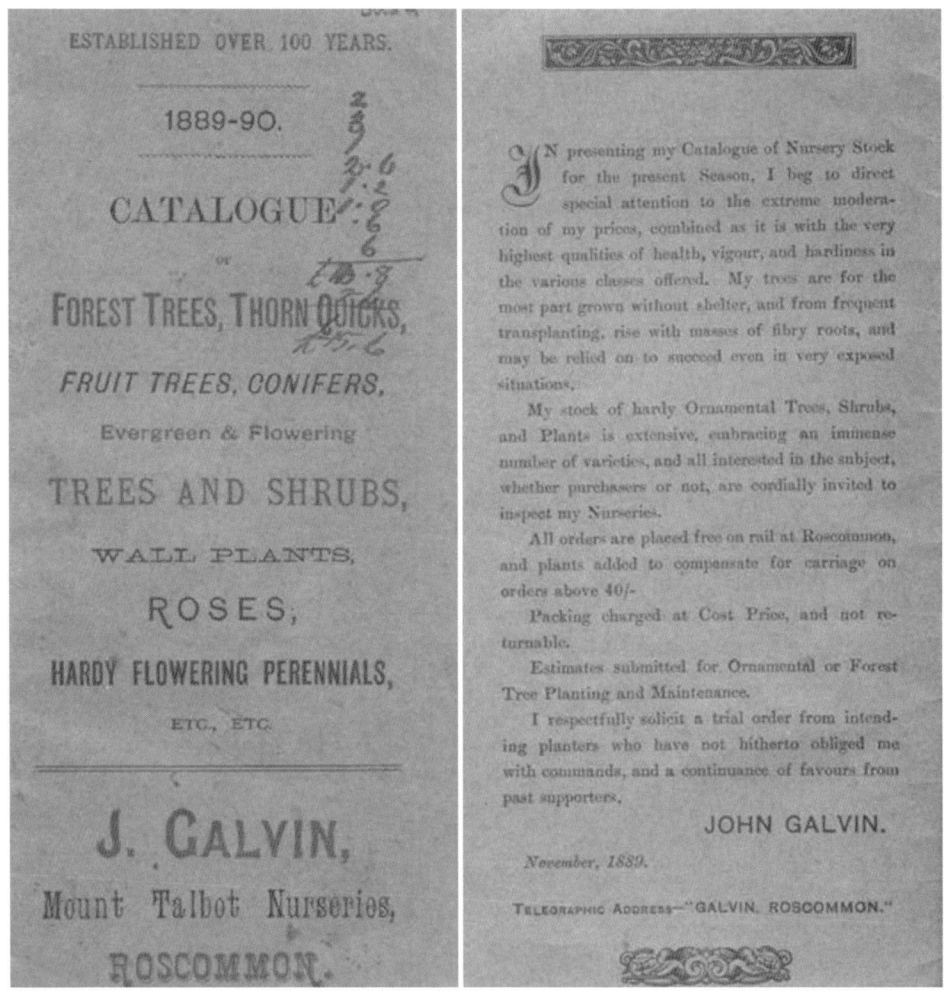

Front cover and inner leaf of a Catalogue from Galvin Nurseries for the planting season 1889-90 (courtesy of NUIG Library, Special Collections).

---

[85] Freemans Journal, June 16th 1891, p7.

Chapter 6 - The 20th Century

The 20th century saw the most dramatic changes in Mount Talbot since the wars of the 17th century, particularly in relation to land ownership. Mount Talbot and its environs changed dramatically both politically and economically during this century but the people of the area certainly did not envisage these changes as the new century dawned. The 1901 and the 1911 census have both survived destruction in their entirety and they provide an excellent snapshot of the village and surrounding areas in the early 20th century.

The 1901 Census

The 1901 census gives details of all the occupants of the houses in Mount Talbot and the surrounding areas. Details listed in the census include the full names of each occupant commencing with the 'Head of Family' and the subsequent names are listed in order of their relationship to the head of the family. Other details of the occupants include age, religion, literacy, occupation, marriage status, place of birth and proficiency in Irish. The inhabitants of Mount Talbot House are listed in the census but the Talbot owners are not included presumably because they were elsewhere when the census was taken.

The population of Mount Talbot (not including the Talbots) in 1901 was 43. From the total of 43 people, 33 people were Catholics, 9 were Protestant and 1 was Presbyterian. 21 of the people listed were born within the locality, 3 were born in County Galway, 1 in Kilkenny, 1 in Laois (then known as Queens county), 1 in Donegal, 1 in Dublin, 1 in Cavan, 1 in Armagh, 2 were born in England and 1 in Scotland. 6 people listed can speak Irish and all children listed above the age of 7 can read and write signifying the important role of the national school in Mount Talbot.

The surnames of the people in Mount Talbot listed in the census include: Lyons, Naughton, Boyle, Finnerty, Hoare, Blackwood, Byrne, Connolly, Galvin, English, Hawkshaw, Reddington, Waletron, Cleeland, Gallergah, McCready, Shannon, Lawlor, Sharman and Meely. The occupations of the people living in Mount Talbot are varied and the list includes: farmers, a national school teacher, servants, a county councillor, a nurseryman, an acting clerk of petty sessions, a veterinary surgeon, a land steward, a shop assistant, gardeners, a footman, a laundry maid, a hospital nurse and a herd. Many of the occupations listed are directly associated with the big house or businesses located within the village.

Roscommon Journal, July 26th 1902, W.H Sharman is shown in the 1901 census as a gardener at Mount Talbot House.

MOUNT TALBOT

FRUIT for eating or home jam to be sold at moderate prices during June and July. Orders booked from now on by

. W. H. SHARMAN,
The Garden,
Mount Talbot.

In the 1901 census there are 23 houses in Cloonakilleg with a total population of 107 people. The surnames of the occupants were: Connolly, Lennon, Collins, Ward, Crehan, Cormican, Mannion, Naughten, Devine, McLoughlin, Galvin, Mullan and Turley.

Cloonlaughnan (including Corrocot) contained 24 houses and had a population of 152 people, their surnames were: Farrell, Kelly, Lennon, Cunniffe, Smyth, Connell, Little, Connor, Healy, Nolan, Byrne, Mulynn, McDonnell, Moran, Galvin, Dolan, Kennedy, Flanaghan, Burke, Killelea, Carroll and Heath.

There were 12 houses in Cloondara with a population of 52 people, their surnames were: Butler, Conboy, Flanagan, Tiernan, Casey, Healy, Curly and Queeney.

Cloonca contained 3 houses with one of these being 'Cloonca House'. This house was owned by the Talbot Crosbie family and their farm manager was John Quinn. The Talbot Crosbies are not listed in the census so they must have been elsewhere on the night the census was taken. John Quinn lived at Cloonca House with his wife Catherine and a housemaid called Lizzie Campbell. Cloonca townland had a population of 13 and their surnames were: Quinn, Campell, Smith and Flanagan.

Cartron contained 7 houses and had a population of 40 people. The surnames of the occupants were: Connolly, Clogher, Boland and Burke.

Lismaha contained 13 houses and had a population of 51. All the people living in Lismaha were Catholic and their surnames were: McConn, Mullen, Healy, Beatty, Cleary, Moylan, Daly, Quirke, Staunton, Conboy, Fallon, Corr, and Neely.

Lisgillalea contained 6 houses and had a population of 23. This townland was also known as 'Bushy Park', named after the large house that existed within the townland and occupied by the Ffrench family. The Ffrenchs leased the house and land at this time from Johnnie Talbot of Mount Talbot House. The surnames of the people living in Lisgillalea were: Cawley, Ffrench, Larkin, Lennon, Fallon, Gavin and Lane.

One house existed within the townland of Garrier and this was occupied by John Naughton who was a member of the Royal Irish Constabulary. Five other family members lived in this house with John and a schoolteacher named Bridget Divine was visiting the house on the day of the census.

Thornfield House is the only residence shown within the townland of Thornfield and 6 people were residing here. The head of the house was Thomas K. Mahon and he lived here with his wife Frances. The 4 other occupants worked as servants within the house.

The 1911 Census

The population of Mount Talbot in the 1911 census is 53 showing an increase of 10 people since the 1901 census. The population includes 31 Catholics, 21 Protestants and 1 Presbyterian giving an increase of 12 people that were Protestants, 2 less Catholics and the same number of Presbyterian's compared to the 1901 census. The occupations of the inhabitants included farmers, gardeners, servants, schoolteachers, a road and labourers foreman, gamekeepers, a land steward, a nursery foreman, a sub post mistress and a retired sergeant with the Royal Irish Constabulary. Many of the occupations listed are attributable to the Big House. The 1911 census indicates that there are many more people living in Mount Talbot from outside the county than existed in 1901. The Counties represented include: Cavan, Wexford, Dublin, Meath, Wicklow, Fermanagh, Derry, Armagh, Antrim, Mayo, Monaghan, Laois and Kildare. Other inhabitants were born in England and one in Scotland. The high number of Protestants and people from Northern Ireland living in Mount Talbot indicate the influence of Johnnie Talbot's wife Julia who favoured servants and farm labourers from her own tradition. The surnames of the inhabitants of Mount Talbot were Farly, Galvin, Hague, Lambert, Naughton, Finnerty, Seaman, McIntyre, Kelly, Lawlor, Blackwood, Hanratty, Kenny, Clelland, Geraghty, Meely and Drimmie.

The number of houses located in the adjoining townlands in the 1911 census are: 13 in Lismaha, 5 in Lisgillalea, 12 in Cloondara, 3 in Cloonca, 23 in Cloonakilleg, 6 in Cartron, 1 in Garrier, 23 in Cloonlaughnan and 1 in Thornfield.

Sports and Pastimes

The beginning of the 20th century saw the arrival of organised sports in Mount Talbot, particularly sports associated with the Gaelic Athletic Association. A Gaelic football team and hurling team were organised in the area during the formative years of the new century and both these teams competed in the County Roscommon GAA championships. The GAA had been formed in Thurles in 1884 and was part of the general re-awakening in Irish culture and heritage that occurred in the latter part of the 19th century. The Gaelic league and the Irish Literary revival also contributed enormously to instil in Irish people a renewed sense of self-belief and pride in their country and its traditions.

A hurling club was formed in 1904 or early 1905 by Matt Heavey who was a schoolteacher in Tisrara National School at this time and the team subsequently became known as the 'Tisrara Maith go Leors'. The Maith go Leors were an exceptionally talented group of players winning three County Roscommon senior championships in a row between the years 1905-07. The fact that the team were so successful within a year after being formed suggests that a strong hurling tradition existed in the area prior to the formation of the club. Local tradition recalls hurling matches between Mount Talbot and Athleague being played in the front lawns of Mount Talbot House throughout the 19th century. These matches took place in a field called 'Crab Park' in front of the big house and was part of an overall sports day involving a variety of track and field events. No written account of this event is currently available but records of similar events taking place in other parts of Ireland suggest that the local landlord picked the teams, arranged the hurling greens and supervised the matches. It seems these events were eagerly anticipated by the local gentry who were known to gamble heavily on the outcome of the hurling match. After the formation of the Maith go Leors Johnnie Talbot provided a training pitch for the team and this was located adjacent to the entrance to the Cloondara road within the townland of Lismaha. The hurling team shared this pitch with the local Gaelic football team. In December 1905, the Freemans Journal newspaper referred to a championship hurling match that was to be played on January 7th 1906 between 'Tisrara and Athleague Gaels'. The match was scheduled to take place in Mount Talbot and this confirms that championship hurling matches took place at the pitch in Lismaha at this time. The Maith go Leors' built up a great rivalry with their near neighbours Athleague who had a very talented team. Athleague hurling club had been formed early in the 20th century by another school teacher, Paddy O'Sullivan from Cork. Araghty Gaels were another hurling team that existed locally at this time. This team was made up of players from the townland of Araghty that adjoins the townlands of Cloondara and Lismaha. In the early 20th century, Araghty townland contained a large number of houses and had a sizable population. The fact that the Maith go Leors and Araghty Gaels contained players from neighbouring townlands added extra intensity to the hurling matches that took place between these sides. Roscommon Gaels also had a very strong team and the annual personal duel between Matt Heavey and Harry Hession at mid-field was eagerly anticipated by all hurling supporters in the county. Roscommon Gaels had won the first 3 Roscommon Senior hurling championships in 1902/03/04. The Maith go Leor hurling panel contained 13 players from Mount Talbot and its environs with 2 players from Four Roads, 1 from Tibarney and another from Coolderry.

An original hurling ball used by the 'Maith go Leor' team during the formative years of the 20th century. This ball or 'sliotar' was made by Tom Connolly of Cloonakilleg.

Matt Heavey was a strict disciplinarian and always ensured that the players were adequately prepared for each championship match. He favoured a direct style of hurling and encouraged the players to move the sliotar at pace on the ground resulting in the opposition finding it difficult to deal with the speed of the game. To allow this style of hurling to be played Heavey needed the correct shaped hurley with a broad heavy heel and he eventually found the perfect 'pattern' from a source in Wexford. Heavey gave the pattern to a local carpenter in Corrocot called James Nolan who took great pride in producing hurleys of exceptional quality. When a sliothar was struck properly with Nolan's hurleys it travelled at great speed and the hurlers could get fantastic height and distance in their ground strokes. The sliotars were also made locally by Tom Connolly of Cloonakilleg, the author's grandfather. The jerseys worn by the Maith go Leors were black in colour with a green stripe running diagonally from shoulder to waist, the collar and cuffs were also green. Mount Talbot National School and the Handball Club wear these same colours today.

Those men of fame won many a game

They were swift but never sore

In cold or heat they're hard to defeat

Those good men Maith-Go-Leor[86]

---

[86]Verse 5 of a contemporary poem by Tom Seavers, this poem was recited from memory by a grandson of Tom Seavers, Marty Smith of Corrocot.

Hurling continued to be played in the area after the Maith go Leors and a very good team emerged in the late 1920's, early 30's and these became known as the 'young mogies'. The centre of hurling shifted from Mount Talbot to the neighbouring village of Four Roads in the 1930's and matches were played in a field belonging to Brian Finnerty of Coolderry. The hurling team at this time became known as Four Roads and the team jerseys were changed to their modern 'blank and amber' colour and style at this time. Training took place at a field at Tumrover in Cloonlaughnan, Kelly's 'pump field' and at a field to the rear of Coyle's public house. Mount Talbot still produced excellent hurlers, Pat Carroll, Joe Galvin and the Cunniffe and Turley brothers were particularly talented. John Cunniffe from Corrocot was an excellent all-round sportsman and played soccer with Arsenal Football Club in London during the 1930's. He worked in London as a young Priest shortly after his ordination from Maynooth seminary[87]. Success at senior level did not arrive until 1945 when the county title was secured after a fantastic performance by Mattie Heavey of Mount Talbot who was a son of the clubs founder, Matt Heavey. Mee's field at Coolderry was first used by the hurling team in 1941 and this remained the centre of hurling in the area until the club moved to Tisrara Community Sports Park near the village of Four Roads in 1995. Four Roads are the most successful club in the history of Roscommon hurling having amassed 32 Roscommon senior titles and 2 Connacht senior club titles over the last 109 years (up to and including 2014). Mount Talbot has a long association with Four Roads hurling club and every team since the time of the 'Tisrara Maith go Leors' has contained players from this area.

This hurley was made by James Nolan in Corrocot for the Maith go Leor hurling team in the early 20th century. It is the last known hurley in existence from this era.

---

[87]Four Roads Hurling Club-A Century of Hurling 1905-2005, from an article written by Tommy Connolly of Cloonakilleg.

The 'Tisrara Maith go Leors' that won three Roscommon County Senior Hurling championships in a row between the years 1905 and 1907. Back row (left to right) Tom Connolly, Tibarney; John Healy, Lismaha; Pakie Naughton, Mount Talbot; Brian Finnerty, Coolderry; Mike Connolly, Cartron. Middle row: Mike Conboy, Cloondara; Tom Treacy, Cloonlaughnan; Arthur Casserly, Four Roads; Mike Gately, Kilnagralta; Pat Kelly, Lisduff. First row: Matt Heavey, Four Roads; Ned Smith, Corrocot; Jack Smith, Mount Talbot; William Finnerty, Coolderry; Joe Fallon, Lismaha. At front: 'Downey' Conboy, Cloondara; Joe Naughton, Mount Talbot.

Photo comparing a Maith go Leor hurley with a modern hurley. This photo highlights the thickness of the 'heel' of the hurleys used by the Maith go Leors. The pattern for these hurleys with the broad heavey heel was sourced in Wexford by Matt Heavey.

A Gaelic football team was organised in Mount Talbot at the turn of the 20th century and this team competed in the Co. Roscommon senior football championship for a number of years. In April 1903 the Freeman's Journal newspaper gave a report on a championship match between Mount Talbot and Roscommon Gaels. This match took place in Roscommon town in front of a large crowd with Roscommon Gaels emerging as eventual winners on a scoreline of 7 points to 2. Mount Talbot continued to field a football team well into the 1930's but the team disbanded after this time. On the 6th of June 1931 an article in the Connacht Tribune's sports section gave a list of Mount Talbot players that took part in a local football tournament, the players were: M. Turley (Captain), T. Cunniffe, P. Carroll, M. Cunniffe, T. Cormaken, J. Galvin, M. Heavahan, N. Heavahan, H. Farrell, J. Clogher, J. Moran, J. Healy, C. Kelly, M Nolan and P. Conboy.

After the disbandment of the local football club Mount Talbot continued to produce some excellent Gaelic footballers, Sean Naughton of Naughton's shop in the village won an All-Ireland minor medal with Roscommon in 1941 and Mattie Heavey was on the panel of the great Roscommon Senior football team of the mid 1940's. Gaelic footballers from the area now play their club football with St. Aidans football club based in the neighbouring village of Ballyforan.

CO. ROSCOMMON FOOTBALL CHAMPIONSHIPS.

A large crowd assembled at Roscommon on Sunday to witness the first matches played for the Championship in the southern portion of the county. The day was beautifully fine, and the field splendidly laid out.

ROSCOMMON GAELS v. MOUNT TALBOT.

The Gaels won the toss, and taking advantage of a slight breeze they worked splendidly, scoring a point in the first three minutes. The game can be easily described up to half time, as the Gaels scarcely ever allowed the ball on their territory, and at the interval had scored 6 points to nil. On resumption the Mount Talbot men played much better, and succeeded in registering a point, which was followed shortly after with another. Mid-field play was the order for some time and nearing the end the Gaels scored a point against the wind. At full time the result was—

ROSCOMMON GAELS .... 7 points
MOUNT TALBOT .... 2 points
Mr. M. Brennan acted as referee.

FOOTBALL

A football tournament was held in Roscommon on Sunday last, when the following teams attended :—Roscommon, Kilbride, Ballygar, Mount Talbot, Athleague, and Fuerty.
The first contest was between Mount Talbot and Kilbride, when, after a well-contested game, the score was :—

Kilbride ... .. 1 goal 2 points.
Mount Talbot .. .. 4 points.

Ballygar and Roscommon next tried conclusions, when, after a good game, the home team was defeated by one point.
Owing to the lateness of the hour and the inclemency of the weather the other matches had to be abandoned.
——o——
A football tournament will be held at Ballygar on Sunday, April 21st. The following clubs have been invited.—Roscommon, Athleague, Fuerty, Mount Talbot, Creggs, Mount Bellew, Moylough, and Cultra. First match at two p m sharp.

Match report from the Freemans Journal dated April 7th 1903 (left) relating to a championship football match between Mount Talbot and Roscommon Gaels. Newspaper report from the Roscommon Messenger (right) showing Mount Talbot footballers involvement in local tournaments.

The Land Question

Land ownership had been a contentious issue in the locality for many generations. All the land in the area was owned by Landlords and the people resented the fact that they had to pay rent for their small holdings to these landlords. The late 19th Century had seen widespread land agitation throughout the country and the 'Land League' brought immense pressure on the British Government to instigate Acts of Parliament to allow tenants to purchase land from the landlord. The area around Mount Talbot seems to have been relatively quiet in relation to land agitation but oral history recalls a group known as the Molly Maguires raided houses locally for firearms[88]. Various Land Acts were eventually passed through the Houses of Parliament including the Ashbourne Act of 1885 and the Balfour Act of 1887 but the strict terms of these acts did not benefit the average tenant. It was not until the Wyndham Land Purchase Act of 1903 that the majority of tenants could actually avail of the tenant purchasing schemes proposed by the British Government. The Wyndham Act differed from the other Acts as it made provisions for the Government paying the difference between the price that the Landlord expected to get for the land and what the tenant was prepared to pay. After the Land Acts were in place the Irish Land Commission developed into a tenant-purchasing commission and assisted in the agreed transfer of freehold farmland from landlord to tenant[89]. The Congested District Board of Ireland (CDB) was established in 1891 to help alleviate poverty and congested living conditions in the west of Ireland. Subsequent to the Wyndham Land Act the CDB was authorised to purchase land from the large estates and redistribute this land to tenants. In 1909 the Congested District Board was authorised to purchase lands by means of Compulsory purchase from landlords that refused to sell parts of their estates. The Local Government (Ireland) Act of 1898 replaced the Grand Jury system with a democratised form of local government. Up to this time landlords had controlled the undemocratic grand juries as membership was based on being a large rate payer. This Act did not include any direct clauses relating to land ownership or land transfer but it allowed the tenantry (who were mostly Catholic) to have strong representation in the new County Councils, thus weakening the stranglehold that the landlords had on local communities.

The transfer of land from landlord to tenant did not occur in Mount Talbot and the surroundings area until the first decade of the 20th century. Since 1870 the Ffrench family had been renting a large quantity of land from the Talbots at Bushy Park and this family purchased all the land in 1907 for £1,644. A Rent Book from the Talbot estate from the early 20th century shows a tenant in Kilnagralta purchased land from Johnnie Talbot on the 1st of November 1907. This tenant was paying £12 per year in rent at the time and he bought the land in question from the landlord for £257. The House and Building Return form (form B1) that is attached to the 1901 and 1911 census show that in 1901, 11 out of a total of 15 houses in Mount Talbot village were owned by the landlord Johnnie Talbot. However by 1911, 10 houses out of a total of 13 were owned by the occupiers of the house. This clearly shows that householders in Mount Talbot were availing of the various land acts to gain ownership of their homesteads and it seems many of these purchases occurred after the introduction of the successful Wyndham Land Purchase Act of 1903. It is worth noting that at the time of Griffiths Valuation of 1857 the Talbots owned every single house in Mount Talbot. On the 18th of November 1912 over 400 acres of the Talbot estate was vested in the Congested District Board for redistribution among the tenantry and this gave an opportunity for some of the tenants with smaller holdings to purchase land. By the 1920's the Talbots estate had been reduced but they still owned a large amount of Land in the area and were unwilling to sell any additional lands to the tenants through the Land Commission or the Congested District Boards, causing resentment and anger among the remaining tenantry. The Talbots also owned a large amount of land in Castlesampson, Curraghboy and parts of Ballyforan at this time.

---

[88] The 'Molly Maguires' or 'Mollies' were later involved in labour activities in the US, up to 20 of this group were executed in the US for organising strikes in the mines of Pennsylvania.

[89] The Land Commission was created in 1881 as a rent fixing commission by the Land Law (Ireland) Act 1881 but concentrated on transferring land after the Ashbourne Land Act of 1885.

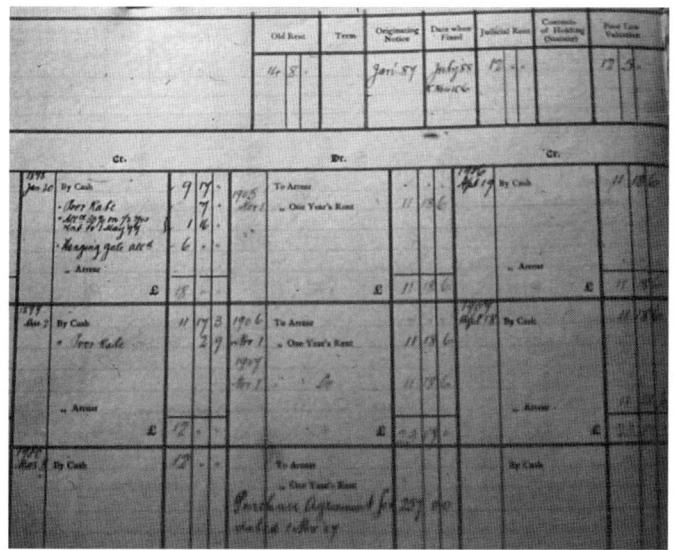

Rent Book from the Talbot estate giving details of the purchase of land by a sitting Tenant (from the Cronin collection).

As mentioned in the previous chapter the Bagotts purchased the lands and Castle at Aughrane from Denis Kelly in 1863. In 1903 the Bagotts put the entire estate up for sale and the 1,600 acres of land was purchased by the Irish Land Commission. The Castle and surrounding demesne were purchased by the Department of Agriculture and Scientific Instruction in 1910. Aughrane Castle or Castle Kelly was inhabited sporadically after this time with the last known occupants being a Mr. Donavan and his family, Mr. Donavan was the local Forester.

St. Patricks Catholic Church in Athleague – The stone section at the front of the church was originally part of the castle at Aughrane. The entire section was moved to this location prior to the demolition of the castle.

The Castle at Aughrane was set on fire and badly damaged by republicans during the War of Independence as it was believed that it was going to be occupied by British Soldiers who were already in occupation of the yards and outbuildings. What remained of the estate was purchased by the State Forestry Commission in 1938. During the mid 1950's the remaining parts of the castle that were still standing were levelled and no trace of this building exists today.

Johnnie Talbot had purchased Garrier and Thornfield from Bagotts in the late 19th century and he continued to lease the house and lands to the Mahons. The Mahons owned Cloonakilleg and after the death of Tom Mahon in 1906 his wife moved back to her family in England. The people of Cloonakilleg pleaded with the landowners to allow sitting tenants to be given the option to buy the land. This started a long and bitter legal case with the tenants at one stage being sued by the landowners but eventually the tenants won the right to purchase the land through the land commission.

On Friday the 14th of April 1916 five families from Cloonakilleg moved to Garrier during the redistribution of the lands by the Land Commission. The families in question were the Cormicans, Turleys, Devines and 2 Collins families. Garrier had contained only 1 house for many years until the arrival of the families from Cloonakilleg as the famine had all but wiped out the population of this townland.

The remaining tenants in Mount Talbot and the surrounding areas had to wait until the early 1920's before the remaining lands in the ownership of the local landlords became available for purchase and redistribution.

This wooden plough is owned by Sean Collins of Garrier. It was brought out to Garrier from Cloonakilleg by Sean's grandfather when the family moved to the area in 1916. The plough dates to the late 19th century (P. Connolly, August 2014).

Landscape with Light

Fields covered by winter floods;
flat *callas* shimmer under latent power
from January sun and stretch to
the tower of Killeroran graveyard.

The water gleams like melted mercury;
billions of rounded diamonds
vibrate and throb in new found glory
over acres of lost grass.

It is the triumph of water over earth
as it was in the beginning. The land
is a massive lake now, but like lakes
on Titan, is not what is seems.

I want to keep this day forever, this light,
this water, this cold January noon;
I know when I return again, the fields
will be greening for summer meadows,

as if nothing had happened at all,
as if nothing has happened to me.
I take my camera from my pocket
and rest on an old whitethorn,

its trunk roped with ivy arms
so that the ivy is a green bush
at the top, revelling in winter's
temporary triumph.

I move my camera across the waterscape,
from Killeroran tower to the slopes
of Cloonakilleg on the opposite side
of the river. Here my grandfather

grew wheat to pay the landlord's rent;
careful, tight-fisted neighbours buried
new sovereigns each autumn
under flagstones of their kitchen floors.

Even when my grandfather left the place,
sold the thatched house and farm
to come to Garrier on this side
of the river, my father and his brothers

kept a boat under the salleys
where the stone wall ended,
and rowed back every Sunday
to the village of their birth.

The row of tall salleys between
the River Field and Slough Field
is there; only the ghost of the wall
my grandfather built remains,

a scatter of white-patched stones
blotched with tufts of black moss.
The fields are different too, moulded
by the markings of the flood.

The water in the Slough Field
is shaped to a long rectangle,
where a marooned hillock
becomes a tree-filled island;

its trees are old and clawed;
their reflection in flood-water
like a light-filled lithograph –
still, stamped, holding eternal pose.

A swan floats by this fluid facsimile,
keeps close to the island's curve,
with wings and feathers puffed
like hoisted ghost-galleon sails.

When she has left my sight,
the photographs are finished.
Roped arms of the ivy press
my back as if wanting to tie

me into their twisted patterns;
to become rooted in this place
forever watching seasons pass
to music of endlessly arguing swans.

Mary Turley-McGrath

Mount Talbot House in the early 20th century

At the beginning of the 20th century Johnnie and Julia Talbot had settled in to married life and were enjoying the comforts of their vast combined wealth. In 1903 Johnnie became High Sheriff of County Armagh suggesting that they divided their time between Mount Talbot and Julia's birthplace, Castle Dillon. Julia purchased a former schoolhouse beside her ancestral home which she named 'Little Castle Dillon'[90]. They also travelled extensively spending time in rented accommodation in England and visiting Europe and America. The Roscommon Journal noted on the 21st of December 1901 that *'Mr. W.J Talbot, DL, Mount Talbot and Mrs Talbot left Ireland last week on a trip to South Africa'*. Johnnie Talbot owned the first motor car in County Roscommon with the registration number D1-1.

As stated in chapter 4, Johnnie Talbot was well liked in the community but his new bride was immensely disliked by the people of Mount Talbot. It seems Julia practically ran the estate and Johnnie had very little say in matters relating to the house or land. Oral history recalls her domineering manner and her mistreatment of staff employed in the house and on the estate. She was given the nickname 'The Major' by the employees presumably because of her military approach to the running of the estate. It is alleged that she rationed the food of the workers and she became even more disliked when she replaced the popular William English as land steward. It seems however that Julia did not ration her own food as her weight increased enormously over the years making her even more intimidating to her staff. A servant who worked at the house at this time later remarked that *'if you were on the right side of her, you were alright, but if you were on the wrong side it was a hell of a long way to get around her'*[91].

However, it seems Julia did show some friendliness to the local population as on the 6th January each year the children from the local national school were invited to a christmas party at the house. The party was held in the 'photo gallery' and the 'coach-house' and these buildings were located in the western wing of the house. The late John Collins of Garrier recalled that the rooms *'would be all lit up and decorated with flowers and a big table covered with presents for the children'*[92]. Every child got a small present, food and drinks were provided and the children were treated very kindly by their hosts, however no party was held at Mount Talbot House after the Easter Rising in 1916.

Julia Talbot was heavily involved in charitable organisations in the area and during the early part of the 20th century she formed the 'Mount Talbot District Nursing Association'. This organisation provided a resident nurse at Mount Talbot to attend the sick in the area. Julia was also involved in fundraising events for ex British Army servicemen being a member of the Soldiers and Sailors Help Society and the Red Cross but these organisations were not very popular in a society where Irish nationalism was on the increase. For her involvement in charitable work relating to ex-servicemen Julia Talbot was awarded an OBE in 1919 by King George V.

---

[90] This remodelled Schoolhouse later became the property of the mother of Field Marshall Montgomery the hero of El Alamein and North Africa in WW2.
[91] Quote taken from article in Roscommon Herald, 5th February 1927.
[92] Mount Talbot School Board of Management, Mount Talbot School, a Window in the Past, 1992, p15.

Mount Talbot District Nursing Association.

TO THE EDITOR OF THE MESSENGER.

DEAR SIR—I should be much obliged if you would kindly let it be known, by the publication of this letter in your paper, that the committee of the above association have decided to hold a Jumble Sale from 12 to 5 p m on 2nd December. Mr Talbot has kindly lent the Photograph House, Mount Talbot, for this object. Friends, both here and in London, have given and collected many attractive things, and different ladies in the neighbourhood have kindly consented to take charge of the stalls. Entrance will be 2d, and everything, new and old, will be sold at popular prices. I may mention that the nurse, who lives in Mount Talbot, works in a large district, which includes Ballygar, Athleague, and the Four Roads. Thanking you before hand for your kindness in inserting this letter.—I am, very truly yours,

JULIA TALBOT.

Mount Talbot, 25th Nov, '04.

DOLL SHOW AT MOUNT TALBOT.

The Doll Show in connection with Miss Goulding's work of distributing toys at Christmas to workhouse children, was held on 22nd December at Mount Talbot. Over forty-five dolls were dressed by ladies in Roscommon and the neighbourhood, and the show was visited by one hundred and sixty grown-up people and children. First prize was won by Mrs Legge and Miss Dillon, Ballygar, who tied, receiving one, a silver hair ornament, the other a silver-mounted scent bottle; second prize, Mrs Brown, Roscommon; third prize, Miss D'Arcy. The judging was by popular vote. Twenty of the dolls were sent at once to the Cork workhouse; others will be distributed in Roscommon workhouse on 6 h inst, and the remainder will be kept for next year.

Letter written by Julia Talbot in November 1904 to the Roscommon Messenger Newspaper highlighting her role in the Mount Talbot District Nursing Association (left). Newspaper report in the Roscommon Messenger relating to a Doll Show held at Mount Talbot House to raise funds for local workhouses (right).

Johnnie and Julia were happiest entertaining guests of their own social status and no expense was spared in relation to these events. Guests were lavishly entertained and many large social events were held within the house and throughout the impressive gardens in the demesne. In August 1907 an open air fete was held in the grounds of Mount Talbot house and all the landed gentry in the area were in attendance. In January 1911 the Talbot's hosted their third shoot of the season at Mount Talbot where over 750 pheasants were shot.

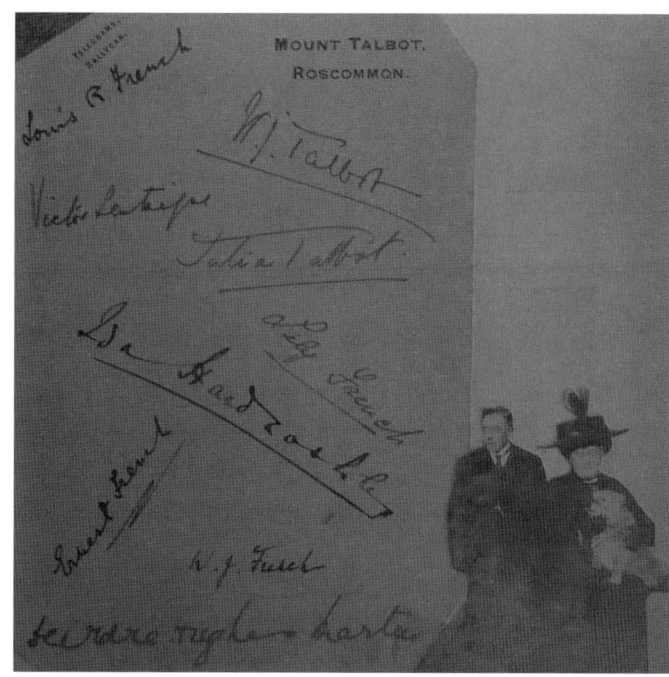

Signatures of people attending a fundraising event for ex-servicemen held at Mount Talbot house in 1918. The hosts, Johnie and Julia Talbot are shown in the lower right corner (courtesy of the National Library of Ireland).

In August 1919 a garden party was hosted by the Talbots to meet the Lord Lieutenant of Ireland, John French the 1st Earl of Ypres. The guest list included some of the most influential people in the country and beyond highlighting the high social standing of the Talbots at this time. Among the many guests were the Duke and Duchess of Staepoole and many high ranking British Military personnel. Also in attendance was Doctor Douglas Hyde who became the first President of the Irish Republic later in the century. One can only imagine the pressure that the servants and staff were under prior to this event as the Talbots reputation as leading party hosts depended on this event going smoothly. Any error, no matter how small, would not have been accepted by the 'Major' and was sure to result in an immediate termination of employment.

GARDEN PARTY AT MOUNT TALBOT.

Mrs. W. J. Talbot gave a garden party at Mount Talbot, Co. Roscommon, on Saturday last, to meet the Lord Lieutenant. Amongst the guests were the following:—Colonel Stenhouse and officers of the Somersetshire Yeomanry, Marie Lady de Freyne, Lady Castlemaine and Hon. Eva Handcock, Sir William and Lady Mahon, Lord de Freyne, Mr. A. St. George Caulfield, the Duke and Duchess de Staepoole and Mrs. McMiking, Major and Mrs. Hall and party, Dr. and Mrs. Douglas Hyde, Colonel and Mrs. Odell, Hon. Arthur and Mrs. Handcock, Mrs. Blake-Kelly and Mrs. Comyn, Mr. and Mrs. Monahan of Newtown, Lord Clonbrock, Mr. and Mrs. Bagot, Miss Mapother and party, Sir Thomas Stafford, Miss O'Rorke and Mrs. Bradford. Hon. Lily and Hon. B. French, Misses Ffolliott, Captain Hon. C. Mulholland, in attendance on His Excellency; Mr. and Mrs. John Godley and party, Sir Gilbert, Lady King and party; Hon. Georgina Dillon, Miss Zoe Strouge, Miss Cust and Miss Higgins, Colonel and Mrs. Kirkwood and party, Major and Lady Cecilie Goff, Major and Mrs. French, Mrs. D'Arcy and party, Canon and Mrs. Forde, Major and Mrs. Murphy and party, Mrs. St. L. Tyrell, Major and Mrs. French, Mrs. and Miss Auchmuty, Canon and Misses French, Rev. Mr. and Mrs. Landy, Mr. and Mrs. A. Walker, Mrs. and Miss Satchwell, Mr. Rice, R.M.; Mr. C. M. Russell, R.M.; Mr. Munro, Mr. W. J. Walpole, J.P.; Mr. and Mrs. Pakenham Mahon and Mrs. King-Harman, Mrs. Henderson, The Manse, Roscommon; Mrs. Shiel, Kilbegnet; Mr. and the Misses Black, Miss Mildred Cartan, Roscommon; and very many others.

Mrs. Talbot previously had a luncheon party, at which the guests were:—Marie Lady de Freyne and Hon. Lily French, Lady Castlemaine and Hon. Eva Handcock, Lord de Freyne, Lord Clonbrock and Hon. G. Dillon, Colonel Stenhouse, and Mr. A. St. G. Caulfield.

The beautiful gardens and grounds of Mount Talbot were thrown open to the visitors. The band of the Somersetshire Yeomanry played throughout the afternoon and during an American tennis tournament, which was arranged by Mr. Hetreed, and played off in the three fine courts in the grounds.

Tea was served to the company in the dining-room, where the floral decorations of scarlet sweet-pea looked particularly well against the old walls and the scarlet leather chairs. All the war workers in the Roscommon district were invited. They wore their badges and decorations, which added much to the interest of the scene.

Newspaper article from the Irish Times dated 30th of August 1919 reporting on the garden party held at Mount Talbot house to meet the Lord Lieutenant of Ireland.

Photo No.1   Photo No.2

Photo No.3

Johnnie and Julia Talbot enjoying a day trip to Galway City accompanied by their friend Alex Eustace. Johnnie is wearing a dark suit in these photos (courtesy of Emmy Eustace).

Photo 1 is taken in the Claddagh, Photo 2 is taken near the Spanish Arch with Quay Street in the background, Photo 3 is taken at the Salmon Weir Bridge.

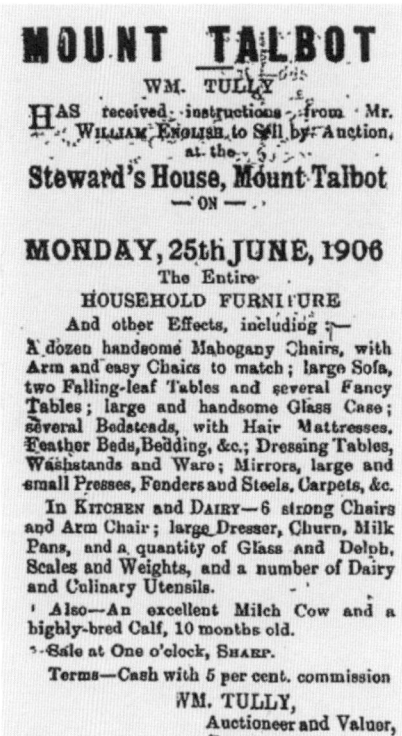

MOUNT TALBOT

WM. TULLY

HAS received instructions from Mr. WILLIAM ENGLISH to Sell by Auction, at the

Steward's House, Mount Talbot

— ON —

MONDAY, 25th JUNE, 1906

The Entire

HOUSEHOLD FURNITURE

And other Effects, including :—

A dozen handsome Mahogany Chairs, with Arm and easy Chairs to match; large Sofa, two Falling-leaf Tables and several Fancy Tables; large and handsome Glass Case; several Bedsteads, with Hair Mattresses. Feather Beds, Bedding, &c.; Dressing Tables, Washstands and Ware; Mirrors, large and small Presses, Fenders and Steels, Carpets, &c.

In KITCHEN and DAIRY—6 strong Chairs and Arm Chair; large Dresser, Churn, Milk Pans, and a quantity of Glass and Delph, Scales and Weights, and a number of Dairy and Culinary Utensils.

Also—An excellent Milch Cow and a highly-bred Calf, 10 months old.

Sale at One o'clock, SHARP.

Terms—Cash with 5 per cent. commission

WM. TULLY,

Auctioneer and Valuer,

Roscommon.

Newspaper Notice giving details of an auction at the Stewards House in Mount Talbot. The occupier of the house, William English had been replaced as land steward, much to the disappointment of the local tenantry. This house later became Flanagans Post Office and it has recently been beautifully restored.

Coming into the 1920's the Talbots were enjoying life to the full, entertaining distinguished guests, travelling extensively, attending equestrian and botanical events, spending time in the oppulance of Castledillon. They must have thought that this enjoyable lifestyle would never cease, but Ireland was changing. The people were now receiving a better and broader education and they started to question the social landscape. For the first time in generations, young men began to feel angry and rebellious. The land question in the later half of the previous century had shown the people what is achieveable by a combination of poitical and physical strength. The Talbots had no idea what was coming but their world and the world of the landlord was going to change forever.

The War of Independence

The Irish Volunteers were established in November 1913 at a public meeting held at the Rotunda Rink in Dublin. They were formed against a background of rising tension in Ireland over the Irish Home Rule Bill of 1912 which was vehemently opposed by Ulster Unionists who had formed the Ulster Volunteer Force. The Irish Volunteers became very popular among the general public and by July 1914 the movement contained 180,000 members. The Volunteers split over their involvement in World War 1 with over 90% favouring participation in the War on the British side to help ensure that the Home Rule Bill was enacted when the war was over. At the outbreak of World War 1 there were approximately 70,000 Irish men in the British Army and 140,000 more men enlisted during the war with many of these new recruits coming from the Irish Volunteers. Some young men from Mount Talbot and the surrounding areas enlisted in the British Army to fight in WW1. During the war the remaining Irish Volunteers who opposed involvement in WW1 rebelled against British occupation in a Dublin rising that was not wholly supported by the Irish people. The British decision to execute the leaders of the rising was yet again a castrotophic decision on their part and resulted in a swell of support for the rebels and their political wing Sinn Fein. Many Irish soldiers returned disillusioned from WW1 after bravely fighting at the Somme and other battlefields and witnessing at first hand the horrendous slaughter that occurred at the western front. Home Rule that had been promised to these soldiers prior to their departure failed to materialise and their dreams of returning to Ireland as heroes never happened. Many of the ex-soldiers from Mount Talbot and the surrounding areas rarely spoke about the Great War and their stories were lost in the swell of nationalism that developed after the failure of Home Rule.

Interesting Letter from Former Mount Talbot Man.

What German Domination Would Mean to Ireland.

TO THE EDITOR OF THE MESSENGER.

Paris, July 12th, 1918.

SIR—I am writing to a cousin of mine in Cloghan, Mount Talbot, giving him some good advice, etc, so I am sending you something and kindly put it in your paper, and I thank you for your past favours. I am in Paris, France, doing war work for the Knights of Columbus. There are about 300 of us over here—some out at the front helping all the soldiers, in every possible way we can, in keeping the spirit within them to lick the Kaiser and his gang. Twenty-three of us landed at —— a week ago, and expect to go to the front in a few days. This organisation of the K of C is wonderful, and is doing what it can to help all soldiers fighting at the front, of any creed, to crush the iron hand of the German Empire, which is the worst enemy the world ever had to contend with. The sooner they are crushed the better it will be for the entire world and permanent peace and a decent place to live. I volunteered my services.

IN THE CAUSE OF FREEDOM AND DEMOCRACY.

You see we are right, so all Ireland should stand by us as the Irish are in America. President Wilson is our guide and the greatest man of the day. Wilson is your friend as he is ours. The Government of United States can rely on the Irish in America no matter what happens. With all the Germans boasting of their kultur if they won in this war they would make a bear garden of Ireland; there is more truth than poetry in that. Don't trust them. America realised that we are not fighting for fun, but for honour and decency. Many things happened to our nuns and sisters in convents in Belgium and France. Germans ravished everything before them like a lot of wild beasts. Is there a drop of blood in a christian's veins could tolerate such an outrage? Germany was preparing 40 years for this war; she had everything complete and nothing undone as far as war was concerned.

GERMANY THOUGHT WHEN SHE STARTED SHE WAS GOING THROUGH HEAVEN AND EARTH TO RULE THE ENTIRE WORLD AND DOMINATE THE UNIVERSE.

God forbid. We would be worse than slaves, and wouldn't want to live any longer and enjoy the pleasures in this world as God intended we should. The Kaiser, Crown Prince, his son, and Hindenburg and others of the Royal family are fanatics on war. Germans are a lot of square-heads; they don't know anything only Kaiser Bill. They idolize him as their God. Germany lied and deceived President Wilson, and what would she do to you? America tried to keep out of this terrible war but could not. The Kaiser promised Wilson he would not sink any more ships with women and children on them, but before the note reached Washington he deliberately repeated the same cowardly act. The Kaiser is like the devil in the night, and his corruptable Government of Germany. God help Ireland if the Kaiser had his say towards her welfare; in my mind there would be no more of the green fields of Erin.

THE SNAKES THAT ST PATRICK DROVE OUT OF IRELAND

would return, and the same fate would follow Ireland as that of poor Belgium. May God give us health and strength in the next few months to crush the monster off the earth.—JOHN J McCORMICK, Cloghan, Mount Talbot, Roscommon, Ireland. (Formerly in America 30 years).

Letter from John J. McCormick, formerly of Cloghan, to the Roscommon Messenger in July 1918 relating to his involvement in World War 1.

Roscommon was to see the first Sinn Fein canditate elected an MP after Count G.N Plunkett won a seat in a by-election in 1917. Sinn Fein leader Eamon De Valera addressed a large gathering at a republican rally in Ballygar in November 1917. Representatives from a Sinn Fein club in Tisrara attended this rally where *'there was a big display of Republican colours and a number of bands were in attendance'*[93]. A further rally took place in Ballygar in 1918 to protest at the imprisonment of local nationalists and a large Military and RIC presence is reported to have been in attendance. This rally seems to have become violent as the authorities were accused of carrying out a bayonet charge on the people attending the rally. A protest rally against the imprisonment of the Sinn Fein leaders was held in Athleague in June 1918 but this seems to have passed off peacefully. In the 1918 general election Sinn Fein won 73 seats out of a total of 105 with Plunkett retaining his seat in North Roscommon and Harry Boland winning another seat for Sinn Fein in South Roscommon[94]. The Sinn Fein MP's refused to take their seat in Westminister and instead created an independent Irish Republic with a parliament called Dail Eireann. The Dail met for the first time on the 21st of January 1919 but many of the members were absent due to imprisonment. The Irish Volunteers swore allegiance to the new Dail and were known from this time as the Irish Republican Army. On the same day as the first Dail met two members of the RIC were ambushed and killed at Soloheadbeg in Co. Tipperary. The Irish War of Independence had begun.

BALLYGAR DISTURBANCE

Another Report of the Scenes on Friday

We have received a letter, signed by a number of residents of Ballygar, Co. Roscommon, protesting against what is described as the misleading report in our issue of Saturday of the violent scenes which occurred in the town on the previous day. The letter states:—

" No crowd assembled until the young men were in the barracks, and then it consisted of about two dozen young men, members of the Volunteers, with a sprinkling of old men, women and girls. There was no baton charge ordered, and none took place. There were no bricks or stones fired. Mr. Rice, R.M., had no difficulty in arriving at the barracks, where the depositions were read, and ont in the Courthouse, as stated in your report. The prisoners were taken directly to the Police Barracks, where the depositions were read : as no trial took place,' and no one was allowed to be present with the exception of Dr. Kielty, P.P., and Mr. P. J. Colleran. No baton charges took place at any time, as alleged in your report, but there were two bayonet charges in the course of an hour.

The letter further states that John Egan was only one of seven injured by bayonet thrusts.

The names signed to the letter are:—

M. Kielty, D.D., P.P.; Thos. Hanley, John Farrell, P. J. Colleran, P. J. McDonnell, John Hughes, John Martyn, Joseph McDonnell, Patk. FitzMaurice, Patk. Pettit, John Egan, John Kelly, D.C.

Newspaper reports relating to rallies held in neighbouring villages in support of local republicans, the Freemans Journal, 19th June and 25th June.

THE POLICE AT BALLYGAR

Military and police attended in force at Athleague, Roscommon, on Sunday afternoon when a meeting of protest against the arrest and imprisonment of members of the Sinn Fein organisation was held. The proceedings passed off quietly.

References were made to the recent bayonet charge at Ballygar, which is only three miles away.

Rev. Dr. Kielty, P.P., said he was surprised the police took such decided action against the people.

Very Rev. Canon Cummins said that in Roscommon the relations between the police and people were of a most cordial character, and he hoped that state of things would continue.

---

[93] Freemans Journal, November 26th 1917, p3.
[94] Harry Boland received a massive 10,685 votes compared to J.P Haydens (Nationalist party) 4,233 votes.

Mount Talbot seems to have been relatively quite for the first year of the war with no major incidents besides 'cattle driving' being reported but in April 1920 after an escalation of military and aqrarian activitiy in the area British Soldiers arrived at Mount Talbot House. The soldiers were billeted in the gardens of the house and the numerous white tents scattered over the lawns gave a clear indication to the local people that the area was in a high state of tension. The military presence at Mount Talbot House caused much discomfort and anxiety to Johnnie Talbot who seems to have spent most of this time at Castledillon in Armagh.

CATTLE-DRIVING AGITATION.

Soldiers have left Athlone for protection duty on farms which were driven during the week, on which the cattle have now been put back.

Cattle have been driven off grass lands in various parts of Roscommon.

As a result of agrarian disputes in the district, military have arrived in the village of Mount Talbot, Co. Roscommon.

Newspaper article announces the arrival of British soldiers at Mount Talbot House, Freemans Journal, April 12th 1920.

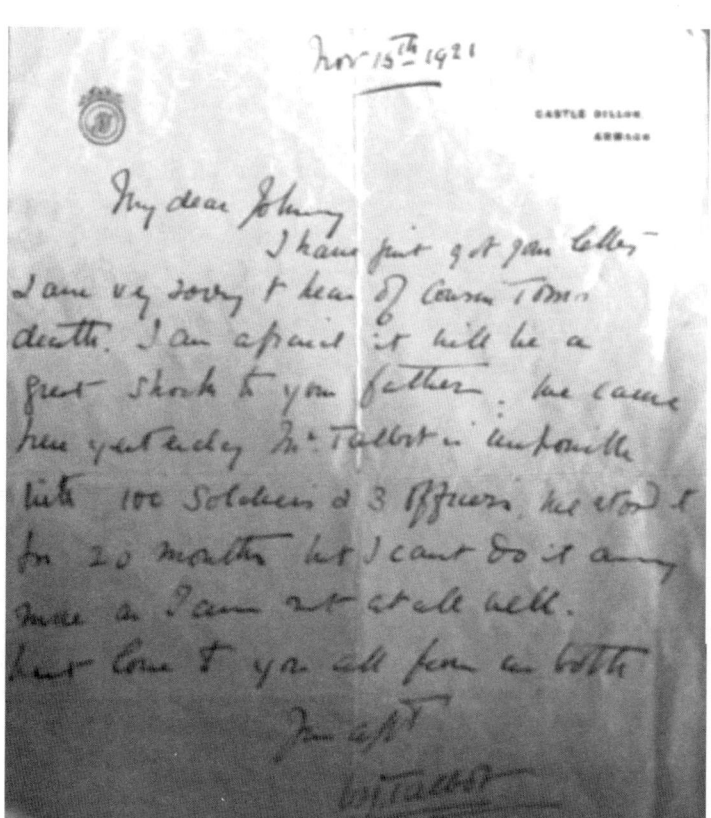

Letter written at Castledillon dated 15th November 1921 from Johnnie Talbot to a friend outlining his concerns about the continued presence of British military personnel at Mount Talbot House (courtesy of the National Library of Ireland).

The British Government were reluctant to fully engage their regular army in the suppresion of the rebels as they believed that this was 'a policemans job supported by military and not vice versa'. The Royal Irish Constabulary (RIC) were under enormous pressure particularly in rural areas where practically all the barracks had been attacked and subsequently abandoned. The Government decided to bolster the RIC numbers by recruiting over 13,000 new members and these were mainly ex-British soldiers demobilised after World War 1. These new recruits rapidly gained a reputation for drunkeness and ill decipline and throughout the war they carried out many unnecessary reprisals on the civilian population. Because of a shortage of official RIC uniforms these men were issued with khaki coloured military clothing and they subsequently became known as the 'Blank-and Tans'. The 'Auxilieries' were an officer class that were recruited to serve in Ireland and they were also immensely disliked within the communities and were known to be utterly ruthless in their dealings with local activists and their supporters. Like the 'Tans' the 'Auxies' were generally recruited from the ranks of de-mobilised ex-servicemen from World War 1. As the war progessed King George V of England expressed his horror to Prime Minister David Lloyd George at the killings and reprisals carried out in his name by the Black and Tans.

Republican activitiy in Mount Talbot and the surrounding areas intensified with the arrival of enemy forces. Most of the Volunteers from the area became members of the Mount Talbot Coy that was attached to the Four Roads Company, 4th Battalion, South Roscommon Brigade of the Irish Republican Army. The South Roscommon Brigade contained 5 companies and this was later increased to 8 when the companies of Ballygar, Kiltoom and Dysart joined the brigade. Two men stand out as being to the forefront in republican resistance in the Mount Talbot area, Joe Galvin of Cloonlaughnan and Tommie Kelly of Corrocot.

Tommie Kelly was born in the village of Corrocot in 1900 and attended Mount Talbot national school. After completing his primary education Tommie began working in his fathers tailoring business in Corrocot. At sixteen years of age he joined the local Sinn Fein branch and during the 1918 general election came to the attention of the Royal Irish Constabulary. He was a captain in the local branch of the Irish Volunteers and after the formation of Dail Eireann he became an active member of the Irish Republican Army gaining the rank of Adjutant to the Knockcroghery Company of the 4th Battalion South Roscommon Brigade[95]. Throughout the War of independence Tommies home was raided on numerous occasions by Crown forces stationed at Mount Talbot House and he spent most of the war 'on the run'. He managed to work at home with his father during business hours but this was only possible due to the co-operation of his neighbours in Corrocot, particularly Paddy Connell who owned a forge across the road from Kellys house. When Paddy heard approaching military vehicles from the big house he immediately changed the hammering sound on his anvil. This warning was subtle but of immense importance as it gave Tommie Kelly time to make his escape through the rear of his fathers premises to a 'safe house' or to one of the many 'dug-outs' located in the surrounding bogs. It was normally the Black and Tans that carried out raids as the British Army generally remained in barracks and only became active if a large scale military engagement was planned. The 'Tans' were detested in the locality and the treatment of Tommie Kellys family and other families in the area during raids was totally unacceptable. They seem to have lacked any humanity or self-decipline and their actions helped enormously in uniting the community behind the

---

[95] Bureau of Military History, 1913-21, Statement by Witness, Document no W.S 701, p6.

republican soldiers. The Auxiliaries also raided Tommie Kellys house on a number of occasions and they bayoneted his dog after being informed that the family pet barked incessantly when Crown forces were approaching. All the family members including the children would have to flee from the house prior to a raid no matter what time the event took place, as the attackers often ransacked the house and anyone found inside would be brutally interrogated about the whereabouts of Tommie. British Army officers however did make attempts throughout the country to restrain the Tans and they generally disciplined the instigators of these unnecessary acts of violence but it seems this did not act as a deterrant as their conduct actually deterioated as the war progressed. The late John Collins of Garrier recalled an incident that occurred when he was going home from school in Mount Talbot during the War of Independence, *'the Black and Tans pulled up at the bridge with a prisoner. His name was Reddington, a shop boy in McDonnells now Petits. They told us to clear home but we went as far as Englishs gate and we were peeping through the rails from there. They put the prisoner in the river but he got under the arches of the bridge and ran for his life and they shooting after him'*.

During times of particularly high levels of enemy raids the local republicans spent the entire time on the run generally hiding in 'dug-outs' that were located in remote areas of the parish. Oral history recalls a dug-out being located in a part of Cloonakilleg known as 'pollglas' and another dug-out existed in Cloondara bog. During this time food had to be brought to the occupants of the dug-outs and this was an extremely dangerous task. It was generally women from 'Cumann na mBan' or local children that carried out this act as they were less likely to arouse suspision. When stopped and questioned by Crown forces the children were told to inform the soldiers that they were bringing food to their fathers who were cutting turf in the bog.

Armed republicans preparing an ambush near Mount Talbot in 1920.

Tommie Kelly was present at an attack that took place in January 1921 on an RIC patrol at Strokestown and he was also involved in the Scramogue Ambush two months later. As mentioned above Tommie was attached to the Knockroghery Company of the IRA and on the 19th June 1921 this area was the scene of an extreme act of violence when Knockcroghery village was burned to the ground by Crown forces. Four lorry loads of Tans, Auxilleries and RIC had left Athlone in the early hours of the morning to seek revenge for the killing two days earlier of General Lambert who was the Chief Commanding Officer of British forces in the west[96]. The people of Knockcroghery were ordered out into the street at gun-point and all the houses were set alight by the attackers. Most of the village burned down with the exception of some bulldings that had slated rather than thatched roofs. This event caused additional hatred and animosity within the local population towards the black and tans as many innocent civilians were effectively homeless. The house that was occupied by the Catholic priest was also burned down and the local Protestant clergyman who was disgusted by the event immediately offered a room in his rectory for the Priest to live in until such time as the parochial house was rebuilt. The feelings of animosity towards the black and tans was not confined to the Catholic population.

Tommie Kelly of Corrocot in Irish Army uniform, mid 1920's (courtesy of Tom Kelly).

---

[96]The Knockcroghery Company of the IRA did not carry out the ambush that resulted in the death of General Lambert, the ambush was actually carried out by the Tubberclair Company from Co. Westmeath.

Tommie Kelly was heavily envolved in most of the engagements with the british military that took place in the area throughout the war including an ambush of crown forces that occurred near Ballygar. The Black and Tans retaliated to this ambush by burning down two houses in Ballygar including a public house that was owned at the time by Jack Egan who was a prominent member of the local IRA. The authorities at Dublin castle however denied this incident was carried out by their forces stating that *'the houses were destroyed by armed and disguised men'[97]*. Tommie Kelly managed to avoid captivity or serious injury throughout the entire War of Independence and this reflects well on his organisational capabilites and also on the soldiers under his command and the co-operation of his neighbours.

Joe Galvin was born in the townland of Cloonlaughnan in 1890 and began his education at Mount Talbot National school 5 years later. In his adolescence he played hurling with Tisrara and football with Mount Talbot and excelled at both sports. Joe was sworn in to the Irish Republican Brotherhood in 1914 and later joined the local Volunteers together with his brother John. He fought in the 1916 rising and fled to Scotland immediately afterwards where he began working in a munitions factory. He subsequently managed to get some arms and ammunition that was manufactured in his workplace to the Volunteers in Dublin. After the formation of Dail Eireann in January 1919 Joe became a member of the Irish Republican Army and soon came to the attention of the RIC. He became Officer in Command of the Mount Talbot Coy that was attached to the Four Roads Company of the 4th Battalion, South Roscommon Brigade[98]. He was actively involved in the organisation attending all the Battalion Council meetings in Rahara and the Brigade meetings in Ballymacurly. Joe accompanied Ernie O'Malley during the early years of the war sourcing arms and ammunition in Ballinasloe and the surrounding areas. Joe made an audacious raid on the military barracks in Athlone where he seized rifle ammunition some of which was used in the Scramogue ambush[99].

Joe Galvin's house was constantly raided by the Black and Tans with 3 raids a day not uncommon during times of high military activity. He was eventually captured in March 1921 and taken to the military post at Mount Talbot House. Later that night he was blindfolded and taken by lorry to the Military Barracks in Roscommon. On the way to Roscommon he was taken out of the lorry and was severely beaten by British Soldiers who wanted to find out where arms were stored and the names of other IRA members in the locality. His captors threatened to shoot him but Joe refused to speak and was put in solitary confinement. After three days he was taken to the detention barracks in Athlone and two weeks later he was moved to the prisoner of war camp at the Curragh, Co. Kildare. He was held at Rath Camp that had been specially prepared to hold a large number of prisoners. It was enclosed by a barbed wire fence that was ten feet high and eight feet wide with a similar fence located 20 feet farther out. Two NCO's and 20 guards manned the entrance with a sentry on each of the 4 corners of the camp. Powerful lights illuminated the boundary area and the prisoners were infomed that anyone approching the fence on lock down would be shot on site. Escape seemed impossible but Joe Galvin instigated an escape plan with other inmates including Jim Brady from Cavan who had worked as a miner at Arigna. They decided to commence digging a tunnel but if

---

[97] Freemans Journal, 8th July 1921, p5.
[98] Bureau of Military History, 1913-21, Statement by Witness, Document no W.S 701, p2.
[99] The Scramogue ambush was carried out by members of the north and south Roscommon Brigades. The 9th Lancers Regiment and some members of the RIC were ambushed at Scramogue (on the Strokestown-longford road) on March 23rd, 1921 resulting in the death of six members of the British forces.

successful they needed a wire cutters to get through the two boundary fences. When a working party of British soldiers arrived to add more wire to the fence they brought with them a number of wire cutters. Joe and some other prisoners managed to get possession of one of these wire cutter and they subsequently began to dig an escape tunnel. The huts in the camp were raised two feet off the ground and this gave them just enough room to crawl under the floors and begin digging. The work was difficult and slow as all they had at their disposel to dig with were knives, spoons and a metal bar. However they eventually completed the tunnel and sent a note out to GHQ in Dublin that they would be out in two days. Unfortunatley the HQ offices were raided by British forces and the plan was uncovered. The occupants of the office managed to escape through the skylight one of whom was IRA Director of Intelligence Michael Collins. The next day an armed party of Scottish Borderers arrived at the camp and found the escape tunnel and afterwards the prisoners were deprived of all rights and privileges. Soldiers dug a four feet wide by four feet deep trench around the camp and they planned to fill this trench with water. The prisoners decided to make another attempt to escape before the trench was flooded and they began digging a new tunnel. The tunnel was only two feet square and they had to dig down four feet before tunnelling horizontally to avoid the recently installed outer trench. Digging the tunnel in such a confined space was extremely difficult and two of the men involved became violently sick due to the shortage of air at the tunnel face. Small outlets to the surface were installed to increase the air supply in the tunnel and after approximately three weeks the tunnel was completed.

The prisoners decided to attempt their escape and at 11.30pm on the 9th of September 1921, Joe Galvin and Jim Brady entered the tunnel. They asked their colleques to wait an hour and a quarter before following them as the final surface excavation needed completion and they had to cut the wire on the inner and outer fence. When they opened the shaft to the surface they discovered that the tunnel did not reach the required distance but as the surrounding trench was to be flooded on the following day they knew that they must continue with the escape plan. The searchlight was shining on them intermittedly and the sentry on duty almost discovered them but was distracted by an officer doing his rounds of the sentry posts. They ran to the inner fence and cut an opening and continued to the outer fence where they cut another opening and found themselves in the Curragh Plain. A thick fog had descended but they managed to make their way through the Curragh racecourse and eventually arrived at the town of Newbridge. They continued towards Naas but had to quickly get off the road when two lorry loads of British Military sped passed having been sent out to recapture the escapees. Joe Galvin found a safe-house in Naas and transport was organised to allow safe passage for Joe and Jim Brady to Dublin. When they arrived in Dublin they were sent to an IRA camp in the Dublin mountains to lie low for a few days before arriving safely back home to their families.

Almost 70 prisoners had escaped from the Curragh camp with many of these from the Roscommon Northern and Southern Brigades. This escape from the Curragh camp was one of the most significant events of the entire war and it was of huge embarrassment to the British Military[100].

---

[100]The details of the Tunnel escape is taken entirely from an interview with Joe Galvin by Michael O'Callaghan. I received a transcript of the interview from the present members of the Galvin family in Cloonlaughnan.

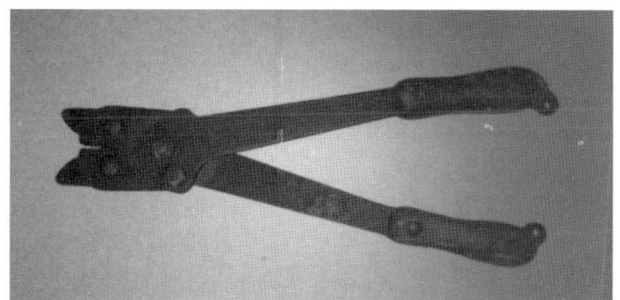

Wire cutter used by Joe Galvin during the escape from the Curragh camp in 1921.

Joe Galvin in Irish Army uniform, mid 1920's (courtesy of the Galvin Family).

Joe Galvin returned to his position as Officer in Command of the Mount Talbot Coy but discovered that a truce had been signed on the 11th of July between the IRA and British Forces. Joe, Tommie Kelly and the other IRA members in the locality awaited political developments and after long and tortuous negotiations a Treaty was signed in London on the 6th of December 1921 causing widespread celebration in the area. The Treaty however was not welcomed by all the members of the IRA as it did not deliver an Irish Republic. Dail Eireann approved the Treaty by 64 votes to 57 and a National Referendum also approved the treaty with the Provisional Irish Government taking over from the British Administration on the 16th of January 1922. British Soldiers began demobilsation and prepared to hand over the Barracks to the new Free-State Army. Athlone Barracks was handed over on the 28th of Febuary with British forces vacating Roscommon Barracks and Mount Talbot House in late March 1922.

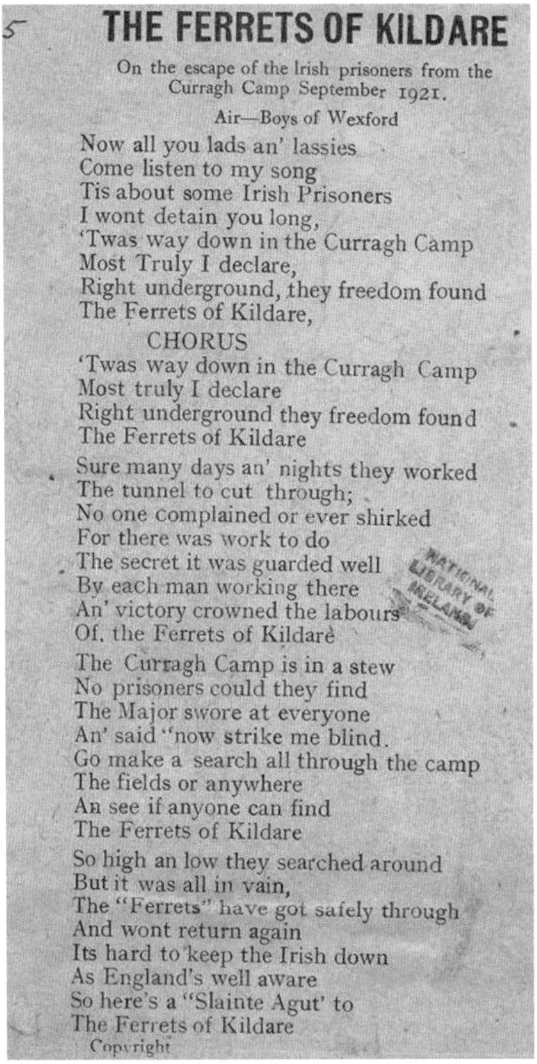

THE FERRETS OF KILDARE

On the escape of the Irish prisoners from the Curragh Camp September 1921.

Air—Boys of Wexford

Now all you lads an' lassies
Come listen to my song
Tis about some Irish Prisoners
I wont detain you long,
'Twas way down in the Curragh Camp
Most Truly I declare,
Right underground, they freedom found
The Ferrets of Kildare,

CHORUS

'Twas way down in the Curragh Camp
Most truly I declare
Right underground they freedom found
The Ferrets of Kildare

Sure many days an' nights they worked
The tunnel to cut through;
No one complained or ever shirked
For there was work to do
The secret it was guarded well
By each man working there
An' victory crowned the labours
Of the Ferrets of Kildare

The Curragh Camp is in a stew
No prisoners could they find
The Major swore at everyone
An' said "now strike me blind.
Go make a search all through the camp
The fields or anywhere
An see if anyone can find
The Ferrets of Kildare

So high an low they searched around
But it was all in vain,
The "Ferrets" have got safely through
And wont return again
Its hard to keep the Irish down
As England's well aware
So here's a "Slainte Agut' to
The Ferrets of Kildare
    Copyright

Song commemorating the escape from the Curragh by republican prisoners in September 1921. Joe Galvin of Cloonlaughnan helped plan and execute this daring escape (courtesy of the National Library of Ireland).

The Irish Republican Army was deeply divided over the Treaty and conflicting views emerged among many of the local Battalions. An Anti-Treaty Army convention was subsequently held in Dublin on the 26th of March 1922, where they refused to recognise the Irish Free State. On the 7th of April 1922 armed Republicans carried out an unsantioned attack on Mount Talbot House. Johnnie Talbot was seized and thrown down the front steps of the house and his life was threatened. Julia Talbot remained inside the house and she heard several shots being fired outside and feared the worst. Tommie Kelly and Joe Galvin managed to persuade the more militant republicans to spare Johnnie

Talbots life. Their chauffeur who was from Northern Ireland was also seized and was tied up and thrown into the river Suck but he managed to survive. The Talbots were given 24 hours to leave the house and on the 8th of April they drove out the avenue and through the 'Grand Gate' for the last time, leaving behind all their possessions and 270 years of Talbot association with the area. Julia brought her husband to a nursing home in Mount Street in Dublin and she then checked into the Shelbourne Hotel on St Stephen's Green. Julia Talbot died in her sleep that night and was found the next morning by hotel staff. Her family and friends believed that she died from shock caused by the attack on Mount Talbot House. Johnnie Talbot survived the attack but was devastated when informed of Julias death.

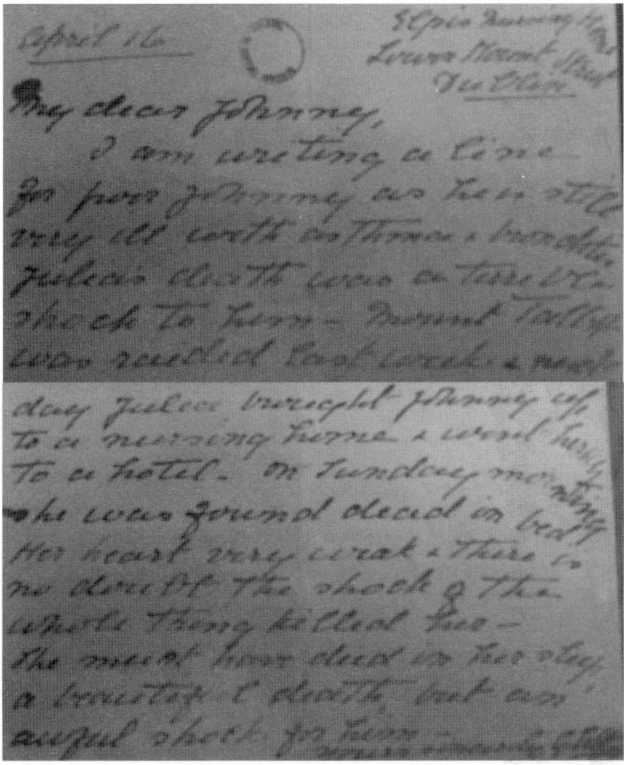

Letter from JohnieTalbots half-sister Gertrude Crofton to a friend confirming the death of Julia Talbot after the raid on Mount Talbot House (courtesy of the National Library of Ireland).

A newspaper report from the 12th of April 1922 stated that *'armed men took sporting ammunition from Mount Talbot House...also Lady Clonbrocks motor car, which was drawn up at the entrance'*[101]. These armed men were IRA volunteers who opposed the Treaty and they subsequently took possession of the unprotected and unoccupied Mount Talbot House. The entire contents of the wine cellar was consumed by the occupiers. The house was also looted at this time and many of the movable furnishings were taken from the house. After a number of days the authorities arrived at

---

[101] Irish Independent, 12th April 1922, p4. Lady Clonbrock was a member of the Dillon family who owned Clonbrock House near Ahascragh, Co. Galway, the Dillon's were close friends of the Talbots.

Mount Talbot and after a fierce gun-battle they managed to remove the Anti-Treaty forces from the house. During this time the words *'To Hell with the Red Cross'* were painted on the demesne wall of the Mount Talbot estate for all passers by to see. This slogan harked back to Julia Talbots involvement with the Red Cross during and after WW1[102]. Johnnie Talbot could take no more and on the 6th of June 1922 he put up for auction what remained of the contents of Mount Talbot House with the livestock and machinery being sold a week earlier. He had obviously decided that he would never return to Mount Talbot. On the 13th of April 1922 Anti-Treaty forces occupied the Four Courts in Dublin and the country tetered on the brink of Civil War.

Newspaper announcement for the Auction that was held at Mount Talbot house on the 6th of June 1922.

Civil War

With no agreement or compromise forthcoming, the Civil War officially began on the 28th of June 1922 when Free State forces attacked the occupied Four Courts in Dublin. National Troops set up a Military Barracks at the vacant Mount Talbot House but County Roscommon remained relatively peaceful. Joe Galvin, Tommie Kelly and many of the local volunteers joined the new National Army but some of their former colleques joined the Anti-Treaty forces or 'Irregulars'[103]. Irregulars from Southeast Galway joined forces with men from South Roscommon to form a flying column and together they took possession of Ballygar Barracks. National Army member Frank Simmons of Roscommon later recalled that *'there was little or no Civil War down here in Roscommon. I had arranged here with some of the fellas on the opposite side that I wouldn't attack them nor they wouldn't attack us..they came along and attacked Mount Talbot and they nearly blew it up...thats what started the Civil War in Roscommon'*[104]. This attack on Mount Talbot House occured on the

---

[102] Roscommon Herald, 29th January 1927 in an article called *'Mount Talbot and its Spooks'*.
[103] Joe Galvin's close friend Jim Brady of Co. Cavan joined the Arigna flying column of the anti-treaty IRA. The two men who masterminded the prison break from the Curragh found themselves on opposing sides in the Civil War.
[104] Kathleen Hegarty Thorne, *They Put the Flag a-Flyin, The Roscommon Volunteers 1916-1923*, 3rd Edition, p145

night of the 8th of July 1922 and involved 100 Irregulars attempting to seize the house from 27 National Troop defenders[105]. Mines were placed by the Irregulars at various locations around the house but only one of the mines actually exploded as the person laying the mines tripped over the wires on his retreat causing the wires to disconnect from the charges. The front entance to the house was badly damaged by the mine that did explode. This explosion also resulted in many of the windows in the house shattering. The fierce gun battle that ensued was heard for miles around but the Irregulars failed to take the house and retreated before daylight. Official reports stated that there was one Anti-Treaty man killed, one injured and another taken prisoner but the amount of blood subsequently noticed in the area by eye-witnesses suggests that this event may have resulted in many more casualties. A temporary treatment room was set up in Naughtons shop in Mount Talbot to treat the injured and this also suggests that more than one combatant suffered injuries during the attack.

ROSCOMMON MANSION MINED

Over 100 Irregulars made an attempt to blow up Mount Talbot House, Roscommon. A mine was laid under the front entrance, and a number of bombs were exploded simultaneously. The entrance, which is of an ornamental character, was greatly damaged. A detached photographic house was destroyed and all the windows in the house, including several stained glass windows, were shattered.

The house had been guarded by about 27 National soldiers, in charge of Commandant Compton, and they succeeded in beating off the attack, taking prisoner an officer of the Irregulars. Hession Brothers, contractors, of Roscommon, estimate the damage to the building at £1,000.

Details of the attack on Mount Talbot house from the Freemans Journal dated July 17th 1922 (left). Bullet-holes from the gun-battle that occurred at Mount Talbot house in July 1922 are still visible on one of the remaining walls of the house (below)

---

[105]There are conflicting figures in the sources relating to the size of the attacking and defending forces with Irish Army military intelligence reports stating that there were 200 attackers and 20 national troops defending the castle.

Later, on the same day as the attack on Mount Talbot House the Irish Army surrounded and attacked the Barracks in Ballygar. This Barracks was occupied by eleven anti-treaty soldiers and they managed to hold their position for a number of hours but at 5pm that evening the occupants of the barracks surrendered and were arrested and detained by the National Troops.

A large section of the bridge at Mount Talbot was blown up by irregulars on the 15th of October 1922, making the bridge impassable and causing widespread disruption in the area. The Anti-Treaty forces were trying to disrupt National army movement in the area.

Mount Talbot Bridge after it was blown up by Irregulars on the 15th of October 1922.

Mount Talbot bridge, which connects the Counties Galway and Roscommon over the Suck near Mount Talbot, was blown up on Sunday morning. Traffic over the bridge is now only possible to pedestrians and cyclists. The bridge was one of the finest in the county, and the charge which blew it up must have been powerful, as the sound of the explosion was heard 12 miles away from the scene.

The incendiaries continue their ruthless campaign.
D..row Abbey, Offaly, a beautiful and historic residence; Spiddal House, Co. Galway, the property of Lord Killanin; Cloncah House, a fine old mansion on the Mount Talbot property, Co. Galway, and the Protestant Schools at Ballydevlin and Goleen, near Schull, Co. Cork, have been given to the flames.

Newspaper reports relating to incidents that occurred in Mount Talbot during the Civil War

The attack on Mount Talbot house was the only full scale military engagement in Mount Talbot throughout the Civil War but some other incidents occured nearby including an attack at Ballygar in Febuary 1923 on two lorry loads of National troops that resulted in one death and two serious injuries. In April 1923 Cloonca House the home of the Talbot-Crosbie family was badly damaged by fire after being set alight by anti-treaty forces, it seems the house was unoccupied at this time. This attack was to be the last incident that occured in the area during the Civil War[106]. The Civil War ended on the 24th of May when Frank Aiken ordered anti-treaty forces to 'dump their arms and return home'.

After the conclusion of the Civil War Joe Galvin remained in the Irish Army where he served in Castlebar and later moved to Athlone Barracks before retiring in 1929. He served as a training officer for the part time Local Defense Force during World War II. Joe Galvin died in 1970 and received a full military funeral in Four Roads cemetary[107]. Tommie Kelly also remained in the Irish Army and he was stationed in Westport where he gained the rank of Commandant. During his time in Co. Mayo he married Kathleen Kelly from Bridge House and they had four children. Tommie Kelly retired from the Army in 1930 through the Voluntary Demobillisation Scheme and moved to London with his family during World War II where he worked in the clothes rationing department . Tommie Kelly died in 1965 at the age of 65 and is buried in North London. Joe Galvins brother John emigrated to London in 1927 and returned to Ireland on reaching retirement. He died in September 1999 aged 106 years and was the last surviving member of the South Roscommon Brigade of the old IRA. John Galvin had served as a dispatch carrier during the War of Independence carrying important intelligence reports and messages between the various IRA companies. He used a motorbike to carry the dispatches and he was targeted many times by the British forces but managed to escape serious injury or capture thoughout the war. He also took an active part in an ambush at Corofin in County Galway in the summer of 1921.

The Mount Talbot area produced many other republican soldiers including Tommie Lennon, Tom Meeley and Bill Carroll. Bill Carroll had been a very active volunteer spending most of the war in County Clare. He had been in the RIC and joined the Mid-Clare brigade of the IRA after handing over the RIC barracks in Ruan to local republicans. The raid on the barracks allowed the local battalion to gain possession of 14 rifles, 14 revolvers, several thousand rounds of ammunition, hand grenades and bicycles. Bill had to go 'on the run' as he was now a wanted man, he had to wear disguises on many occasions to avoid capture and was known to have dressed as a priest and even a nun. A song was later written about his time on the run entitled *'where has Bill Carroll gone'*. He managed to avoid being captured and was subsequently involved in many engagements during the war. He was injured during the Monreal ambush in West Clare in December 1920. Bill Carroll returned to live in the townland of Cloonlaughnan after the war and his house was located a short distance down the Cloonakilleg road. A lot of unknown faces were noticed at his funeral in Four Roads cemetary, it seems many of his former comrades from County Clare made the trip to Roscommon to pay their respects to their old friend. Tom Meeley was also an active volunteer and he was highly respected by his comrades. On his death he received a full military funeral in Four Roads cemetary.

When the Civil war ended the Irish people were facing an uncertain future. Independence had been achieved but the country was in physical and financial ruin. Former comrades and friends had fought against each other resulting in a bitterness and resentment that took many years to heal. The people of Mount Talbot were happy that the War was over and they could now concentrate on getting the area back to normal. However many local people had to find alternative employment

---

[106] Freemans Journal, 28th April 1923, p7
[107] Joe Galvin refused a pension from the state for his participation in the War of Independence stating that he fought to free his Country, not for any monetary gain.

due to the departure of the Talbots. The Irish Army vacated Mount Talbot House and the newly formed unarmed police force called the 'Civic Guard' or 'an Garda Siochana' began establishing police barracks in the villages adjacent to Mount Talbot.

Johnnie Talbot had died in London on the 7th of June 1923 at 14 Wimpole Street, aged 64 years. He died without issue and the trustees of his will sold Mount Talbot House and lands to the Land Commission under the 1923 Land Act for an undisclosed sum. In the years leading up to the War of Independence Johnnie Talbot had brought a younger member of the Talbot Crosbie family to Mount Talbot with a view to taking over the Talbot estate on his death. The Talbot Crosbies had died out at Cloonca House but there were many more members of that extended family still residing in Ardfert in County Kerry where they owned an enormous amount of land. John Darnley Coke Talbot was born on the 5th of December 1910 and moved at a young age to Mount Talbot House. He was educated at Bradfield College in Reading, England. John was only 13 years old when his cousin Johnnie Talbot died so he was too young to inherit the house and lands. The trustess of the will decided that the best option was to sell Mount Talbot House and lands much to the annoyance of the young inheritor. John Darnley Coke Talbot went on to gain the rank of Major in the British Army and he was decorated with the award of the Territorial Decoration. He ended up living in Glocestershire and remained there for the rest of his life. His father Maurice Bertie Talbot Crosbie had fought in World War 1 as Lieutenant in the service of the Royal Artillery. His grandfather Lindsey Bertie Talbot Crosbie had held the offices of Justice of the Peace, High Sheriff and Deputy Lieutenant for County Kerry. Unusually for a very large landowner Lindsey had made numerous attempts to solve the land question at the start of the 20th century and many commentators credit him with being the instigator of the very successful Wyndham Land Act of 1903.

March 12th 1945.

Menzaleh,
Eden Road,
Glenageary,
Co Dublin.

My dear John,

You must think that I have a very short memory! Of course I recollect perfectly you and your charming wife coming to see us at Wimbledon, many years ago.

Poor Mount Talbot is a sad sight now, I passed it last summer, and it is in ruins, in fact they are pulling it down to use the stones in building new houses. John Talbot told me he was very sad about the trustees having sold it during his minority, as his one dream was to live in Ireland and hunt. The very same thing is going on now at our family place, Mote, the Trustees are selling to the Land Commission, while my cousin, aged 18, who adores the place, is at sea. The same fate has befallen all the places round about, there is hardly one left. Our family have lived at Mote without a break, ever since Elizabeth's day, so it is rather a bitter pill to see it go.

Part of a letter sent from Gertrude Crofton (who was Johnnie Talbots half sister) to a friend in 1945, this letter states that a John Talbot (John Darnley Coke Talbot) had hoped to live at Mount Talbot House. He had been left the house by Johnnie Talbot but the Trustee's had sold the house during his minority (courtesy of the National Library of Ireland).

Most of the land that had belonged to the Talbots in the area was redistributed among the local population by the Land Commission in the following years. Mount Talbot House and 158 acres of surrounding demesne land were advertised for sale by the Land Commission on Dec 17th 1927. The newspaper advertisement suggests that Mount Talbot House was to be sold as a habitable residence. Oral history recalls that the house was a ruin after the attack by Anti-Treaty forces but it is now evident that it was still intact at the time of the sale by the Land Commission. Photographs from 1929 clearly show that the house is standing however the windows are boarded up and the entrance to the front door seems to have been damaged by the mine exploded by Anti-Treaty forces. The cost of getting the house back to its former grandeur would have been excessive, particularly at a time when the country and most of its people were in dire financial difficulty. Mount Talbot House and 158 acres of surrounding lands was purchased from the Land Commission in early 1928 by W.J Kelly from Ballygar for £1,300. It is ironic that after 270 years this land was now owned by a family with the surname 'Kelly' who were most likely descendants of the original owners, the O'Kelly's of Hy-Many.

The Irish Land Commission invite Tenders for the purchase of

Mount Talbot House,

with Out-Offices and Lands adjoining same, containing 158 acres Statute Measure or thereabouts.

The Mansion, beautifully situated, overlooking the River Suck, is approached by two main avenues, with a back evenue leading to farm yard. It consists of three storeys, with basement and contains spacious Hall, Drawing Room, Dining Room, Library, Billiard Room, Sitting Room, 14 Bedrooms, 3 Dressing Rooms, 3 Bath Rooms, 4 W.C.'s, Airing Press, Kitchen, Scullery, etc., Butler's and Housekeeper's Rooms, Wine Cellar, Strong Room, Central Heating Plant and Lift for Luggage and Fuel to all floors. The Out-offices substantially built of stone, slated and well arranged in two yards, provide stabling for 17 horses, ties for 60 cattle, also Garage, Harness-room, Dairy, Piggery, large Corn Barn with Loft, Hayshed, Turf shed, etc., and Acetylene Gas Plant.

The pleasure grounds are well laid out and well timbered with well stocked walled in garden, 3½ acres in extent, with 4 green houses. There are two tennis courts (hard and soft).

Conditions of Sale and Forms of Tender may be obtained on application to the Offices of the Irish Land Commission, 24 Upper Merrion Street, Dublin, where a Map of the lands can be inspected.

Tenders on the prescribed form should be addressed to the Secretary, Irish Land Commission, 24 Upper Merrion Street, Dublin, and should reach that address not later than 12 o'clock noon on the 18th January, 1928.

The Land Commission will not be bound to accept the highest or any Tender.

28/S.2722   3245-24127   W.H.co.

The Irish Land Commission advertise for sale Mount Talbot House and 158 acres of surrounding land.

View of the entrance front of Mount Talbot House from 1929 showing damage at the entrance porch from the explosion that occurred during the Civil War. The car in the photograph was owned by the Baleys of Ballyarthur, Co. Wicklow (courtesy of Emmy Eustace).

View of the outbuildings at Mount Talbot House from 1929. This photo was taken from the tower of Mount Talbot House (courtesy of Emmy Eustace).

View of the gardens of Mount Talbot House from 1929 (courtesy of Emmy Eustace).

View of the garden front of Mount Talbot House from 1929 (courtesy of Emmy Eustace).

Throughout the 1930's Mount Talbot House continued to fall into ruin and the roof and walls became unstable. On the 10th of January 1938 a public auction was held at the house. The auction sale included 6,000 blue banger slates, timbers from the roof, water tanks, skylights, marble and slate mantels, orginal windows and doors, stairs, floor tiles and the remaining contents of the kitchens and restrooms. A quantity of furniture and a small amount of farm equipment was also sold. With the roof removed, the house detiorated further and the walls began to crumble with tree's and foliage enveloping the structure. One can imagine a fine hotel and golf course on these grounds but as stated earlier in this chapter no one was in a position at that time to provide the necessary funding. Hotels and golf courses were far from everyones mind with the country trying to lift itself out of economic and physical ruin.

MOUNT TALBOT, CO. ROSCOMMON.

SALE BY PUBLIC AUCTION AT MOUNT TALBOT OF

Slates, Corrugated Iron,

ROOFING TIMBER, DOORS, GATES, Etc.

I will sell at Mount Talbot Castle, Ballygar, on MONDAY, JANUARY 10th, 1938, at 12 o'clock sharp, the contents of above including 6,000 Blue Bangor Slates all sizes; Corrugated Iron, Sheds, Roofing Timber, Flooring, Joists, Pinewood Beams (6' to 20' lengths), 3 Large Steel Water Tanks, Sky Lights, Marble and Slate Mantels, Wooden do., Window Frames, Sashes, Panel Doors and Frames, Staircases, Water Heating Radiators, Baths, Copper Cylinders, Washups, Galvanised Tanks, W.C.'s, Steel and Lead Piping, Floor Tiles glazed surrounds, 1 Large Heating Boiler, 1 Kitchen Range, Fire Grates, Firewood, etc.; Mower, Pulper, and Hay Kicker.

Also a quantity of Furniture: 1 Chesterfield Suite, Diningroom Suite, Dining Tables, Chairs, Overmantles, Sofas, Chests Drawers, Hall Stands, Bedsteads, etc.; 4 Pony Traps (rubber tyred), 1 Donkey do., 4 Sets Harness and various other articles. .

Terms—Cash and, five per cent. commission.

M. J. KELLY, M.I.A.A

Auctioneer and Valuer, Ballygar and Athlone.

Newspaper notice giving details of Auction on the 10th January 1938 at Mount Talbot House.

The early years of the Irish Free State

The formative years of the new Irish Free State were all about getting the country back on its feet after the War of Independence and the destruction of the Civil War. During this time the people of Mount Talbot worked hard to get the area moving again and attendance at fairs and at other local events increased. The bridge at Mount Talbot was repaired in August 1924 by the County Council and soon the village began to return to normality.

CLOSING OF ROAD

On and after Monday, August 4th, 1924, the road from BALLYGAR to ROSCOMMON via Mount Talbot will be closed to all vehicular traffic until repairs to Mount Talbot Bridge are completed. Pedestrians and cyclists will be able to pass. The alternate route is by Rookwood and Athleague.

By Order,
MICHAEL NERNEY. B.E.,
County Surveyor. Roscommon.

Details of a road closure at Mount Talbot bridge to allow repair work to be completed, Irish Independent, 29th July 1924.

After the difficulty of the previous decade the people needed to enjoy their new found freedom and various sporting groups were formed and social events were organised in the area. A handball alley was constructed in 1929 at the Fair Green by Tim Cormican and Martin Turley of Garrier. The idea of a handball alley had materialised after a sum of money had been collected by local men through an exceptionally long series of card games at Naughtons house in Mount Talbot. A travelling family had camped in the Fair Green in late 1927 and had in their possession a bantom cock. When they were moving on they were unable to catch the bird and left without him. He caused much disruption to the local chicken population and eventually made his way into Naughton's yard and took up residency among their domestic fowl. One night at a card game in Naughtons it was decided a game of cards would be played for the bantom cock as Mrs Naughton was keen to off-load her uninvited guest. The card players that night were Patrick Naughton, Andrew Finnerty, Tom and Michael Cunniffe and Joe Galvin and they paid 6 pence each for the card game. The winner of the game however did not want the bird either so another game was played and this continued until a considerable sum of money had been collected. Mrs Naughton's attempt to get rid of her troublesome chicken was not proving successful and a more direct approach was needed and duly carried out. The question then arose over what would be done with the 'cock money' and it was decided to build a ball-alley. Dances were held locally and the money raised was added to the money already collected from the card game.

The ball-alley was completed in 1929 using sand from Finnerty's field nearby. The walls however had to be raised in 1930 as too many balls were being lost in the adjacent fields. Soon tournaments were held in Mount Talbot and a number of gold medals were played for with many players coming great distances to take part. It cost 6 pence for adults and 3 pence for children to play hand-ball and the local people spent many long evenings at the new ball-alley[108].

---

[108] Taken from an article written by the late Sean Naughton of Garrier in: Tisrara Heritage Society, A History of Tisrara, 1997, p110.

People Who Saw the Ghosts.

Our Roscommon representative writes:—On Monday evening four Roscommon men motoring along the Mount Talbot road saw the driverless car come across the fields, and over the road right in front of their car and through the back gate of the estate. This gate is locked and barred and has not been opened for years. One of these men fainted, and was only brought round with considerable difficulty after being brought in to Ballygar. A Hollygrove resident saw two cars come up the bog road and continue in a straight line across country and enter the Mount Talbot grounds. The first car had neither driver nor passengers, and the second had two passengers at the back but no driver.

A young lady at Lismaha saw the phantom car with some horrible figure in the front seat. This lady fainted away and is even yet too distressed to give a clear account of what she saw.

There are reports of several flights of driverless cars over the walls. The general impression conveyed by the accounts from the Rockwood side is that the flights and visitations are the penances of unhappy souls condemned to restore to Mount Talbot the looted goods. They come and go in this driverless car restoring, and yet never having restored, for as soon as the articles are deposited on the lawn they fly away again, and some authorities assert that the journey back and forth must be repeated a million times

From Hollygrove and the moving bog country the stories all point to the ghost being that of the "Minor" who is supposed to be collecting his stolen property. The visitations around Athleague are all concerned with large groups of ghosts, and the theory is advanced on good authority there that the shades of the departed who were exterminated, with cruelty amounting to the borders of barbarity, from the rich lands of Mount Talbot, are now coming to rejoice that the breed of the exterminators is no more, and that the lands are being divided amongst the descendants of their original owners.

There is one eye witness who still asserts that the visitant is a ghostess, and that her mission is to cause the paintings on the walls of the Demesne to be removed. "To Hell with the Red Cross," is the slogan which excites her particular anger.

On Tuesday evening an appearance of the phantom car surprised two men who followed its flight to a point opposite the site of the old wooden bridge which was torn away in the time of the cattle drives. On approaching the spot a strong smell of Brimstone could be detected. Other people were called to the spot, and the noxious fumes are testified to by all of them.

(From A Correspondent.)

Startling reports concerning the reappearance in the Mount Talbot district, Ballygar, of the Phantom Car continue to pour in, and the consternation caused by its frequent appearance has reached to such an incredible extent that every available vehicle is being chartered nightly by investigators of the incident, for the purpose of witnessing this unearthly spectre.

Innumerable and astounding reports and rumours are afloat in an attempt to find a solution or cause for this strange appearance, and with the number of investigators increasing nightly and pouring in from the adjoining villages of Athleague, Creggs and Roscommon, the number of reliable witnesses is also increasing with the result that more satisfactory information is now to hand.

The district of Mount Talbot which is situate about a mile from Ballygar, has a fine list of tales of ghosts to its credit, but none has evoked the public interest to such an unbelievable degree as this, the latest "ghost," which is masquerading in the guise of a motor car.

PHANTOM MOTOR CAR.

Curious Report from Ballygar.

A correspondent writes:

Sensational reports are to hand from Ballygar district concerning the nocturnal visits of a mysterious motor which negotiates hedges and ditches at an abnormal pace and with two weird-looking occupants sitting behind. The alarming item of the incident is the fact that witnesses of the spectre have been unable to perceive a driver and maintain that the car or "tank" is driverless.

The scene of the incident has, no doubt, an eerie history, and a witness of the apparition gives in detail the history connected with the district in which this "automobile apparition" took place. In the district stands a house which suffered during the civil war regime in Ireland by being bereft of its furniture. This ghastly looking and dazzling car appeared on several nights within this last fortnight, and as the report goes, it actually contained furniture. Apart from the authenticity of the furniture item, the outstanding mystery in the locality, and which created consternation, is how this mystery motor could cross fields and hedges at such a rate and driverless. Pressmen and reporters have visited the place and find the inhabitants are quite confident that this appearance cannot be accounted for.

Newspaper reports from the Connact Tribune referring to a 'Phantom Car' that was reportedly seen in the Mount Talbot area in Janruary and February 1927. These humorous articles caused quite a stir locally and in the neighbouring towns and villages.

The Economic War occured in Ireland from 1933 to 1938 and it brought much hardship to the local community. The Free State Government had refused to repay the 'land annuities' to Britain and the British Government responded by imposing a 20% tariff on Irish exports. The most important Irish export was beef and the price of cattle tumbled. The fair at Mount Talbot witnessed record low prices for cattle and local farmers were finding it very difficult to earn a living. Local history recalls that some farmers actually gave calves away for nothing as they could not afford to rear them.

The formative years of the Irish Free State proved difficult for the people in the area but they worked very hard through this testing time to ensure the survival of their newly aquired freedom. By the end of the 1930's the outlook seemed brighter for the people of Mount Talbot. However, storm clouds were gathering over mainland Europe and the sound of marching soldiers echoed through the streets of the cities and towns. The powers of Europe were again arming for war.

New Year, 1932

i

Gabriel looked from the gate of Heaven
And saw the world on its journey driven,
Like a snowflake borne on a wintry wind,
By Time's dark forces which none can bind;
And he heard carols come echoing clear
Through the dusk that shrouded the dying year –
"Peace and goodwill, Peace and Goodwill,
Peace upon earth, goodwill to men!"

ii

But Gabriel turned, for he heard a cry
At the threshold of gold where he stood on high,
Some shadowy figures were crouching there,
Sobbing and weeping in wild despair.
Gently he asked what their grief might be,
And thus they answered him piteously,

iii

"we are the souls that shall come to birth
In the new-born year on the distant earth,
And this is the night that we look below
To see the homes where we soon must go-
We gazed with hope through the misty gloom,
But now we shudder to think of our doom.

iv

The peoples of earth are arming for war,
Though they sing of peace as they sang before;
And some are starving, and some are strong
And eager to harry the weak with wrong;
The nations are seething with hatred and fear
And we dread to be born on the earth this year.

v

Must our innocent childhood wither and fade
At the breath of the poisons that men have made?
Must we perish by famine and plague, or die
In the blazing destruction men rain from the sky?
Oh, Gabriel, pity our terror and pain –
Go, bear them the message of peace again."

vi

Gabriel sighed as he shook his head –
"a bootless errand 'twould be," he said,
"yet still there is hope, for yourselves shall bear
the message of peace to your kindred there,
Your infant voices shall plead with them,
And tell them the message of Bethlehem.

vii

If they hearken not to the wordless plea
Of the babies that they welcomed so joyfully,
Read no appeal in those innocent eyes,
No prayer for mercy and love in the cries
of their own little children, helpless and weak –
Then they will not hear, though an angel speak –
'Peace and goodwill, Peace and goodwill,
Peace upon earth, goodwill to men'".

Noelle Davies of Bushy Park, 1932

The Second World War began on Speptember 1st 1939 and it had an enormous effect on the people of Mount Talbot. Ireland had remained neutral but this did not stop the worldwide economic turmoil from reaching our shores. A state of emergency was declared on the 2nd of September 1939 and the Emergency Powers Act was enacted on the following day. This gave important powers to the government such as internment, censorship and complete governmental control over the economy. Rationing was put in place to help overcome the shortages brought about by the drastic reduction in supplies being shipped into the country. A Minister for Supplies was appointed by the Government and ration books were issued to every member of a household including the children. Most food was rationed and fresh bread was in short supply, tea was rationed to ½ oz per week for each person in a household including children. This resulted in large families having an ample supply of tea and the excess tea was often bartered for some other item that was badly needed in the house. Bacon was also in short supply and this often resulted in a pig being killed and the bacon cured. The authorities would not have been made aware that such an event took place as bacon was also rationed. Petrol became extremely scarce and soon the only cars on the road were those belonging to people that provided essential services such as the doctor, vet, hackney drivers and the local Priest but their supplies were also severely rationed. The scarcity of petrol resulted in the bicycle regaining its place as the most popular mode of transport but tyres were almost impossible to locate. Various methods of re-using tyres and tubes were carried out including the use of two or more tyres on the same wheel. Paraffin oil and candles were the main source of internal lighting in the locality and they became very scarce, very quickly. The 'Scared Heart' lamp was sometimes the only light available in houses. Old methods of illumination were re-introduced such as 'rush candles'. These consisted of peeled rushes that were dried and soaked in fat or dripping and these candles could provide light for over an hour. Turf and timber were however in plentiful supply and these provided sufficient lighting to rooms with open fires. Local people recall that all the windows of the houses were 'blackened out' during the hours of darkness to avoid targeting by stray aircraft.

In 1941 coal imports fell dramatically and the government looked to the bogs to provide the countries fuel. Hugo Flynn TD was appointed turf controller and he immediately gave control of the bogs to the County Councils. Bogs adjacent to Mount Talbot were taken over by Roscommon County Council, including Cloonakilleg bog. An enormous amount of turf was cut in the bogs under the supervision of a Council Engineer and many young men in the locality were employed in turf production. Payment of up to £2 per week was available to locals who were involved in the production of turf. This was the biggest government employment initiative provided locally since the Suck Drainage Scheme at the end of the 19th century. When the turf was 'saved' it was piled on the side of the bog roads in 'reeks' awaiting transport to the large towns and cities throughout the country. At one stage during the war the main road in the Phoenix Park in Dublin was lined by huge banks of turf that measured up to thirty feet in height. Some of this turf came from the bog in Cloonakilleg and other bogs in the area. Trees were also felled in Mount Talbot and its environs to provide additional fuel to the towns and cities. Timber was used primarily to power trains at this time.

Charcoal was produced in large quantities behind the ball-alley in Mount Talbot during the war years and also at the forests at Cloonca and Aughrane. Charcoal was manufactured by gathering waste timber and piling it into heaps which were then set alight, when the fire was burning throughout the entire pile a steel dome was placed over the fire. The fire was left to smoulder and after a length of time the fire was quenched and cooled and this process produced charcoal. The cooled charcoal was then taken to a fuel merchant and it was primarily used to power trucks and heavy machinery[109].

---

[109] Killian-Killeroran Historical Society (1984), *Newbridge, Ballygar, Toghergar News,* p 57 to 63.

All of the farmers in the locality were subject to a 'Compulsory Tillage Order'. Every farmer even if he had never tilled land previously had to sow a certain amount of crops on his land and this was policed by government inspectors. Kathleen Connor-McGrath (formerly of Corrocot) later recalled: *'Compulsory tillage was introduced and it was back to the land in a big way. Everyone in the area grew their own vegetables and people reared their own fowl'[110].*

Some men in the locality joined the Local Defence Force (L.D.F) or the Local Security Force (L.S.F) and a number of women joined the Red Cross. The local Red Cross was based at Ballygar and their leader was Rosamund Ffrench of Bushy Park House. Training and lectures were held in the Temperance Hall and the Old Preaching House in Ballygar and training was also held occasionally at Bushy Park House. This branch of the Red Cross took part in the 'Presidents Trophy' that was held each year to reward the most efficient Red Cross branches in the country. The local branch came 4th in 1946, 3rd in 1947 and 2nd in 1948. During the war a number of holes were dug along the top of Mount Talbot bridge to allow mines to be installed if an attack was imminent, the purpose of this was to slow down the movement of an invasion force by blowing up the bridge. This was part of a nationwide procedure instigated by the government to prepare against a possible (but improbable) invasion. Thankfully the holes at Mount Talbot bridge were not required and remained free of explosives.

The war ended in 1945 but the emergency did not conclude until the following year and the ration books were gladly discarded by the people of Mount Talbot. The economy began to slowly recover but there was still little in the way of direct employment available in the area. A large number of young men and women left Mount Talbot for England in the years after the war finding employment in the rebuilding of the major towns and cities after the extensive damage caused during the Blitz. Construction workers and nurses in particular were urgently required by the British Government and a whole new generation of people were lost to the locality.

Shops and Businesses

A number of shops existed in Mount Talbot throughout the 20th Century. Naughton's was the largest shop in the village providing a wide range of goods to the people in the area. All the essential grocery items, animal feed and hardware were available to buy together with boots and working clothes. A bar was set up in a circular shaped outbuilding at Naughton's during fair days in Mount Talbot, providing refreshments to the local farmers and many difficult 'deals' were struck at the bar counter. Keane's pub in Athleague and occasionally Kenny's in Ballygar ran the bar during this time. Fairs ended in Mount Talbot in the summer of 1955, thus bringing the curtain down on a long and very successful event that began in 1712 when the Talbots first received a licence to hold a fair at Mount Talbot. Initially 4 fairs were held yearly but by the 1950's this had been reduced to 2 and these were held on the 8th of May and the 1st of November. One of the most popular attractions at the fair was the 'stand' operated by Miss Fullard from Roscommon town. Miss Fullards stand was located beside the village pump where she sold a wide variety of sweets with her biggest sales coming from 'Peggies Legs' that were sold at 1p each. Sonny Hoey from Ballyforan was the last

---

[110] Mount Talbot School Board of Management (1992), *A Centenary Publication of Mount Talbot School in Co. Roscommon*, Boyle, p42.

person to attend the fair in Mount Talbot, he brought a couple of sheep to the fair in his horse and cart but found on arrival that he was the only person attending the fair. Better prices could be obtained at the fairs in Ballygar and Roscommon and this resulted in the fair at Mount Talbot being disbanded.

A shop existed at Flanagan's Post Office where the basic grocery items could also be purchased. The post office was of huge importance to the people at this time as it kept them in touch with loved ones abroad, later a pay phone was installed and this proved very popular at a time when few people had telephones at home. Kate Carr had a shop in Mount Talbot adjacent to the entrance to the Cloonca road. The shop was located in a room to the right of the front door and contained a fine selection of sweets that went down very well with the schoolchildren at the time. Another small shop existed in the townland of Lismaha on the Athleague side of the Bushy Park road and this was owned by Jimmy Nolan. Cigarettes, sweets and newspapers were sold in this shop together with some basic household items.

Johnnie Kelly had a carpentry business in Mount Talbot throughout the mid 20th century. This was located a short distance down the Four Roads road on the same site as a Forge that had existed in the previous century. The forge had been operated by Charles Lyons who was a relative through marriage of Johnnie Kelly.

Photo's of Naughtons Shop, Mount Talbot. The photo on the left dates to the early 1960's, the late Martin Joe Moran from Ballygar is shown sitting on the car bonnet. The photo on the right dates to the late 1960's or early 70's (courtesy of Pat Naughton).

136

Receipts for goods purchased at Naughtons Shop in Mount Talbot. The receipt on the left is dated November 1966 and the goods listed are mainly feedstuffs for farm animals. The receipt on the right is earlier and dates to September 1951, the items on this receipt are general household goods.

Naughtons shop was sold to Pakie Collins in 1972, Pakie was originally from Cloonakilleg and bought the shop and some land in Mount Talbot after returning from America with his wife and family. The family remained in the area until 1982 when they sold the shop and returned the US. The shop was subsequently operated by Eamon Hannon but closed permanently a few years later. All the shops that had existed in Mount Talbot were closed by the mid 1980's and the last post office closed in 2003. This post office had been opened by Eileen Kelly in the mid 1980's after Flanagans post office next door had closed down. Kelly's post office was located in the same building that was used as a post office by the Blackwood family in the early 20th century.

The closing of local businesses was generally caused by an increase in the availability and use of motorcars. Cars allowed the people in the locality to travel further to purchase goods required for the house or on the farms. People that did not have cars could however take advantage of the 'travelling shop' where a shopkeeper from the neighbouring villages or towns would travel to the more rural areas in a large van packed with essential household items. This van would call to individual houses in the area and each householder could then purchase their required weekly groceries directly from the shopkeeper. Martin Heavey operated one of these travelling shops as did

Kilgarriffs shop in Ballygar. This essential service was provided to the rural community up until the late 1980's.

Carr's house in the village of Mount Talbot, a small shop existed here during the mid 20th century and the 'herd' on the Talbot estate lived in this house during the mid 19th century (P. Connolly, June 2014).

Corrocot was a hive of activity during the mid 20th century with a number of workshops existing within the village. Frank Rourke had a Forge in Corrocot and he was known to have been an excellent blacksmith. Frank was originally from County Down and had replaced Paddy Connell as the local blacksmith in 1924 after Paddy emigrated to America. James Nolan operated a carpentry business next door to Frank Rourke's Forge and he is remembered in the area as being one of the best wheelwrights in the trade. After he completed a cart-wheel James teamed up with his neighbour Frank Rourke to carry out the difficult task of placing the iron rim around the wheel using fire and water. People that had the privilege to witness this amazing spectacle were overawed by the skill displayed by the participants. James excelled at all types of carpentry and his work could be seen internally and externally in most houses in the area. As mentioned previously in this chapter James made the hurleys for the 'Maith go Leor' hurling team in the early part of the 20th century. He died in 1968 aged 91 years after witnessing enormous changes in the locality.

Across the road from the Forge and the carpentry shop was Willie Kelly's tailoring business. He had taken over the tailoring business from his father Thomas earlier in the century and was known locally as 'Tailor Kelly'. Kitty Nolan ran a small grocery shop in Corrocot earlier in the 20th century and this was located on the main road adjacent to the entrance to Corrocot Village.

This '10 spoke' cart-wheel was made by James Nolan in his carpentry shop in Corrocot in the 1950's for his neighbour, Marty Smith (P. Connolly, September 2014).

The workshops of the tradesmen in Corrocot and Mount Talbot were a hive of activity throughout the 1940's and 50's. They were a very important part of the local community, performing a social function as well as a practical function with local men often congregating in these workshops to discuss local and international events. School kids from the area loved to call in and observe the skilled workmanship that was on display. Children from Cloonakilleg and Corrocot passed by 4 workshops on their way to and from school and were captivated by the different sounds and smells emanating from these magical places.

Mount Talbot National School – Group Photo 1955 (from the Cronin Collection).

Mount Talbot National School group photo 1962 (Cronin).

Mount Talbot National School group photo 1962. The boys prepare to practice their hurling skills (Cronin).

Ned McLoughlin's house in Cloonakilleg in the late 1970's, this was one of the last thatched cottages in the locality (Cronin).

The 'Metal Bridge' across the river Suck that links the townland of Mount Talbot to Cloonruff. The railings shown at the side of the bridge have since rusted away (Cronin, 1970's).

Mount Talbot village in 1979 looking from the village pump towards Four Roads, this photo was taken just hours before the popular 'chestnut trees' were removed as part of a road widening scheme (Cronin).

A View of Mount Talbot village in the 1960's looking towards Athleague (Cronin).

The late Bernie Fallon cycling down Cloonca road with his dog on a beautiful autumn evening in the late 1970's (Cronin).

The gate-house that once stood across from the entrance gates to Araghty House. The Shaw family lived here in the early 20th century and the children attended Mount Talbot National School. This photo was taken in the late 1970's. No trace of this house exists today (Cronin).

School group at Mount Talbot National School in 1979 (Cronin).

The towerhouse at Cloghan, the home of the powerful Donnellan family throughout the Late Medieval Period. The Donnellan's owned the townland of Cloonlaughnan up to the mid 19th century (Cronin).

The single arched stone bridge that existed over the Millrace stream on the 'Togher' in Cloonakilleg. This bridge was replaced with a precast concrete bridge in the 1980's (Cronin).

The remains of a 'ford' that once linked Garrier and Cloonakilleg is still visible in the river Suck at Connollys callow during very dry summers (Gerry Connolly, 1994**).**

The other 'Big Houses' in the area

Mount Talbot House was not the only 'Big House' in the area. 3 other houses existed within a couple of miles of Mount Talbot and all of these houses were inhabited well into the 20th century with one of them inhabited up until recent times. The houses in question are Bushy Park, Cloonca and Thornfield.

Bushy Park House

Bushy Park House was originally built on lands owned by the Talbots in circa 1721 as a charity school with a Reverand McGloughlin as its headmaster[111]. The school must have been in existance for a very short time as the Elphin Census of 1749 shows the house being occupied by a farmer called William Lennon. The House was known in its formative years as Dundermot House named after the townland on which it was built. The house was subsequently renamed Bushy Park House and the townland became known as Lisgillilea. Later the townland also became known as Bushy Park. After the charity school was disbanded the Talbots regained possession of the lands and began leasing the house and surrounding farmland to various families throughout the following century. As stated above William Lennon seems to have been the first sitting tenant and he was closely followed by Parson Hicks who opened a school here for the sons of Protestant Clergymen. John Barlow leased Bushy Park House and lands from the mid 1820's until the 1850's and he also worked as a Land Agent on the Talbot estate. John carried out various alterations and additions to Bushy Park House including the construction of the Georgian front that exists today. The Barlows were a wealthy family and lavishly entertained guests. They also owned a large pack of hounds and held many hunts at Bushy Park. It seems the Barlows entertained too lavishly though as they lost all their money and emigrated to Australia. Reverend George Knox took up residency at Bushy Park House after the departure of the Barlows. A rent book from the Talbot estate from 1864 to 1870 shows that Rev. Knox paid a yearly rent to the Talbots of £114 and 50 shillings, an enormous amount of money at the time. The rent book also shows the acreage of land involved, with 113 acres and 15 roods in the townland of Lisgillilea, 11 acres in Derrinlerrig and 1 acre in Cloonca.

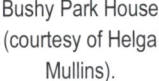

Bushy Park House
(courtesy of Helga
Mullins).

---

[111] Charity Schools were also known as 'Charter Schools' and they were set up by the British Government to offer free education to Catholic children. Children entering these schools were removed from Catholic influences, were brought up in the Protestant faith and were to be apprenticed only to Protestants. These schools failed to gain any foothold in Ireland and most were disbanded by the early 19th century.

Talbot Estate Rent Book from 1864 to 1870 relating to lands rented by Rev. George Knox of Bushy Park House (courtesy of John English).

The Frenches came to Bushy Park from Monivea in the early 1870's replacing Rev Knox as sitting tenants. The Frenches were tillage and cattle farmers and they immediately began to carry out drainage works on the estate opening up previously unusable land to crop sowing and grazing. Tom Ffrench came to Bushy Park with his parents and uncles at 10 years of age and took over the running of the estate on the death of his father. Four years after the passing through Parliament of the Wyndham Land Purchase Act of 1903, Tom Ffrench bought Bushy Park House and lands from Johnie Talbot for £1,644. Tom was known to have been an excellent farmer. He rented land near Dublin to fatten cattle prior to selling them at markets in Manchester and other cities in the north of England. The 1913 lockout at Dublin docks brought difficult times to Bushy Park as all shipping to England was interrupted, but the War years from 1914-18 brought great prosperity as Irish beef was in huge demand in England. Tom had a genuine interest in the countryside and its people and learnt Irish as a child from his neighbours in Monivea. Tom Ffrench married Georgina May Kennedy and they had two daughters, Noelle born on Christmas day 1899 and Rosamund born in August 1901. Georgina May Ffrench spent a large part of her formative years in Germany and England working as a 'Companion-Help'. During her time in Germany she developed a keen interest in music and in England she became an accomplished wood carver.

Social gathering at Bushy Park House, early 20th century (courtesy of Helga Mullins).

Georgina May Ffrench of Bushy Park - 1940

(courtesy of Helga Mullins).

Rosamund and Noelle Ffrench - circa 1904-05

Rosamund enjoyed farming immensely and spent all of her spare time and school breaks helping her father in the fields around Bushy Park. Noelle was an academic and this was evident from a very early age. She was writing short stories and poetry at the age of eleven. Noelle was educated at the

French School in Bray, County Wicklow and Trinity College Dublin. She graduated in 1922 from TCD with Double First Class Honours, two Gold Medals and the Brook prize in Classics[112].

Rosamund (left) and Noelle Ffrench (right) in their early adult years (courtesy of Helga Mullins).

During her time at Trinity College she is known to have become aquainted with republican leader Michael Collins and it seems she fully supported the War of Independence. A beech tree in the grounds of Bushy Park House contains a message that was carved into the tree on the 6th of December 1922 to commemorate the formation of the Irish Free State. The message was written by Noelle and Rosamond Ffrench with Noelle's initials (NF) carved into the tree directly above Rosamonds (RF). The message is written in Irish and is still legible today. It reads:

saorstát

éireann

bail o Ḋa air

6/12/22

Buíochas le dia   **NF**

                                                                        RF

---

[112] Mount Talbot School Board of Management, *Mount Talbot School - a window on the past*, 1992, p54

This message commemorating the formation of the Irish Free State is carved into a beech tree in the front field of Bushy Park House, adjacent to the avenue that leads to the bushy park road (P. Connolly, May 2014).

Noelle and Rosamond's mother Georgina was a fervent nationalist who instilled a deep love of Ireland in her two daughters. In her memoirs Noelle writes: *"once when we were driving in the pony-trap, an English governess of ours, Mrs Balderstone, asked her what was this Irish poem 'the wearing of the green' which, she had been told, moved crowds to tears, and my mother thereupon repeated it for her with a quiet fire which kindled such an answering flame in my nine-year-old heart"*. It is known that the British military based at Mount Talbot House visited Bushy Park House during the War of Independence and questioned the family about republican activity in the area. The army had been wrongly informed that the Ffrench's were harbouring volunteers in Bushy Park House. When the army officer arrived at the door he was greeted by Rosamond and he immediately noticed a large painting hanging in the front hallway depicting a British Army Officer in full uniform. His questioning immediately ceased after he saw the family painting and he apologised for the inconveniance caused.

Noelle Ffrench was devastated when Michael Collins was killed in an ambush at Béal na Bláth in August 1922. She wrote three unpublished short poems about him after his death and the content of these poems suggest that they had become friends. She is known to have regularly visited Glasnevin cemetary to spend time at his grave. A photograph of Collins in Irish Army uniform was found among Noelle's personel belongings after her death.

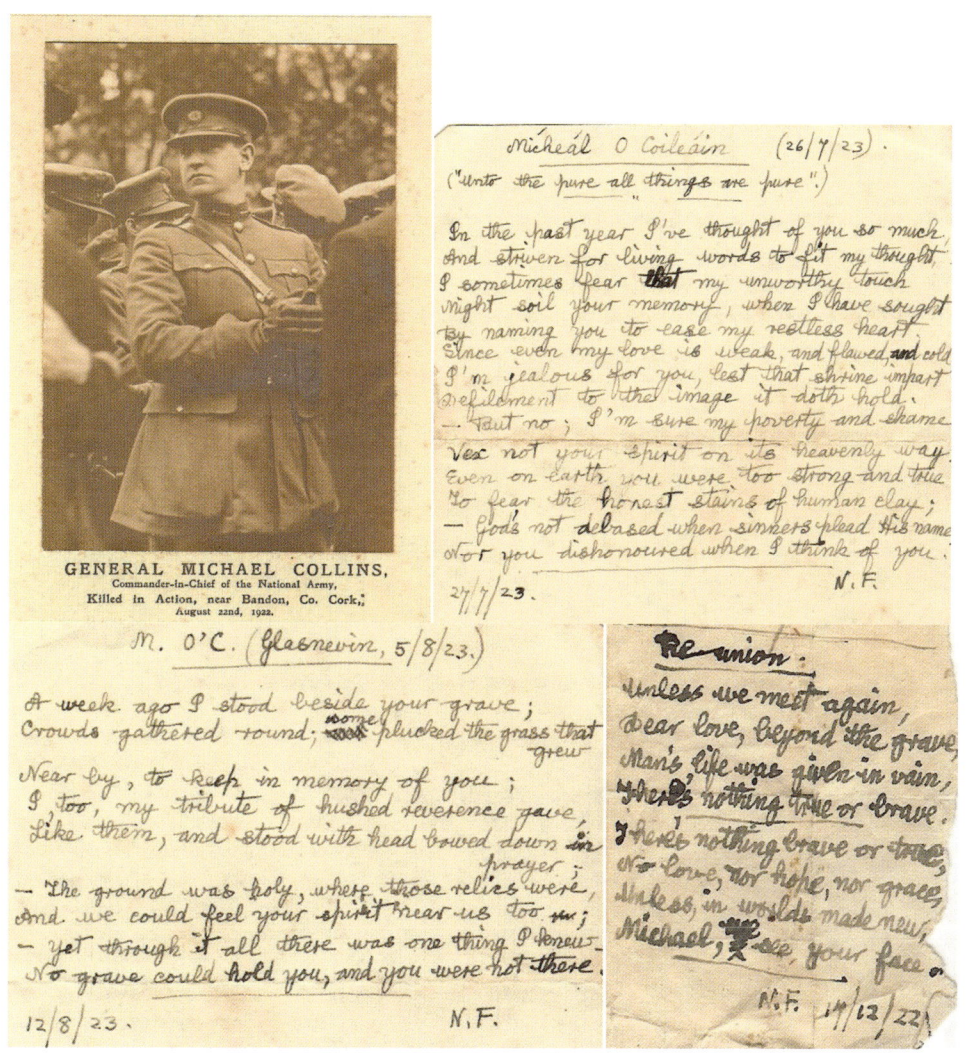

Poems written about General Michael Collins after his death by Noelle Ffrench of Bushy Park House. The photo shown above of Collins was found among Noelle's personal possessions after her death in 1983 (courtesy of Helga Mullins).

Noelle Ffrench met David James Davies from Wales at the International People's College in Elsinore, Denmark in 1924 and they instantly became inseperable. Noelle always called him 'Dai'. They shared the same political and social beliefs and they married in Milltown, Dublin in 1925. Dai and Noelle were very interested in the Folk School movement and attempted to open a folk school in Ireland but their attempt proved unsuccessful[113]. Dai had left school at a young age but his new bride encouraged him to finish his education. With Noelle's academic and financial assistance he graduated from Aberystwyh University in Wales with a Bachelor of Arts in Economics in 1928, a Masters of Arts in 1930 and a Doctor of Philosophy in 1931 and went on to win consecutive awards at the National Eisteddfod of Wales in 1930, 1931, 1932 and 1934 on essays on economics and politics. In 1932 Noelle and Dai bought the Pantybeiliau mansion at Gilwern in Monmouthshire and made another attempt to establish a Folk School but again this proved unsuccessful. Both Noelle and Dai became members of the Welsh Nationalist Party, 'Plaid Cymru' when it was founded in 1925 and continued to actively support the party throughout the following decades. Dai died in 1956 and Noelle returned home to Ireland and lived in Greystones, County Wicklow with her relatives.

Wedding photo of Noelle Ffrench and David James Davies in 1925. Mrs Ffrench is seated second from left and Rosamund is seated second from right (courtesy of Helga Mullins).

---

[113] Folk Schools originated in Denmark in the late 19th century, the idea was to give the peasantry and other people from the lower echelons of society a higher education through personal development. The focus was not on formal education but on popular education and enlightenment. The language and history of the country, its constitution and industries (mainly farming in Ireland) along with folk songs were the guiding principles of an education based on a Christian framework.

Tom French died in 1940, his wife passed way in 1941 and Rosamund subsequently took over the running of the farm. Noelle had remained very close to her sister and visited Bushy Park regularly during her time in Greystones. Both sisters were involved in charitable organisations, Rosamund was heavily involved in the Irish Red Cross and Noelle became very active in Amnesty International and the Co-Operative Movement. After the Second World War ended in 1945 Germany lay in ruins and many of the civilian population were in serious difficulty with food and other essential items becoming increasingly scarce. In 1946 the Red Cross began sending children to Ireland from Germany while the bomb damaged cities were being re-built and essential infrastructure was reinstated. One thousand children came to Ireland during this time and one of these was seven year old Helga Weiss from Essen in the industrial north-west. Essen had been bombed by the allies on numerous occasions during the war due to its importance to the German war effort, particularly the Krupp factory where panzer tanks and other armaments were produced. Many civilians were killed during these raids and very few buildings were standing in the city at the end of the war. Helga was sent to Ireland with her brother Walter by her parents in 1946 as they were finding it impossible to provide for their children. Prior to the departure of Helga and Walter, their father purchased rosary beads and put them around his childrens necks. The family were Lutherans and Helgas father believed they had a better chance of being fostered in Ireland if the local people believed them to be Catholic. After they arrived in Ireland it was soon discovered that Helga and Walter were not Catholics but it did not cause any problems. Rosamund Ffrench of Bushy Park House had become aware of the arrival of these two Lutheran children into Ireland and immediately arranged to foster them. She collected them in Dublin and brought them by train to Roscommon. During the journey Rosamund bought some oranges and bananas for her new guests. Helga remembers eating both an orange and a banana without peeling them as she had never seen fruit before. She missed her family but was in awe of the greeness and unspoilt beauty of the Irish countryside. Her young mind could not understand how all the buildings were standing and air raids and gas-masks were non existant. She remembers sitting in the hallway of Bushy Park House staring at the massive oak door (formerly located at Mount Talbot House) and being amazed at the size of her new home. She was terrified that she would get lost in this enormous house with six flights of stairs. Helga could not speak any English but began to pick up words quickly and within a few months she was conversing freely with her foster parent and house staff.

After two and a half years Helga and Walter returned to Essen to live with their parents. The city was partially re-built and functioning again. Helga however found it very difficult to re-adapt to city life and yearned for the freedom of Bushy Park. She had also forgotten how to speak German but eventually Helga settled back to life in her native country. Within two years of their return Rosamond Ffrench wrote to Walter and Helga's father to see if he would allow Walter to return to Bushy Park with the understanding that Walter would eventually inherit the house and farm. Their father agreed and Walter returned to Bushy Park. Helga missed her brother enormously as they had never been apart. All throughout the war and during their stay in Ireland they had supported and looked out for each other. Helga's parents realised this and allowed her to return to Ireland for a second time to be re-united with her brother and also with Rosamund Ffrench who she had also missed enormously. Helga returned to Bushy Park and later in the year she went to boarding school in Sligo and Walter attended school in Galway City. Walter became restless after he finished his secondary education and decided to move to England leaving Rosamund with no one to manage the farm at Bushy Park. She hired a farm manager called Larry Mullins from Barnaderg in County Galway who immediately began to modernise and improve the farm. A relationship developed between Helga and Larry and they married in 1957. Within a few years the sound of childrens feet could be heard again on the old timber floors of Bushy Park House. Rosamund Ffrench became ill in 1964 and Noelle moved home temporarily to Bushy Park to look after her sister. Rosamund died in 1965 and is buried with her family at Mount Talbot cemetary. She is remembered with fondness and affection in the area.

Photo from 1961 taken on the steps of Bushy Park House showing Larry and Helga Mullins and their family, Noelle Davies is shown on the left of back row beside Mrs. Weiss (Helgas mother). Rosamund Ffrench is shown in the front between Larry and Helga (Courtesy of Helga Mullins)

Larry and Helga inherited Bushy Park House and lands after Rosamund passed away. Noelle moved back permanently to Bushy Park when she became ill in the late 1970's and she passed away on February 14th 1983. She is buried with her sister and parents in the Ffrench plot at Mount Talbot cemetary. The National Library of Wales contains an enormous amount of papers and documents that were written by Noelle between the years 1926 to 1979 and nineteen boxes of material are available to view in the library. The material was donated in three groups: Prof. A. O. H. Jarman, Cardiff, in November 1983; by Helga Mullins of Bushy Park in March 1987; and by Dr Ceinwen Thomas, Cardiff, in September 1987. Her poetry was taught to us when we attended Mount Talbot National School by the late Tim Cronin who greatly admired her wonderfully descriptive poems that often related to the people that lived around her in Bushy Park.

Bushy Park

Jewel of Hope with its beckoning light

Jewel of joy inexplicably bright

Jewel of peace where no fears can appal

Jewel of Memory, dearest of all

(Noelle Davies, 1981)

154

Cloonca House

Cloonca House was built in the late 1870's or early 1880's by Johnnie Talbot for his cousins the Talbot Crosbies of Ardfert in County Kerry. The house was unique in the area as many parts of the external stucture was constructed entirely from bright cream coloured brick. The bricks were manufactured by 'J & M Craig' in Kilmarnock, Scotland and their importation suggests that no expense was spared by Johnnie Talbot during the construction of the house.

Early photo of Cloonca House from the 1880's (courtesy of Donald Cameron).

William David Talbot Crosbie lived at Cloonca House in the late 19th and early 20th Centuries. He was born on 17th of June 1849 and married Kathleen Sophia Coke on the 3rd of October 1874. They farmed over a thousand acres in the locality. Cloonca House was re-modelled by David and Kathleen and part of the front of the house was removed and additonal sections were built to the rear of the house. David Talbot Crosbie acted as Land Agent on the Talbot estate and oral tradition recalls an incident that occurred when he tried to remove an elderly woman from her house for not paying rent. The woman refused to leave the house and replied *'hoult I have Crosbie, and hoult Ill keep'*[114]. He was also very eager to evict the Ffrench's from Bushy Park House prior to the eventual purchase of the house and lands by Tom Ffrench in 1907. David Talbot Crosbie left Cloonca in 1912 after his health had deteriorated and he died on the 19th of November 1915. The house seems to have been owned at this time by Johnnie Talbot and it was inhabited after the Talbot Crosbies departed by Andrew McIntyre and his family. Andrew was the Land Steward on the Talbot estate and moved to Cloonca House from a house in Mount Talbot village. The house he vacated became Flanagans Post

---

[114] From the Memoirs of Noelle Davies of Bushy Park House, courtesy of Helga Mullins.

Office later in the century. The association of the Talbot Crosbies with Cloonca House ended permanently with the death of David Talbot Crosbie as David and his wife Kathleen did not have any children.

Mr W. D Talbot-Crosbie, Clooncagh, Mount Talbot, had a narrow escape from what might have been a serious accident in Roscommon on Saturday last. When proceeding home on horseback from his office the animal which he was riding got suddenly frightened in Abbey street at some passing object, and losing complete control of its limbs, fell helpless to the ground. Mr Crosbie was thrown to the ground in front of the horse, but beyond a severe shaking escaped injury, his feet being instantly released from the stirrups. The horse, which was badly cut and bruised in a few places, was brought back to his owner's premises at the rere of the Estates Office and the services of Mr Byrne, V S, immediately requisitioned. The gentleman thought it necessary to have the animal removed in a float to his own residence at Castlestrange where his injuries will be attended to under his own personal supervision.

Newspaper reports from the Roscommon Messenger relating to William David Talbot Crosbie of Cloonca House, dated July 1907.

THE TALBOT ESTATE

A deputation representing the tenants on this estate waited on the landlord, Mr W J Talbot, D L, and his agent, Mr W D Talbot Crosbie, at Mount Talbot last week, to ascertain the views of Mr Talbot regarding the sale of his property. The matter having been discussed at length, no arrangement was come to in face of the refusa of the landlord to dispose of the grass lands for divison amongst the small tenants and their families.

David Talbot Crosbie, late 19th century (left). David with Dolly Brierley seated on a horse also called 'Dolly' on the grounds of Cloonca House (right), early 20th century (courtesy of Donald Cameron).

Kathleen Talbot Crosbie (nee Coke) with her sister-in-law Charlotte Talbot Crosbie in the 'salon' at Cloonca House, late 19th century (courtesy of Donald Cameron).

David Talbot Crosbie and his wife Kathleen at the tennis courts of Cloonca House, late 19th century (courtesy of Donald Cameron),

David Talbot Crosbie feeding a calf on the grounds of Cloonca House, early 20th century. The front of the house had been re-modelled by this time (courtesy of Donald Cameron).

Cloonca House was attacked by irregulars during the Civil War and it was badly damaged by fire. The charred remains of flooring joists are still visible today. This beautiful and unique house was only in existence for approximately 40 years. The large amount of money spent on its construction and its re-modelling together with the cost of its elaborate internal decoration was extravagant but it all was to prove wasteful. Cloonca house was the only 'big house' in the area other than Mount Talbot House to have been attacked during the turbulance of the early 1920's. It is ironic that Cloonca House was targeted by Republicans as the previous owner of Cloonca House, David Talbot Crosbie seems to have had nationalist sympathies. Part of a letter he wrote to the Irish Independent in 1905 stated: '*We in the west, have had a brilliant outbursts of oratory of late, but reading column after column, the only remedy, apparently, suggested is this one word, 'Compulsion', a word hateful to all true lovers of liberty and going back to the old methods of class conflict, which we hoped had been left in the 19th century. And that with the 20th century had dawned on a united Ireland, whose first work was to produce the last Land Purchase Act, not by compulsion, but by inducement, and if there is again a united Ireland I am convinced, with the added help of the Irish Reform Assocation, we shall be able to settle the western difficulty on the same lines. Surely we can never awaken our people to the true meaning of liberty by giving them abject lessons in compulsion and coercion....'*.

Photos from the early 20th century showing the rear (left photo) and the front (right photo) of Cloonca House (courtesy of Donald Cameron).

David Talbot Crosbie with two young horses that are in the process of being trained. Records exist of David Talbot Crosbie winning prizes for his thoroughbred horses the Dublin Horse Show at this time (courtesy of Donald Cameron).

The horses 'Trap' used by the Talbot Crosbie land agents to travel around to collect rents from tenants on the Talbot estate was still visable in the abandoned coach house at Cloonca well into the 1960's. They also collected rents at one of the out offices at Cloonca House during the early 20th century. In this instance the tenantry came to the land agent and not vice versa. Cloonca House was known locally as the 'Agents House'.

Cloonca House is now a ruin but there is enough of the fabric of the building still standing to imagine how imposing this house must have been in its prime. The once impressive gardens are wild and overgrown but some of the exotic and unusual plants and trees still come to life every spring. To the modern observer the Anti-Treaty attack on this house seems unnecessary and wasteful. The Civil War was practically over at this time and it seems the attack was carried out to settle old scores rather then to gain any military advantage. After the Civil War ended the uninhabitable house and the surrounding lands were purchased by the Land Commission and distributed out among the former tenantry, bringing to an end a brief but eventful period in the history of this townland.

Modern Photos of what remains of the once impressive Cloonca House. The charred remains of a flooring joist may be seen in the photo on the right, the result of a fire that occured here during the Civil War (P. Connolly, June 2014).

Modern view of Cloonca House looking from the east, the cream coloured brick used in the construction of this house came from Kilmarnock in Scotland (P. Connolly, June 2014).

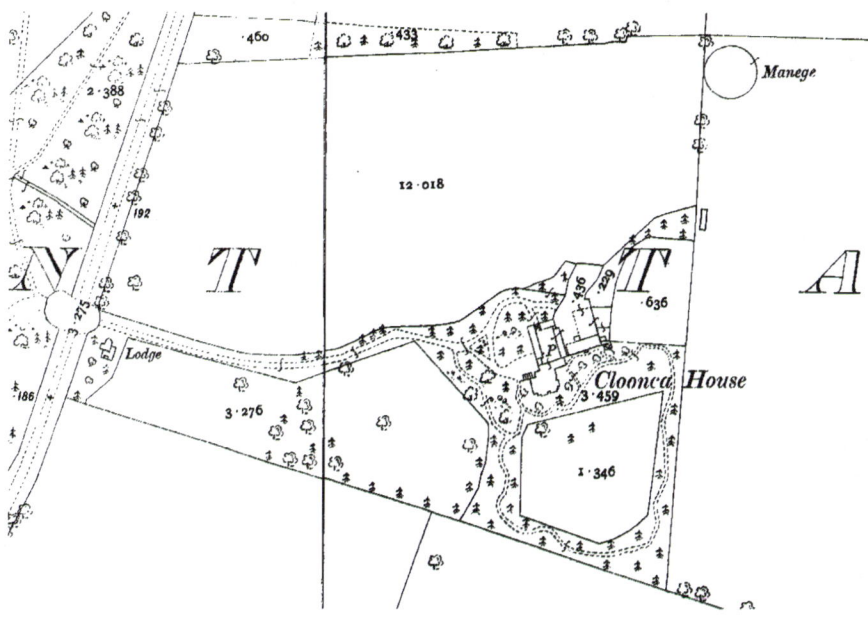

Map from the early 20th century showing the layout of Cloonca House, the outbuildings and grounds. The 'Manege' shown to the north east was used to train the prize winning horses that were owned by the Talbot Crosbie family. The 'Lodge' was located across from the 'Grand Gate' that led into Mount Talbot House. The 'Maith go Leor' hurler Jack Smith lived at the lodge with his family throughout the first half of the 20th century (OSI, Licence number 2010/15CCMA/Galway County Council).

Thornfield House

Thornfield House was constructed in the late 18th century on the Galway side of the river Suck adjacent to Mount Talbot Bridge. The house was constructed in the townland of 'Srahaunnagort' but after the house was completed the townland subsequently became known as Thornfield. The lands were owned by the Kellys of Castle Kelly (Aughrane) and they leased out the house and lands to various tenants throughout the following century. The first recorded owner of Thornfield was Doctor Terence McDermott who lived here in the 1780's and 90's. The island in the river Suck that is located in front of Thornfield House subsequently became known as 'Doctors Island'.

Front view of Thornfield House. The house contained 23 rooms and the yards contained 30 out-buildings
(courtesy of John English).

In 1828 the local Vicar Reverend Henry Marcus Crofton is recorded as living at Thornfield and he also leased the adjoining lands from the Kellys. The longest serving residents of Thornfield House were the Mahons. In 1831 John Mahon of Upper Gardiner Street, Dublin married his cousin Leonara Kelly who was a daughter of the Reverend Armstrong Kelly of Castle Kelly[115]. In 1834 John and Leonara Mahon took up residence at Thornfield and were given a lease of the house by the new bride's father and her brother Denis Henry Kelly[116]. The Mahons also leased the lands at Thornfield, Garrier and Tully from the Kelly's. Leonara was Armstrong Kelly's only daughter and he was particularly

---

[115]John Mahon was a brother of Captain Denis Mahon of Strokestown house. Denis Mahon evicted over 3,000 tenants on his estate during the great famine and this terrible event led to his assassination by one of the evicted tenants on the 2nd of November 1847.
[116]Galway County Council Archives, Kelly Papers, G00/04/153. This document gives details of the lease between the Kelly's and John Mahon including the amount of land involved.

happy that she was living close by as it gave him an opportunity to 'keep an eye' on her new husband. The Mahons and Kellys families became very close and this friendship continued into the next generation with the Mahons adding the name Kelly to their surnames. In 1876 Thomas Kelly Mahon of Thornfield House owned 947 acres in County Galway and 584 acres in County Roscommon. It is worth noting that this family never actually owned Thornfield House or the surrounding lands with all the lands in their ownership being located outside of their base at Thornfield.

After the sale of Denis Kelly's lands by the Landed Estates Court in 1863, the Mahon Kelly family leased the land from the new owner of the Aughrane estate, Christopher Neville Bagott[117]. The advertisement for the sale of Thornfield House stated that the Desmesne *'contained richly wooded and ornamated lands, good rich pasture, and prime tillage, with house, offices and garden, laid out in the most modern style, and on which several thousand pounds have been expended….this lot adjoins the beautiful desmesne of Mount Talbot from which it is seperated by the River Suck[118]'*. Later in the 19th century Johnnie Talbot bought the house and lands from the Bagotts and continued to lease the estate to the Mahons. The Mahons were excellent farmers and they employed many people on their farm particularly during the busy months from May to August. They also maintained a large amount of domestic staff and treated all their employees very well. They were known to kill a cow every month and a sheep every week to provide food for their indoor and outdoor staff[119].

The last members of the Mahon family to reside at Thornfield house were Thomas K. Mahon (known locally as Tom) and his wife Frances who had been a governess to Tom's sister. Tom Mahon died in 1906 aged 73 and Frances returned to her family in England and put Thornfield house and the surrounding lands up for sale in 1907. The estate was purchased by Henry English who was a son of William English, a former land steward at Mount Talbot House. The 1911 census show Henry living in Thornfield with his son John Latimor English who was known as Jack. Jack was studying medicine at Trinity College Dublin when he contracted pneumonia and the illness resulted in his untimely death at the age of 24 in 1926. Henry English lived at Thornfield House through the turbulent times of the early 1920's and did not leave the area until the early 1950's when he sold Thornfield to his neighbour Patrick Naughton of Naughton's shop in Mount Talbot.

Henry English died on the 5th of May 1955 and is buried in the family plot at Mount Talbot cemetery. The Naughtons lived briefly at Thornfield House during refurbishment works at their house and shop in the village. Thornfield had become practically uninhabitable with dampness seeping through the walls, it was known to have been a particularly cold house. Thornfield House was knocked down in the 1950's and some of the stone was used to build an extension to the church at Ballygar. Some of the outbuildings and garden walls still stand today. The gate house and the impressive entrance gate also exist giving the modern observer a glimpse of the former grandeur that existed within this townland.

---

[117] The Mahon's purchased the townland of Cloonakilleg and also Ballybaun House and estate (near Newbridge) from Denis Kelly in 1863 but they did not purchase Thornfield.
[118] Mary C. Lyons, *Illustrated Encumbered Estates, Ireland, 1850-1905*, Co. Clare 1993, p219-223.
[119] From the memoirs of Noelle Davies of Bushy Park House, courtesy of Helga Mullins.

Jack English on his pony outside Thornfield House, circa 1918 (courtesy of John English).

Henry English, the last long term occupant of Thornfield House (courtesy of John English).

Modern photo of the original entrance gates to Thornfield House (P. Connolly, June 2014)

Modern photo of the gate-house of Thornfield House in the townland of Garrier (P. Connolly, June 2014).

Waterlines

I am the river bed.
You flow over me,
a seamless robe
of endless shifting shades;
opalescent, mercurial, opaque.
You bear alluvium to fields
flattened by generations of hay-makers.
These calla lands that stretch
west to distant bogs and the tower
of Killeroran graveyard.

I am the river bed.
Through you I glimpse
the sun in autumn.
Against its south-west glow
wigeon, teal and mallard rise
from sighing sedge
or black refracted sloping reeds.
Water-hens rummage for food
under the fallen salley,
its trunk a blackened shaft.

As autumn deepens
your currents build
and force against the banks.
They seep out where
the land has dipped,
find life in new levels
as sinuous streams.
They adsorb the low grass, feed
one another and then conjoin
in a mirage of mirror glass.

Now I do not know you.
spread across the fields you engulf acres, find
an empire of your own.
Obliterated divisions leave
a deep-silver mass, solder
fusing towards the winter sky
of endless mist and rain
broken by curlew cries
and flocks of wild geese

When Spring days warm,
floods fold back,
the time of growth begins.
I feel your force return.
You find your course, obey
the bank's restraint, the season
of free-floods spent. Soon
water-lily pads carry green
and golden bulbs, yellow irises
crown your bank.

By the longest day
you feign forgetfulness,
drop your guard and
shrink to half your width.
I see for myself
the pure blue sky and walls
of black-mossed stones dredged
from my depths a century ago.
Part of me belongs to the land
like remnants of a lost domain.

I am the river bed.
You flow over me.
Late in summer I see myself,
a palette of gravel,
stones and sand. In this tapestry
are the atoms of my being,
minuscule woven pixels
multiplied in millions,
bedded together
by the weight of water.

Mary Turley-McGrath

Chapter 7 – The 21st Century

The changes that have occurred in Mount Talbot and its environs, particularly over the 20th century have been phenonemal and the arrival of the new millennium heralded the start of another chapter in the history of Mount Talbot.

Mount Talbot still contains a thriving and active community. The local shops and businesses that existed in the previous century have now closed but the amount of houses in the village has actually increased over the last decade. The school is still providing an exceptional education to the children in the area. 4 and 5 generations of some of the local families have now attended this school. In August 2009 a new handball club was formed in Mount Talbot by local enthusiasts and it has become a phenomenal success bringing crowds of people back into Mount Talbot that have not been seen in the area since the great fairs ended in the 1950's. The original handball alley has been restored and extended, providing an impressive approach to the village for people crossing the bridge from the Galway side. The location of the orginal back-gate to the big house beside the re-burbished ball-alley is a wonderful example of an item from the past being renewed and reinvigorated within a modern context. The old Protestant church is currently being renovated and now contains a fine new roof thus ensuring its preservation. The cemetery is also being renewed and a large amount of foliage has been cut back and removed form the site. The ruins of the Vestry are also visible again after ivy and other foliage were removed from the structure. The old Stewards House in Mount Talbot has been beautifully restored with the original stone and brick surround exposed for passers by to admire. This building also served as the village post office for many years. The old gate-house has withstood the test of time and is perfectly preserved by the Flynn family. This house may date back to the formation of the village in the mid-18th century. Many other old and important buildings remain an intergral part of the village and some of these have now witnessed 3 centuries of habitation. The people involved in the Mount Talbot Village Enhancement Scheme ensure that the village is well maintained for the local population to enjoy and for passers-by to admire.

Mount Talbot has witnessed some extraordinary events in its long and colourful history, from forest clearance for farming during the late Stone Age, population expansion and metal working in the Bronze Age, the rise of the powerful O'Kelly family during the Medievel Period, the bloody wars of the 17th century, the rise of landlordism and religious persecution of the 18th century, the horrendous loss of life during the terrible famine in the 19th century, the fight for freedom and the painful birth of a new nation in the 20th century and the entrance into the digital age of the 21st century. Through all of this the people of Mount Talbot and the surrounding areas have remained steadfast and resolute. Everything they have done in the past and are doing now is for the benefit of the area and this extraordinary appreciation of their birthplace will ensure that this village will continue to be a place of importance for future generations to appreciate and enjoy.

Flynns house is the oldest inhabited house in Mount Talbot. It served as a gate-house to Mount Talbot House when the 'Grand Gate' was located across the road during the mid 19th century (P. Connolly, June 2014).

A modern view of the approach to Mount Talbot from the Galway side of the bridge (P. Connolly, June 2014).

The Church at Mount Talbot, constructed in 1766. This church served the local Protestant community until the 1960's.

The 'Grand Gate' at Mount Talbot (P. Connolly, July 2014).

The cemetery at Mount Talbot carpeted in bluebells. The ruinous Talbot mausoleum is shown to the right (P. Connolly, May 2014).

The Talbot mausoleum at Mount Talbot Cemetery (P. Connolly, May 2014).

Mount Talbot House, the last remaining tower stands defiant against the ruinous effects of time (M. Connaughton, June 2014).

The original plasterwork that adorned the front of Mount Talbot House is still visible among the ruins today (M. Connaughton, June 2014).

The ornate frieze that adorned the underside of a ceiling is still visible in one of the rooms of Mount Talbot House (M. Connaughton, June 2014).

One of the last remaining pieces of original plasterwork at Mount Talbot House clings to an internal wall (M. Connaughton, June 2014).

This chair is one of a set of 18 that were originally commissioned specifically for Mount Talbot House in the late 17th or early 18th centuries. The chairs contain the Talbot and Talbot-Crosbie family crests. 3 of these chairs may be seen in the photo below from the late 19th century taken in the dining room of Mount Talbot House.

Every spring daffodils still bloom along the edges of what was once the avenue that lead from the Grand Gate to Mount Talbot House (Sarah Connolly, March 2014).

The ball-alley at Mount Talbot has been fully restored by Mount Talbot Handball Club and the area around the former 'fair-green' has been beautifully refurbished (P. Connolly, March 2014).

Modern view of Mount Talbot National School (P. Connolly, June 2014).

A modern view of the rear entrance gate to Mount Talbot house with the 18th century stone arched bridge in the background (P. Connolly, June 2014).

The original rear entrance gate to Mount Talbot house is located adjacent to the modern ball-alley and is still in remarkably good condition (P. Connolly, June 2014).

Modern view of the village pump with the ruins of Mount Talbot House in the background (P. Connolly, June 2014).

Stone kerbing near the former entrance gates to Thornfield House. These kerbs were part of a footpath that linked Mount Talbot to Ballygar. It was constructed during the 19th century for the exclusive use of the gentry in the area (P. Connolly, June 2014).

The footbridge at Cloondara that links this townland with Cloonruff on the Galway side of the river Suck (P. Connolly, October 2014).

Clooneleen, this area is located on the approach to Mount Talbot from Athleague. The parapets of a single arch stone bridge dating to the 18th century may be seen in the foreground and the tower of Mount Talbot Church that was constructed in 1766 may be seen in the distance. A large village existed here in the 18th century having developed around a water-mill that had been constructed by Brian Og O'Kelly in the early 17th century. A skirmish occured here during the Cromwellian War when local O'Kelly confederate soldiers engaged parliamentarian forces. The parliamentarians were marching under Captain Ormsby from Athleague to Galway, this skirmish resulted in many injuries and at least one parliamentarian fatality (P. Connolly, August 2014).

Contemporary painting of Cromwells parliamentarian soldiers during the English Civil War. A similar army marched through Clooneleen in 1646 and met with fierce resistance from the O'Kellys.

The circular mound near the ruins of Mount Talbot House. This mound or tumulus was used for burials during the Early Bronze Age, see chapter 1 (M. Connaughton, June 2014).

View of the river suck from Mount Talbot Bridge looking upstream towards Cloonruff. The ruins of Mount Talbot House may be seen in the background on the right (P. Connolly, June 2014).

The remaining outbuildings at Cloonca House, the chimneys from the ruined house may be seen in the background (P. Connolly, June 2014).

The 18th century 12 arch bridge at Mount Talbot. This bridge replaced an earlier ford that had existed close to this location. Part of the bridge was blown up by Anti-Treaty forces during the Civil War. This bridge now forms part of the N63, Roscommon to Galway road (P. Connolly, August 2014)

The ruins of James Nolan's carpentry shop in Corrocot. James made the hurley's for the 'Maith go Leor' hurling team and he was also known to have been an excellent wheelwright (P. Connolly, October 2014).

Photo showing an original 'Maith go Leor' hurley made by James Nolan at his carpentry shop in Corrocot. This photo compares a modern hurley with the Nolan hurley from circa 1904.

The remains of a bridge abutment within the townland of Cloondara. A footbridge was located here that allowed access to 'Lady Anne's Island'. The island was named after Lady Anne Crosbie who married William Talbot of Mount Talbot in May 1775. The island is now known as Sally island, named after the sally tree's that grow in abundance on the island. The orginal hunting lodge for Mount Talbot House was located close to this footbridge (P. Connolly, March 2014).

Large stone pillars and an original gate that once formed part of an avenue that led through the Talbot estate. This avenue is now part the Suck Valley Way that goes through part of the original demesne of Mount Talbot House (P. Connolly, March 2014).

Artists impression of the entrance front of Mount Talbot House in the early 20th century.

Brian Scanlon 2014

Modern photo showing the ruins of the entrance front of Mount Talbot House (M. Connaughton, June 2014).

A Memory

"God be with the old times!" – so you used to say,
sitting in your cottage in the evening of the day,
and telling of the happy scenes your childhood used to know,
and of the friends and kindred that you played with long ago.
Some of them were far away, and some of them were dead –
"God be with the old times!" – you sighed and bowed your head.

As we sat and listened, we saw upon your face
a glimmering reflection of girlhood's vanished grace;
A light of memory in your eyes like autumn sunset gone;
Age had brought no bitterness to mar that shining look;
Still you kept the child-like trust that sorrow never shook.

Time had never touched us; we were children yet;
But in your tone was something that we could not quite forget;
Through that old familiar saying of the Irish country-side
there spoke a living love and faith that could not be belied.
And so it lingers in my heart, while changing years go past,
an echo from old times, remembered to the last.

"God be with the old times!" – I have learnt to see
deeper meaning in your words than once they had for me;
They tell of an immortal hope – God has them in his care,
those lovely vanished days – not lost, although we thought they were –
and those we loved long since, when we come home to Paradise,
as of old, shall meet us with welcome in their eyes.

Noelle Davies of Bushy Park

Appendix 1- Lineage of the leading historic families in the area

Direct paternal lineage of the O'Kellys of Cluain na gCloidhe (Mount Talbot)

Maeleachlainn Ó Ceallaigh, b. 1326 in Gailey Castle, d. 1401. Was Chief of Hy-Many.

Brian Ó Ceallaigh, d.1393 son of Maeleachlainn, was Tanist under his father but died in his father's lifetime so never became Chief of Hy-Many.

Aedh "Hugh" Ó Ceallaigh of Athleague, d. 1467, son of Brian, 27th chief of Hy-Many

Donnchadh Ó Ceallaigh of Lecan, son of Aedh.

Brian Ó Ceallaigh of Turrock, son of Donnchadh.

Malachy Ó Ceallaigh of Turrock, son of Brian, slain by the McDermott's of Boyle and the O'Kellys of Lisdalon in 1545

Brian O'Kelly, son of Malachy**,** first of Turrock and then of Attiknockan and Cluain na gCloidhe. Attacked the O'Kelly chiefs of Hy-Many at Lisdalon to avenge his father's death, this started a bloody and bitter O'Kelly civil war.

Brian Og McBrien O'Kelly of Cluain na gCloidhe, son of Brian, fought with the Irish at Kinsale and stayed after the battle with Donal Cam O'Sullivan Beare in Kerry. He later went to Spain, joined the English Army in the Netherlands and later returned to Cluain na gCloidhe. He was given the rank Colonel in the confederate army in Connacht during the Cromwellian War. All his lands were taken from him at the end of the war and given to Sir Henry Talbot who was transplanted to the area in the Act of Settlement of 1652.

Direct paternal lineage of the Talbots of Mount Talbot

Sir Henry Talbot, born at Templeogue Castle, married Margaret Talbot, transplanted to Cluain na gCloidhe after the Cromwellian war.

James Talbot, d 1691, son of Sir Henry, married Bridget Bermingham, gained rank of Colonel in the service of King James II, killed at battle of Aughrim on the 12th of July 1691, died without male issue, changed name of Cluain na gCloidhe to Mount Talbot.

William Talbot, brother of James, married Lucy Hamilton, d 1692, had ownership of lands at Mount Talbot for only one year.

Henry Talbot, son of William, married Isabella Forward, d 1729, held the office of High Sheriff of County Roscommon.

William Talbot, son of Henry, married Sarah Rose on 30th May 1739, d 1787, held the office of High Sheriff of County Roscommon, built Mount Talbot House (shown below in red military coat).

William John Talbot, son of William, married firstly Elizabeth Margaret Rose on 2nd October 1765, married secondly Lady Anne Crosbie on 24th May 1775, (shown above in blue jacket and coat).

William Talbot, son of William John, married Susannah Kemmis on 20th December 1802, d 1851, held the office of Justice of the Peace for County Roscommon also held the office of High Sheriff of County Roscommon, died without male issue.

John Talbot, b 1818, married firstly Marianne McCausland on 2nd January 1845, married secondly Gertrude Caroline Bayly on 15th October 1858, d 1859, nephew of William Talbot, son of Reverend John Crosbie (formerly Talbot) of Ardfert in Co .Kerry, name legally changed to Talbot by Royal Licence, divorced his first wife Marianne McCausland by Act of Parliament, held the office of High Sheriff of County Roscommon and also held the office of Deputy Lieutenant of County Roscommon, officer in 35th Regiment.

William John Talbot (Johnnie), b 1859, d 1923, son of John, married Julia Elizabeth Mary Molyneux on 14th August 1897, known as Johnnie, held the office's of High Sheriff, Justice of the Peace and Deputy Lieutenant for County Roscommon, held the office of High Sheriff of County Armagh, held the office of Deputy Lieutenant of County Galway, gained rank of Captain in the service of the 7th Brigade South Irish Division of the Royal Artillery, died without issue.

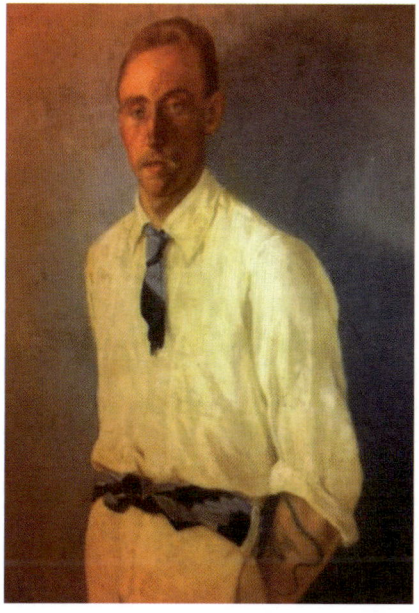

Potrait of Johnnie Talbot of Mount Talbot painted during his early adult years. He is dressed in cricket clothing in the colours of his former school, Eton. A tattoo is shown on his left arm, tattoos were popular among the upper classes throughout the latter half of the 19th century (Courtesy of Donald Cameron)

Direct paternal lineage of the O'Kellys of Aughrane (Castlekelly)

Maeleachlainn Ó Ceallaigh, b. 1326 in Gailey Castle, d. 1401. Was Chief of Hy-Many.

Brian Ó Ceallaigh, d.1393, son of Maeleachlainn. Was Tanist under his father but died in his father's lifetime so never became Chief of Hy-Many.

Maghnus Ó Ceallaigh, son of Brian, born in Skreen (Scrine) and became the first 'Lord of the Manor of Screen'

Domhnaill "Daniel" Ó Ceallaigh, son of Maghnus, 2nd Lord of the Manor of Screen

Donnehadh "Denis" Ó Ceallaigh, son of Domhnaill, 3rd Lord of the Manor of Screen.

Aedh "Hugh" Ó Ceallaigh, son of Donnehadh, 4th Lord of the Manor Screen.

Tadhg "Teige or Timothy" O'Kelly, son of Aedh, first of this family to reside at Aughrane, 5th Lord of the Manor of Screen. Was Sheriff of Roscommon.

Ruaidhri "Rory or Roger" O'Kelly, son of Tadhg, 6th Lord of the Manor of Screen, was Sheriff of Roscommon. Lived at Aughrane.

Colla O'Kelly, d.1615, son of Ruaidhri, 7th Lord of the Manor of Screen. Lived at Scrine.

John Kelly, d. 1674, son of Colla, 8th Lord of the Manor of Screen, fought against Cromwellian forces, surrendered Jamestown to parliamentarians. Lived first at Correbeg and Scrine and then at Aughrane.

Colonel Charles O'Kelly, son of John, 9th Lord of the Manor of Screen, fought for King James II in Williamite Wars, held the title of Knight of the Shire for the County of Roscommon. Lived at Correbeg and later at Aughrane.

Captain Denis O'Kelly, d. 1740, son of Charles, 10th Lord of the Manor of Screen, fought alongside his father in Williamite Wars, owned Aughrane but lived in various locations in Leinster. Died without issue and left his lands to his cousin John Kelly of Cloonlyon.

John Kelly, d. 1748, cousin of Denis, 11th Lord of the Manor of Screen, moved from Cloonlyon to Aughrane after inheriting the Castle and lands from Denis, first of the family to convert to the Protestant religion.

Denis Kelly, b. 1730, son of John, 12th and last Lord of the Manor of Screen.

Rev Andrew Armstrong Kelly, b. 1763, son of Denis.

Denis Henry Kelly, b. 1797, d. 1877 son of Rev Andrew Armstrong, Magistrate for both of the Counties of Roscommon and Galway, DL, MP for Co. Roscommon 1820-21, had to sell all the ancestral lands through the landed estates court due to financial difficulties.

The family crest of Denis Henry Kelly, the last of the O'Kellys of Aughrane (formerly of Scrine). Denis believed he was the legitimate leader of the O'Kellys and next in line to be Chief of Hy-Many.

Appendix 2 - Townlands and Place Names

An enormous amount of information may be obtained about a specific area by examining the place names. Many place names are very old and date back to the early medieval period and sometimes even into the Iron Age. The following is a list of all the townlands that are relevant to this publication together with their meanings:

Townlands:

Mount Talbot – The village and town land of Mount Talbot are named after the Talbot family who resided in the area from 1652 until 1922.

Mount Talbot was known as *Cluain na gCloidhe* prior to the arrival of the Talbot's and earlier it was known as '*Beal an Atha*' and '*Ath an Malthuch*'.

Cluain na gCloidhe (Cluain na gClaí) - The walled meadow or the meadow of the ditches/hedges.

Beal an Atha or *Beal an Atha Ui Cheallaigh*[120] - The mouth of the ford or mouth of the O'Kelly ford. A ford existed across the River Suck between the modern town lands of Mount Talbot and Garrier. This ford was of immense importance throughout the medieval period as it was one of the only navigable crossing points of the Suck during the winter months. The exact position of this ford is unknown but it was probably in the vicinity of the modern bridge.

Ath an Malthuch or *Ath an Molhooey*[121] – the ford of the horseman.

Cloondara – The meadow of the two raths. This townland contained two large adjoining ring forts that were located on the banks of the river suck. Part of one of these forts still exists today.

Lismaha – Matthew's fort.

Lisgillalea – Killalea's fort.

Both the townlands of Lismaha and Lisgillilea were part of an earlier townland known as Dundermott or Dundiarmuid.

Dundermott- Dermot's fort. This townland also extended into parts of the modern townlands of Lisduff and Derrinlerrig. It is not recorded as a townland after the Cromwellian settlement of 1652. The word 'Dun' signifies a fortified structure and suggests that it was an important fort inhabited by a leading member of the local Gaelic family. The 'Dermot' referred to was probably an O'Kelly Chief who resided within the fort.

Cloonca – The meadow of the battle. No battle is recorded here in the early texts but it may date back to the O'Kelly occupation of the area. It is unknown what the area was called prior to the

---

[120] Ordnance Survey, name books for Co. Roscommon, p215.
[121] Ibid.

battle. This townland is located along an ancient road that was in use during the medieval period and it continued to be used until the construction of the modern Mount Talbot to Four Roads road in the late 18th century.

Cloonakilleg – The meadow of the place of the flag stones. Flag stones still exist across the callow to a ford over the river Suck that led into the townland of Garrier.

Cloonlaughnan – Loughnane's meadow.

Cartron – The word Cartron was a land measurement, it was used in place of the word 'ceathru' after the arrival of the Normans in the 12th century.

Srahaunnagort – The holm of the field, this townland is now known as Thornfield.

Garrier or Garreer - The enclosure to the east. A large ring fort existed within this townland during the medieval period and this was probably the enclosure that gave the townland its name.

Placenames:

The Corlann (Oileann na gCutharlán) – The island of the pig-nuts. This area was once an island on the River Suck that became part of the main land after drainage works were carried out on the river in the late 19th century. Although this area is no longer an island some fields along the river are still known as 'the islands'.

Corrocot – The turn of the boat. This name was given to a village near Mount Talbot in the townland of Cloonlaughnan. It is possible that the occupants of this area used a boat to gain access to the island of Corlann.

The Togher – is a raised road linking Cloonakilleg to the main Mount Talbot to Four Roads road. This togher was required as Cloonakilleg was effectively an island being surrounded by the river, bog and marshland with no natural high ground linking it to the road. It is unknown when the first togher was built at this location but as Cloonakilleg is an ancient and historically important townland it is clear that access to the area was required from at least the 13th century. The togher replaced the ford (referred to above in the section dealing with Cloonakilleg) as the main access route into the townland.

Bothar Buí – the yellow road. This is located approximately mid-way along the Bushy Park road. It got its name 2 or 3 centuries ago from the colour of the road during times of flooding when yellowish underground clay seeped upwards through the surface.

Linn na nÉain – the pool of the birds, this part of the river Suck is located downstream of the metal bridge. The river is very wide at this location and the water is still and calm. Large numbers of wild-fowl gather here throughout the winter months.

Baile Thoir and Baile na Mona – these names were given to two distinct groups of houses that existed in Cloonakilleg. Baile na Mona was located nearest to the bog and across from the village of Muckinagh on the Galway side of the river Suck.

Clooneleen – The ridge of the meadow, this is a small area located at the Mount Talbot end of the Bushy Park road. A stream of the same name flows though here and a beautiful single arched stone bridge spans the stream. A very important late medieval watermill was located here. A village grew around the mill and by the mid 18th century this village contained 32 houses. Mount Talbot replaced Clooneleen as the centre of population during the latter half of the 18th century.

Bibliography

Books and Journals

Ordnance Survey, name books for County Roscommon.

Mary Turley-McGrath, *New Grass under Snow*, Summer Palace Press. Donegal 2003.

Mary Turley-McGrath, *Forget the lake*. Arlen House 2014.

S.J. Connolly, *Contested Island, Ireland 1460-1630*. Oxford University Press, 2007.

Nuala O'Faolain, *My Dream of You*. London 2001.

T.W. Moody F.X. Martin F.J. Byrne (ed). *A New History of Ireland, iii, Early Modern Ireland 1534-1691*. Royal Irish Academy, 1991 (third impression).

The Military History Society of Ireland, *Irishmen in War, from the Crusades to 1798*. Dublin 2006.

Murray, J. *Letters to and from Henrietta, Countess of Suffolk and her second husband the Hon. George Berkeley from 1712 to 1767, Volume 1*. London 1824.

Patricia Kilroy, *Fall of the Gaelic Lords – 1534-1616*, Dublin 2008.

Simington, R.C. *The Transplantation to Connacht 1654-58*, Irish Manuscripts Commission. 1970.

S. Lewis, *A Topographical Dictionary of Ireland*. 1837.

Statutes Passed in the Parliaments Held in Ireland Vol. V. *From the Fifth Year of George III.A.D 1761 to the Eleventh and Twelfth Years of George III. A.D 1771-2 inclusive*. Dublin 1795.

The Journal of the Kilkenny and South-East of Ireland Archaeological Society 1856-67,Vols 1-6, Royal Society of Antiquaries of Ireland.

T. Davis, *The Patriot Parliament of 1689*, 3rd edition. Dublin.

Simington R.C (ed). *Books of Survey and Distribution, Roscommon*. Dublin 1949.

Mount Talbot School Board of Management, *Mount Talbot School - A Window on the Past*, 1992.

Kathleen Hegarty Thorne, *They Put the Flag a-Flyin, The Roscommon Volunteers 1916-1923*, 3rd Edition.

Marie Louise Legg, (ed). *The Census of Elphin 1749*, Dublin: Irish Manuscripts Commission, 2004.

Michael Herity, (ed). *Ordnance Survey Letters Roscommon*. Fourmasters Press, Dublin.

Edmund Curtis, *Calendar of Ormond Deeds 1172-1350 A.D*, Dublin: Irish Manuscripts Commission, 1932.

Killian-Killeroran Historical Society, Newbridge Ballygar Tohergar News. 1981 (and 1984).

House of Commons, Paper No:717, *Return of Number of Retail Spirit Licenses In Ireland* . HMSO, 1837-1838.

House of Commons, Paper No:230, *Return from Clerks of Peace in Ireland of Transcripts of Rules and Regulations of Loan Funds* . HMSO, 1836.

House of Commons, Paper No:458, *Account of Schedules Customs, Tolls and Duties delivered to Clerks of Peace of Counties, Cities and Towns of Ireland*. HMSO, 1823.

Four Roads Hurling Club, *A Century of Hurling*, 1995.

Tisrara Heritage Society, *A History of the Parish of Tisrara*, 1997.

D. Broderick, *The First Toll Roads: Irelands turnpike roads, 1729-1858*. Cork, 2002.

Websites

www.osi.ie , www.nli.ie , www.nationalarchives.ie , www.tcd.ie , www.nuig.ie , www.balyd.com , www.nationalarchives.gov.uk , www.askaboutireland.ie , www.galway.ie , www.iarc.ie , www.buildingsofireland.ie , www.nobodyhome.ie , www.heritagecouncil.ie , www.igs.ie , www.irisharchaeology.ie , www.iai.ie , www.museum.ie , www.archaeology.ie , www.irishhistoryonline.ie , www.irishhistoricalstudies.ie , www.historyireland.ie , www.ucc.ie/celt , www.irishnewsarchive.com , www.irishtimes.com/archive , www.dipam.ac.uk , www.logainm.ie , www.focloir.ie , www.focal.ie

Newspapers

Roscommon Champion, Roscommon Herald, Roscommon Messenger, Roscommon Journal, Connacht Tribune, Freemans Journal, Irish Independent, Irish Press, Irish Times, London Times, Farmers journal, Longford Leader, Morning Post

In memory of Michael Connolly

of Cloonakilleg, Mount Talbot and of Bushy Park, Mount Talbot

1932 – 2013

Rest in Peace

Lord, when he comes to Heaven's portal,
Give him no alien crown of gold,
But let him see thy spring immortal
Crowning those fields he loved of old.

Noelle Davies